Also available from Continuum:

Joanna Baker and Heather Westrup: *English Language Teacher's Handbook: How to Teach Large Classes with Few Resources*
Ray Cattell: *Children's Language: Consensus and Controversy*
Manjula Datta (ed.): *Bilinguality and Literacy*
Jun Liu: *Reflective Teaching in the ESL/EFL Classroom*
Len Unsworth (ed.): *Researching Language in Schools and Communities: Functional Linguistics Perspectives*

LEARNING STRATEGIES IN FOREIGN AND SECOND LANGUAGE CLASSROOMS

Ernesto Macaro

CONTINUUM
London and New York

Continuum
The Tower Building
11 York Road
London SE1 7NX

370 Lexington Avenue
New York
NY 10017–6503

British Library Cataloguing-in-Publication Data
A catalogue record for this book is available from the British Library.

ISBN   0–8264–5134–9 (hardback)
        0–8264–5135–7 (paperback)

Designed and typeset by Ben Cracknell Studios
Printed and bound in Great Britain by CPD, Ebbw Vale

Contents

To Gabriella

Acknowledgements

I am very much indebted to Lynn Erler and Vee Harris for their invaluable comments on early drafts of this manuscript and for the encouragement they gave me with some of the more difficult sections and chapters. I'd also like to thank Michèle Deane for providing me with so many ideas on how to adopt a distance learning style of writing, something 1 had not attempted before. In this respect I am also grateful to Anthony Haynes for his positive response when I suggested a departure from a more academic style while nevertheless maintaining, I hope, a high level of theoretical and research content. My thanks also go to Susan Dunsmore for her patient editing and her common-sense suggestions.

The two research projects described in this book were enabled by the funding received from the European Commission (Lingua) and from the University of Oxford Research Committee. Without this funding the research would not have been possible. I would like to thank Gianfranco Conti for sharing with me his expertise on writing strategies and for helping with the writing strategies research project.

There are many teachers of foreign languages who have been involved with the various learner strategy research and I am greatly indebted to them for allowing me into their classrooms and for encouraging their students to become involved with strategy training. Particularly I would like to thank Belinda Bartley, Robert D'Ambrosio, Ros Weller, Mary Haynes and Giuseppina Maria Brandi for their insights, innovative ideas and perseverance.

I'd also like to thank Cynthia Martin for one of the songs contained in this book.

Finally, I would like to acknowledge the invaluable help given to me directly or indirectly by the pre-service student teachers at the University of Oxford and elsewhere who have assisted me in the formulation of the concepts and for keeping me on the straight and narrow in my attempts to reconcile theory and practice.

Introduction

I wanted to call this book *Strategies in the Foreign and Second Language Classroom: Teachers and Students Learning to Learn* but the editors wouldn't let me! Looking back on this now, I think they were right. The title would have been just a tad too long. Nevertheless, I do want to start off with the concept of 'learning to learn'. This may seem an unusual phrase to some of you. Isn't learning a language an end in itself, you may be asking. Let me reassure you from the outset that, as far as this author is concerned, the main purpose of language teaching and learning is for students to become increasingly competent at speaking and writing a second or foreign language. However, the phrase 'learning to learn' originates from an increasing recognition that language learning involves much more than teachers and learners simply interacting with one another and then sitting back and observing how well the learners have soaked it all up. The teacher's input does not automatically lead to the learner's output. If it did, life would be simple and there wouldn't be any need for the constellation of journals under the various headings of applied linguistics, second language acquisition and language pedagogy. If all the learners had to do, in order to make rapid progress with language learning, was carry out the teacher's instructions, there wouldn't be any need for this book. But in educational contexts as varied as learning English as a second language in a Swedish upper secondary school or maintaining first language Urdu outside school hours in Britain, a language teacher's life does not seem to be that simple. Some learners do well and choose to carry on with their language studies even when they don't have to. Other learners appear demotivated at a relatively early stage and can't wait for the moment when they no longer have to endure the tedium of learning a language which, as far as they are concerned, they do not need.

The reaction to this lack of simplicity in the past has been to blame the teaching methods and, by implication, the teachers. At first, the criticism was that methods were based too heavily on the *translation* of written sentences and the explanation of *grammar* rules. How could learners possibly learn to speak by donning surgical gloves and mask and dissecting the stiffened corpse of the language? No, what they needed was the living body of the language, to talk in the classroom in the way that real people in the target country talked to each other. So learners began to be drilled entirely in the foreign language. But teachers were then criticized for aggressively marching the learners up and down to the tune of barked questions and predictable answers, that the teacher-dominated parade ground of the *direct method* was still a far cry from the place where people spoke to each other in the normal course of their everyday lives. Then came technology and so there was an opportunity for the teacher to be, in part, replaced by the tape recorder. But there was to be disapproval here too. The criticism was that learners were being made to 'ape' the pre-constructed sentences of the tape recorder on a given signal. The condemnation of this, the *audio-lingual method*, was based on the recognition that learners were humans with a predisposition to create their own language not animals that performed memorized language tricks when stimulated to do so. And so it came to pass that *Communicative Language Teaching* (CLT) became the general approach adopted by most teachers in most countries of the world and CLT was to last for many years because it allowed teachers so much flexibility. However, because it was a flexible and general approach and not a strict method, it was adapted for national and local consumption and this soon opened the gates to local and national criticisms about how CLT was being misinterpreted by teachers. In England, for example, the criticism became that teachers used too much first language (L1) in the classroom. How could learners ever experience the communicative 'essence' of the language they were learning if the teacher was not constantly communicating with them and they with each other using the second language? The simple solution, then, was to banish the L1 from the CLT classroom. Then the criticism was re-focused to throw the spotlight on the content of the curriculum. How could learners possibly be interested in a curriculum which just taught them how to carry out the transactions they needed for a short holiday in the foreign country? However, as this criticism was not levelled at teachers but at curriculum planners and examining boards, it was not long before it swung its spotlight back to the teaching method. How could learners make progress with language learning if they were not taught properly the grammar of the second language (L2)? And so we came full circle.

This cycle of blame and retribution is framed by the context of language learning in England simply because that is the context I know best. But it need not be. Language teachers all over the world have experienced the same kinds of criticisms, faced the same accusations and been given the same reasons for their supposed failure. The only difference is that the phases of the cycle may have happened at slightly different times.

The reaction to the lack of simplicity of the task facing language teachers has rarely been to find out what barriers or obstacles the learners might be facing. This is understandable as learners are many and disparate and teachers are few and relatively homogenous. Furthermore, it is extremely difficult to get inside the learners' heads whereas it is relatively easy to observe teachers, see the results of their teaching and then ask language educators what they think. But perhaps we now need to react differently to this lack of simplicity. So much research evidence suggests that learners have different learning styles that it seems obvious that we should be inclusive in the methods that we use rather than exclusive, that we should rarely point to things which should not be done but often remind ourselves of things we are not doing or perhaps have not done for some time. Once relieved of the burden of worrying about what is right and what is wrong we can devote more energy to thinking about how individual learners learn and how they might, as individuals, learn better.

This book, therefore, is primarily concerned with the students and the way that they go about the process of learning a second or foreign language. It asks whether it is possible to improve the way that learners learn by offering them a number of practical suggestions as to how they might do so. The intention is to find ways of encouraging learners to help themselves rather than coming up with yet another new and exciting teaching method. That is not to say that what I am advocating is that teachers should start 'boring their students into learning more effectively' but that the excitement of learning a language should come from the learner's self-realization and their estimation that real progress is being made rather than the fact that they are being entertained. Learning to learn, then, is one of the first major steps towards that elusive concept that everyone talks about but nobody ever really defines: autonomy. In this book I do not eschew the concepts of learners' autonomy and independent learning, quite the contrary. However,

I attempt to suggest that these concepts are achieved through a series of practical steps which the learner needs to be guided through, a series of strategies that they need to be exposed to, encouraged to try out and evaluate. Only that way can the learner begin to develop self-questioning and the language learning skills that will, hopefully, last a lifetime.

'So this book is about learning strategies?', I hear you say. 'There are lots of those already.' Both these statements are true. Learning strategies do pervade this book and, yes, there are a number of other authors who have written extensively on this theme. This book, I therefore need to persuade you, is different in three ways.

First, it is not aimed at teachers or learners or researchers or teacher educators (trainers). It is aimed at all four. This is simply because I cannot see how they can be separated. Whereas other books have tried to separate the strategies that learners use from the way that teachers teach, I have found it impossible so to do. I believe that the two are directly interlinked in a mutual dynamic and I hope that I will be able to convince you of this if you decide to read on. Whereas some authors have been almost exclusively interested in research findings and have addressed the implications for the classroom almost as an afterthought, I have found it impossible to maintain that imbalance. Good research feeds directly off the data that the classroom provides and good practice is informed by research. Finally, I have not been able to separate teacher development from teaching, learning and research. To do so would be to provide you with a body of knowledge without the framework of action through which change can be brought about. In addition to teachers using this book on their own, teacher educators will be able to use the information and tasks in this book to work both with student teachers and with language mentors in schools as a way of exploring practice and developing a common language for the description of the way students learn languages.

This brings me to the second way in which this book is different. If you, the teacher, decide to read this book you will need to commit yourself to undertaking a kind of learning programme yourself. In a sense you too will be learning to learn. But your learning will include how to achieve an understanding of yourself as a teacher and former learner as well as acquiring the skills to carry out a systematic exploration of the learners in your classroom. In order to do this I will be asking you to try out strategies to improve the learning you would expect to get from a book such as this one. This is why you may, at times, find this book repeats certain ideas and themes.

Although the book is aimed at a number of different types of reader it is essentially designed for practising teachers, student teachers or teacher educators who have direct contact with classrooms. To be able to carry out some of the guided thinking and the tasks in this book (don't worry, they're not too onerous), you will need to be able to refer to real language learners. In that sense the book offers a kind of distance learning programme for teachers based on the notion of action research, research into one's own classroom. You don't *have* to carry out the action research with your students, you can simply stop and reflect on some questions which I formulate at various points in each of the chapters. You don't even have to stop and reflect in depth on some of the issues. However, some of the reflective tasks do have some learning strategies embedded in them so that you are, in fact, being encouraged to operate on a number of levels. Well, then, you are free to read the book as you wish. All I ask is that you have a pen and paper to hand to take a few notes and, very importantly, that you do build up a simple list of learning strategies that you can refer to as you progress through the book. If, in addition, you are able to discuss some of the questions raised in the various chapters with a language teaching colleague, that would be even better. Indeed, the reflective tasks can even be used as in-service or development aids for language departments or 'teams' of teachers to work together on.

The book is structured to follow an action research cycle by doing the following:

1. Identifying learning problems in the L2 classroom.
2. Raising your awareness and knowledge of the literature on learning strategies.
3. Providing you with examples of strategy training.
4. Encouraging you to adopt a strategy training programme adaptable to your own teaching context.
5. Providing you with the research instruments with which you can evaluate the success of strategy training in solving the learning problems.

Third, this book is one of the first to put forward a feasible and rational programme of training, one which focuses on what would appear to be coherent and appropriate combinations of learning strategies rather than individual strategies.

This book tries to address many types of language learning contexts. The words in the title 'Foreign and Second Language Classrooms' suggest differences rather than similarities. I actually believe that the differences are overstated. One distinction is where the second language is being learnt in the target country (the country where the language is spoken) whereas a foreign language is not. However, in 'the literature' this is not always so clear-cut. Sometimes the term 'a second language' is merely meant to refer (wrongly, in my opinion) to the learning of English because of its status in some countries in particular and in the world in general. Unless I state it explicitly, the issue or strategy that we are dealing with at any particular time is applicable to both foreign and second language contexts. In other words, at the heart of the book is a core of fundamental principles related to *learning to learn* which are the same for all language learners. Indeed, some of the ideas regarding the development of learning skills can easily be transferred to subjects other than second language learning. However, the emphasis will be on the formal L2 classroom situation and, particularly, the classroom where adolescents are learning a foreign or a second language. Examples, figures and artefacts of students' work are provided in English, French and Italian. For those readers who only speak English I have, therefore, in places where the meaning is not clear from the context, provided a translation or an explanation, either in the body of the text or in the Appendix.

Structure of the book

The chapters of the book are designed in such a way as to reflect the cycle of action research mentioned above. Chapter 1 starts by formulating a number of problems encountered in the languages classroom and asks you to relate these to the manner in which your students go about learning an L2. In this way we start our list of learning strategies and simultaneously explore the research background they are set against. With this in mind we examine how teaching methods and strategies can impact on the learner's use of strategies. In order to whet your appetite to read on, the chapter ends with an initial overview of how strategies have been researched and what the research is beginning to tell us about how students learn to learn.

Chapter 2 provides greater detail of the ways that learning strategies have been investigated in the past using some real examples of 'research instruments'. The difficulty of trying to get 'inside the learner's head' is discussed along with ways of overcoming this problem. The chapter then invites you to consider the possibilities of exploring, in your own classroom, the strategies that your students are using.

In Chapter 3 we examine the work of researchers who have merely sought to *describe* the strategies used by language learners. The fundamental question here is, what are successful learners doing that unsuccessful learners are not doing? After a brief overview of this work dealing with strategies in general, we look in detail at descriptive studies involving listening and reading strategies.

Chapter 4 provides, again through a report on previous studies, an introduction to *intervention studies*. By this is meant ways of training your students to experiment with a greater range of strategies and to use them in combination with one another in order to see if their language learning improves. In other words, how can students learn to learn better? We look specifically at the strategies that can be deployed in *oral interaction* and at techniques for improving *memorization* of language.

Chapter 5 continues with the theme of intervention. This time we look in depth at one particular study, carried out by the author, which investigated the process of *writing* in the foreign language. We examine case studies of two adolescent learners and see whether strategy training led to improved written output by them.

After a brief discussion about how to go about deciding what shape your strategy training programme should take, Chapter 6 offers a wide range of practical ideas and materials for raising the awareness of learners, modelling strategies and for encouraging learners to adopt combinations of strategies.

Chapter 7 explores how you might go about following up a programme of strategy training via student self-evaluation and teacher monitoring. I propose that you will want to put in place an ongoing system of monitoring as well as a more long-term framework which will inform you of your students' strategy use over time. In order for you to evaluate the effectiveness of the programme you will gradually have to withdraw the strategy support you are giving your students.

Chapter 8 rounds off the book by offering a conclusion and a number of recommendations. These include an outline of a programme of strategy training, from beginner to advanced, which is designed to be flexible and adaptable for most language learning contexts.

Throughout the book a number of themes and issues which impinge on how students can learn to learn are discussed. Perhaps the two most important are learner autonomy and the role that the first language plays in the learning of a second language. I have already dealt briefly with reasons for including the former. The latter has been a controversial subject ever since Communicative Language Teaching took hold as the predominant instructional approach in schools, colleges and universities. I believe this issue to be so important that at the end of virtually every chapter there is a discussion about the use of the first language in the student's learning process and its implications for strategy training.

The two studies described in the greatest detail in this book are referred to as the Lingua Project and the Oxford Writing Strategies Project. These are two research and development projects on learner strategies that I have been involved with. The first compared groups of 13- and 14-year-old learners in England and Italy and was funded by the European Commission (Socrates: Lingua). The second involved 14–15-year-old students in the Oxfordshire area and was funded by the University of Oxford's research committee. I am grateful to both these bodies for their support.

A note on terminology and metalanguage

I have tried whenever and wherever possible to put across the ideas contained in my own work and in the work of others as clearly and as simply as the complexity of the material allows. However, I have not avoided the terminology that is a common currency in the world of applied linguistics, second language acquisition and language pedagogy. I believe that we do need to develop and share a common language that describes, clearly and succinctly, the subject we teach. We need to develop and use a *metalanguage*. However, I have tried at all times to provide a gloss of the metalinguistic term as there is no assumption made that the reader will already be confident and conversant in the literature of learner strategies research.

I very much hope that you will enjoy reading this book and that in using it with your students or student teachers you will gain valuable insights about language learning that will help to shape your future teaching.

CHAPTER 1

The Learner's Strategies and the Teacher's Strategies

In this chapter we will be doing the following:

1. Looking at some of the problems encountered in the languages classroom.
2. Reviewing some definitions of strategies and some categories of strategies.
3. Discovering some of the strategies learners may use when learning a foreign language.
4. Thinking about how teaching and learning interrelate.
5. Understanding the background to learner strategy research.

Some problems encountered in the languages classroom

I give my students written homework but so many of them seem to do it badly . . . there's that lack of care and attention to detail which I find so frustrating.

It's the business of looking up word for word which basically means they don't understand the whole idea of language . . . they will have a sentence in English and they will just put it into French word for word and it will be total rubbish.

I mark the students' written work . . . spend hours providing them with careful corrections but it doesn't seem to make any difference . . . the mistakes remain . . . the corrections just don't seem to get into their heads.

You can bang on and on and on about . . . you know, about a particular language point and then when they get to actually use that, it's gone out of the window.

There are so many students in my class . . . I can't possibly ask them all to speak every lesson . . . I sometimes wonder what the others are thinking about when I ask questions of individuals . . . It's difficult . . . pair and group work helps but you can't do that all the time.

I can't ask them to read on their own . . . they just give up and say 'I don't understand any of this.' They don't seem to have a method for setting about reading a text on their own . . . I have to constantly give them exercises . . . but that's not like real life . . . you don't get exercises when you read an article in a magazine.

One of the greatest frustrations is they have these wonderful imaginations and they're very creative and they get frustrated because they can't put it into French and then that makes them feel they know nothing.

There's so much vocabulary to learn when you're learning a foreign language . . . and there's so much pressure from exams to get it learnt quickly . . . so they just have to memorize chunks . . . there's no way round it . . . but how? . . . They find it so difficult.

Language learning is about creating new sentences not just repeating memorized chunks they've heard me use . . . but how can I encourage my students to do this more often? . . . There's so little time in language lessons.

They find listening difficult . . . I don't know whether it's because they just can't concentrate or maybe they're getting stuck on a word.

PAUSE FOR THOUGHT

If possible discuss the above quotes with a language teaching colleague and then look at the questions below. If that isn't possible, try to answer some of the following questions yourself:

1. Can I identify with any of the above quotes?
2. Which ones?
3. What are my reactions when these thoughts come into my head?

4. Do I:

(a)   Give up in despair?
(b)   Blame myself as a teacher?
(c)   Blame the learners as 'hopeless compared to what I was like'?
(d)   Blame the school or the teaching situation?
(e)   Blame the teaching approach currently in vogue?
(f)   Devise new teaching strategies in the hope that I might one day 'find the right formula'?

The above quotes are either from recorded interviews on the two main research studies described in this book (see Introduction), or personal communications to me from teachers. They are representative of problems that many of us have encountered in the languages classroom. No matter how dynamic a teacher we try to be, we are often disappointed with the performance of some or all of our learners. No matter how much we try to keep abreast of developments in language teaching by reading articles or books written by 'experts in the field', many of us experience the sensation that there must be something not quite right about the teaching and the learning. When we encounter these responses or problems we react in a number of ways. It is unlikely that your reactions will have been too often like (a)–(f) above, otherwise you wouldn't be reading this book. Negative reactions to problems in the classroom don't do us much good either pedagogically or healthwise. But is reaction (f) the only possible 'good' answer? Could it be that none of us know enough about the ways that students learn a second language or a foreign language to make a 'good' decision about what to do when things do not seem to be going as well as we would want them to?

Some learners' strategies during three common language learning activities

One important aim of this chapter, therefore, is for us to explore how adolescent learners go about learning a second or foreign language (henceforth abbreviated only to L2). Let us look inside an L2 classroom by examining three fairly common activities that students are asked to carry out:

1.   Questioning sequences
2.   Understanding a written text
3.   A writing task at home

Questioning sequences

In this activity the teacher has introduced some new language (English L2) to the class and is in the process of 'practising' it by asking individual pupils to answer questions. For example, the dialogue might go something like this:

T: Jim, do you help around the house at weekends?
   (Teacher points to a picture of someone washing up)

Jim: Yes, I do the washing up.

T: Sally, do you help around the house at weekends?
   (Teacher points to a different picture)

Sally: Yes, I do the vacuuming.

T: Amanda, do you help around the house at weekends?
   (Teacher points to a different picture)

Amanda:*(hesitates)* Yes, I . . .

T: Do you wash the car or wash the windows?
   (Teacher again points to the picture)

Amanda:I wash the windows.

(and so on)

PAUSE FOR THOUGHT

In the above questioning sequence ask yourself:

1. What are the *mental processes* that might be going on inside the learners' heads?
2. How do I know what these mental processes are?

You may have written down some of the following 'mental processes'. The students who are called upon to answer are:

1. *Checking that the question conforms* with what they were expecting from *the context* of the activity. In this case, as it is an activity which occurs often in L2 classrooms, they are likely to recognize it quite quickly. Generally, they will be trying to understand what the teacher is up to.
2. *Trying to hold the sound of the teacher's words* in their heads in order to 'work on the meaning of it'.

3. *Retrieving* the words or phrase from their memory. They may do this 'back-loaded' and in 'chunks'. That is, they might retrieve 'the vacuuming' or 'the washing up' first and then add the 'I do'. Others might have tried to *store* each of the phrases in its entirety as a chunk of language. Some might have done both: stored it in cut-up chunks where there was a pattern and in larger chunks when there was no pattern. It may be that this is why Amanda hesitated with her answer. Perhaps she had not gone through that mental process of *compartmentalizing* the language (sorry, I can't resist the pun as it is one strategy for storing the word) as she was storing it for later retrieval.
4. Preparing to speak by a quick *rehearsal* in their heads (and *monitoring* that it makes sense; perhaps checking that it is correct using some kind of system they have developed for themselves).
5. Preparing to speak by quickly *saying the words under their breath* (and *monitoring* that it sounds right).
6. Looking out for signs (from the teacher) that their answer was correct. That feedback would either *confirm* what they thought was right or make them *revise* what they thought was right.
7. Listening to their fellow students' answers and *holding in their heads* the ones that they accepted as correct.

But what of the learners who were not being nominated to answer the question? Were they going through all seven (or more) mental processes or were they just drifting off and hoping that they would not be asked? They may have looked attentive but how do we know that they were practising getting ready to speak (retrieving, rehearsing, monitoring, revising, confirming) or were they doing it all quickly if and when asked? Of course, the answer is that from the front of the class it is very difficult to tell. In later chapters we will explore ways of trying to solve the problem of how we find out what is going inside the heads of the learners. What we have done for now, however, is to identify *strategies* that some or all of the learners might be bringing to the task. Let us now look at another activity.

Understanding a written text

For this activity you have provided your learners with a written text in the foreign language which contains about 30 per cent of words which they haven't come across before. You ask them to read it quietly to themselves and to try to understand as much as possible before doing an exercise, for example, an exercise with 10 multiple choice questions in the L2.

PAUSE FOR THOUGHT

1. What are the mental processes going on inside the learners' heads as they try to *decipher* the text?
2. How might they best *apply* those mental processes in order to achieve the objective of understanding what is written down in front of them?
3. How will they *decide* whether to use those processes again in the future?

To help you with this, try to find a foreign language text in a language that you don't know very well, a text that is rather difficult for you, and see what you can make of it by trying to translate it into your L1. Do so out loud, all the time trying to articulate the mental processes that you are going through to try to understand it. It might be helpful to get a colleague to listen to you as you do this and jot down what your 'strategies for decoding the text' are. Or, you might want to record yourself on tape and keep it for use in the classroom (see Chapter 6).

Here are some mental processes that the students might have used (and perhaps you also might have used) in order to make sense of the text:

1. They might *skim* the text and try to get an initial impression.
2. They might *look at the text* and see if there are any visual clues that might *confirm* that initial impression (e.g. photos, titles, paragraph headings).
3. They might think of ways of not getting 'uptight' if they think it looks rather difficult – having the right *attitude* to the text.
4. They might divide the text up into manageable pieces and start *analysing* one piece at a time, perhaps by paragraph or by series of sentences.
5. They might scan for all the words or chunks of language that *they already know.*
6. They might look for words that look like words in their L1, *the cognates.*
7. They might *infer the meaning* of some words from the context and from the words they have understood.
8. They might *predict* some of the language that is going to come up from what they have already understood.
9. They might see if some of the *syntactic clues* in the text, or the

order that the words are in, helps them to understand.

10. They might try to *sound out* the words to see if this brings back memories of having heard the word before – *making phoneme-grapheme associations.*

11. They might simply try to *translate* the text word for word.

Once again, it is difficult to know whether some or all the students are actually applying these strategies. It is even more difficult to ascertain *how* they are applying these strategies. That is, in what combination and to what extent? The approach that you adopt to your teaching may make it easier or harder to 'get into the learners' heads' in order to find out their strategy use and we shall be returning to this theme throughout the book. Let us look at a final task that you might set your students.

A writing task at home

For this task you have asked your English (L1) learners to go home and write a letter to a hotel in Italy, booking a room for them and their family. You have already introduced them to words like: *bagno* (bathroom), *camere* (rooms), *doccia* (shower), and so on. About two months ago you did a similar activity with 'booking a campsite'.

PAUSE FOR THOUGHT

1. What preparation activities might the students carry out before settling down to the task?
2. What are the mental processes going on inside the learners' heads as they try to write the letter?
3. What might they do to help themselves with those mental processes in order to achieve their objective?
4. How will they decide whether to use those processes again in the future?

Of course, you might wish to protest at this stage that you would give them a lot more help in the form of materials, lists of phrases and vocabulary, reminders about beginnings and endings to formal letters, a writing framework, and you would be quite right to do so. Even so, one would imagine that your students will have some decision-making to do. That decision-making will contribute to their growing independence as writers.

Here are some strategies that they might use. They might:

1. Make sure that the room in which they are working is quiet and conducive to working well.
2. Clear their desk of all other things apart from the things they need.
3. Arrange on the desk their dictionary, the vocabulary you have given them, their previous letter on camping, their favourite cuddly toy.
4. Look at the precise instructions you have given them for the task and work out roughly how many words will go into each paragraph.
5. *Brainstorm* all the Italian (L2) phrases they know which might be useful for the task.
6. *Re-combine* some or all of these phrases for the purposes of the new task context.
7. Decide (probably as they write) which words or phrases they will need to look up in the dictionary.
8. Decide (probably as they write) which phrases/sentences they will try to *translate* directly from English (L1) and which phrases they will go for directly in Italian.
9. *Evaluate* whether the strategies outlined in 5, 6 and 7 are working for them.
10. *Monitor* their work as they write (perhaps after each sentence).
11. *Back-translate* (perhaps after each paragraph) in order to see if what they have written makes sense.
12. Read through out loud at the end to *check* that it sounds right.
13. Ask their older sibling to help them give the letter one more check through.

These are only some of the possible strategies that the students might deploy and you will no doubt have thought of many more. Most of these strategies are quite *conscious* strategies. If asked when they were doing the task, the student would probably not have too much trouble telling you about them. Contrast this with the strategies we thought they might be using in the other two tasks. These strategies were much more directly related to the language as it switches quickly from inside the learner's head to outside the learner's head. Perhaps these strategies were more at a *subconscious* level and would therefore be more difficult for the student to articulate if asked.

PAUSE FOR THOUGHT

Let us try to summarize our understanding of what learner strategies are by doing two things:

1. Make an initial list of all the words so far in this chapter which are in *italics* (you've probably picked this up as a strategy to follow anyway).
2. Compare your list with the 'terminology' (sometimes called *metalanguage*) that some authors use as they try to provide definitions of what strategies are (see below).

Some definitions of learner strategies

Learning Strategies are the behaviours and thoughts that a learner engages in during learning that are intended to influence the learner's encoding[1] process. (Weinstein and Mayer 1986)

Learning Strategies are techniques, approaches or deliberate actions that students take in order to facilitate the learning and recall of both linguistic and content area information. (Chamot 1987: 71)

Learner strategies refers to language learning behaviours learners actually engage in to learn and regulate the learning of a second language . . . what they know about the strategies they use . . . what they know about aspects of their language learning other than the strategies they use. (Wenden 1987: 6)

Second language learner strategies encompass both second language learning and second language use strategies. Taken together they constitute the steps or actions consciously selected by learners either for the learning of a second language, the use of it, or both. (Cohen 1998: 5)

Specific actions taken by the learner to make learning easier, faster, more enjoyable, more self-directed, more effective and more transferable to new situations. (Oxford 1990: 8)

Background to learner strategy research

Did you notice the absence of two words in particular? When I first started reading and hearing about learner strategies I was struck by the absence of the words 'teacher' and 'teaching'. This caused me some anxiety at first. If it was only about learners, why should I, as a teacher, get involved? Would I be interfering with the learners' private lives? What would my role become as a teacher? We shall be returning to this theme of the teacher's reaction and role later when we listen to what teachers on the two projects (the Lingua project and the Oxford Writing Strategies project) have to say. First, a little historical context.

People have been researching and writing about learner strategies for about 20 years now. However, what learner strategies actually are has been difficult to define at an international level and with full consensus. Steven McDonough (1995), for example, sees a number of terms as overlapping with the concept of strategies. He identifies language skills, language processes, mechanisms to compensate for lack of language, action plans, all as terms used at various times to discuss learner strategies. As we have seen above, one of the tasks of researchers and writers has been to try to come up with clear definitions of what strategies are. Inevitably these definitions are linked to the researcher's or author's main sphere of interest. Some relate to a psycholinguistic domain (the link between the way the brain functions and the language it encounters), some to a more pedagogical one (the way that students appear to learn in general and learn languages in particular).

When we consider the authors' definitions above there seems to be a lack of consensus as to whether learning strategies should include *communication strategies* (language in use). These are the strategies that learners use in order to put across meaning when they are sometimes having difficulty because of insufficient competence in the language. Some authors limit learner strategies to receptive skills and to processes such as, for example, memorizing, practising, preparing oneself to speak, organizing one's learning, etc. (that is, language learning). On the one hand, it would be difficult to deny that there is a process of learning going on simultaneously with the process of communicating. By learning to maintain communication through various strategies we keep the conversation going and therefore end up talking more than if we just clammed up. On the other hand, it could be argued that, in a conversation, you are only learning *through the feedback* from others. Simply saying something in a different way, or using more words because you can't say exactly what you want to say, (*circumlocution*) increases neither your store of language nor your competence in expressing yourself. It is only if others correct you, or suggest alternatives, or simply provide you with more exposure to the language, that you learn. In this book we are primarily concerned with learning and not particularly with the strategies that students can use in order to 'get by' while they are communicating with others in the foreign language. However, we will be exploring the strategies that students can use in order to maximize their opportunities to talk in order to build up confidence, get feedback and bring about exposure to the L2 from more competent speakers.

We will also notice from the above quotations that, in the past, authors have used 'language learning strategies' while others have used 'learner strategies'. You may react to this by saying that 'this is just semantics' and 'all they are doing is playing with words'. It is true that both appear in the literature to be synonymous and interchangeable. In the text so far I have used them both quite deliberately. However, sometimes by making distinctions we understand a problem better. Let us therefore at this point attempt a distinction. One possible distinction between these two terms might be that learner strategies are those used by learners to help with the accomplishment of all language-related tasks. For example, a reading strategy such as *referring to the context* of a newspaper article helps the accomplishment of a clearly defined language activity, understanding the article. However, having inferred the meaning of an unknown word from the context, the reader may now try to commit that word to memory. This would be a learning strategy. Similarly, *noticing* a new pattern in language while someone was speaking may not be related to any recognizable language task. This would be more of a learning strategy. Both kinds would be pro-active strategies where a definite effort (not to say 'conscious') had been made by the learner to help himself or herself accomplish the task or to learn something new. If we use this distinction, learner strategies will often subsume learning strategies. In this book I have tried to make this distinction wherever possible. However, there is another reason for wishing to retain both terms. I would also argue that the term *learner strategies* seems to capture more effectively the emphasis which I would want to place on the learner as *the active participant* in the process of learning. The learner, I would argue, is not simply a performer who responds to the requirements of 'teaching strategies' but 'a problem solver and reflective organiser of the knowledge and skills on offer in the language exposure and required for effective language use' (McDonough 1999: 2). Finally, we need to observe that the term 'language learning strategies' refers more specifically to the process of language learning whereas learner strategies might be interpreted as techniques in the learning of any subject. The latter is not my intention. This book is entirely concerned with providing ideas, techniques and materials for foreign language learning. However, some of the techniques embedded in the materials of this book could be used in the learning of other subjects.

We will also notice, in the authors' quotes, references to making language learning more 'self-directed', to students 'selecting' steps or actions. In other words, there appears to be a close link between the concept of learner strategies and that of learner autonomy. Many current national curricula point to a need to develop learner autonomy in language learning. This need has also been expressed in various research publications and statements of policy at the European level.[2] It is argued that it is unlikely that schoolchildren will be able to achieve fluency and competence merely within the confines of the secondary languages classroom. Moreover, within a constantly changing global context it is impossible for learners to predict which language or languages they will need in their future careers. As a consequence, it is of paramount importance to offer learners the opportunity to develop independent language learning skills while at the same time learning a first or second foreign language. While acknowledging that this link exists, this book will try to demonstrate that the concept of learner strategies, for teachers, is a much more definable, accessible and operational concept than that of learner autonomy. Autonomy as a learning concept is not taking root in schools as quickly as some educators would wish. Perhaps this is because it requires fairly major changes in teaching styles and in the deployment of language resources. But it may also be because it is a somewhat vague concept, much more difficult to grasp than the concrete and recognizable steps that learners can be encouraged to take in order to develop more control of the learning process.

PAUSE FOR THOUGHT

We have explored a number of mental processes that learners use. We have begun to call these processes *strategies*. We have also identified a number of actions (organizing your desk) and also called these strategies. We will explore the difference in a moment. For now, let's gauge your reaction to what you have read so far. Has the discussion been:

(a) informative?
(b) obvious?
(c) surprising?
(d) familiar?

In what ways are learner strategies different from teaching strategies? What is your reaction to seeing them as different concepts?

   Have you started your list of learner strategies (see Introduction)?

How memory works

Let us return to the quotations above and explore a little further the network of words and ideas used. Let us look, for example, at 'deliberate' and 'consciously'. It is assumed by a number of authors that strategy use in language learning is conscious behaviour. If strategies are not conscious behaviour, how could learners possibly acknowledge that they use them? If some strategies were so deeply buried in the subconscious and therefore impossible to articulate by learners, how could an observer detect them? For example, if a student were observed to look up every time a teacher asked the class a question (regardless of whether the teacher was directing the question at that student), an observer could infer that the student was formulating an answer in their head, but the observer could not assert that this was the case. A number of researchers (Oxford 1990; McDonough 1995) seem to be acknowledging the fact that not all strategies may be conscious. As we saw in one of our tasks, a strategy that learners appear to use when reading in a foreign language is *making inferences* from certain elements in the text. Making an inference by matching a single known word with the context of the text might be done with little conscious effort – the learner is not aware that they are doing it. There is no consensus in the literature as to whether strategies can clearly be defined as conscious or subconscious and therefore it may be helpful to see strategies as part of a subconscious to conscious continuum. Linking a word to a visual image may well be at the subconscious end of the continuum but planning a week's revision would be at the conscious end. However, all learners are different and it is impossible to say whether all strategies can be articulated by learners, or whether all learners can articulate any one strategy (see Skehan 1989: 80).

Theories underpinning strategy research

The study of strategies is linked to the theory of *cognition*. Cognition is the way the brain holds information for short periods of time, stores information, selects and retrieves information and processes information (see Figure 1.1). In order to do this, two processes take place in different areas of the brain: the working memory and the long-term memory (LTM). The LTM can store an enormous amount of language information and, unless there is degeneration or damage to the brain, for indefinite periods of time. However, language information in the brain is not held as language as it is in the outside world of sounds and squiggles. It is stored in the 'nodes' of the brain as meaning or 'ideas' (sometimes called 'propositions'). The working memory can only hold information for very brief periods of time (countable in seconds only) but it is the working memory that does all the work of selecting, converting, finding ways of storing and retrieving language from long-term memory. As the learner becomes more and more proficient with a linguistic item (e.g. present tense endings of regular verbs), the speed with which the working memory retrieves it from the LTM becomes faster and faster until it appears to be 'automatic'. The retrieval of the linguistic item is no longer 'controlled' by the fact that the learner has to refer to explicit knowledge about the pattern they have noticed or have been taught.

Figure 1.1   *Cognition processes*

The memory and learner strategies

In the same way that a linguistic item operates between the LTM and the 'outside world' through the help of the working memory, so do learner strategies. Strategies such as saying language under your breath in order to remember it (subvocalization) may start off as 'controlled' ways of improving memorization and then become automatic.

The above is only a very brief overview of the theory of cognition but it is important to have some understanding of it in order to better grasp the idea of strategies. That is why some authors (for example, O'Malley and Chamot 1990) talk of *cognitive strategies* and *meta-cognitive strategies*. Cognitive strategies are more like the sorts of (almost subconscious) things that the learner might have been doing in task 1 (above). Metacognitive strategies are more like the planning, organizing and evaluating strategies that we identified in task 3. They *support* the cognitive strategies. O'Malley and Chamot (1990) provide a further two categories of strategies bringing their classification system to four:

1. cognitive strategies
2. metacognitive strategies
3. social strategies
4. affective strategies

Social strategies and affective strategies are often treated as 'a broad grouping' (ibid.: 45) which involves either interaction with another person or the control of one's feelings with regard to language learning. Thus co-operation on a language task, seeking help from a teacher, discussing your feelings with someone else or convincing yourself that you can do a language task are all examples of strategies from this group.

Another way of classifying strategies is to describe them as Direct Strategies (memorizing, cognitive processing, compensation) and others as Indirect Strategies (metacognitive, social and affective). This is a classification offered by Rebecca Oxford (1990: 16). All these authors have tried to come up with definitive lists of strategies which fit into their categories.

Whether it is very important to come up with a definitive and clear classification is debatable, whether it be for learners or for teachers. However, it has some importance in carrying out research in that comparisons about strategy use can be made and if you are planning to investigate the strategies that your learners use, it is essential to have some sort of list and useful to have categories. Moreover, to try to come up with a definitive list is useful in the sense that then we would be sure that we were not ignoring some of those which were being used by learners but which might be very important to them, or, that we had a strategy in our list which the students were not aware of. As we examine the results of some research in this book, we will refer to a classification based on the idea of a continuum. I have adopted this approach for two reasons, first, there is considerable overlap between cognitive and metacognitive strategies. This overlap is usually brought about by the situation in which the strategy is taking place (see, for example, Susan Bacon's strategies (1992: 165)). Second, if we adopt the approach of only referring to them as cognitive, metacognitive, social and affective, though this would be more anchored in a recognizable theory of cognitive learning, the approach deprives the reader of alternative ways of representing these strategies. It may be that pedagogically we have to conceptualize them, both as teachers and as learners, in different ways. Let us consider these different ways of conceptualizing them (see Figure 1.2).

I have opted for a continuum of subconscious (or 'less conscious') and direct strategies at one end and conscious and indirect strategies at the other because a clear dividing line between what is conscious and what is subconscious is not easy to identify. We can therefore say that those strategies at one end tend to be deployed in direct relationship to the learning task, usually in immediate response to teaching instructions

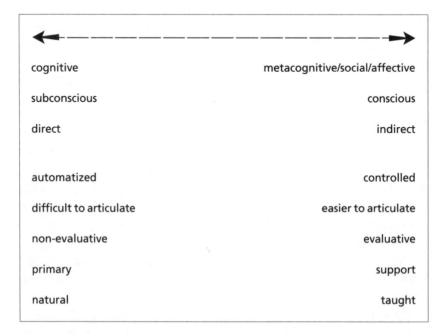

cognitive	metacognitive/social/affective
subconscious	conscious
direct	indirect
automatized	controlled
difficult to articulate	easier to articulate
non-evaluative	evaluative
primary	support
natural	taught

Figure 1.2   *Categories of strategies along a continuum*

or to written or spoken text. Those at the other end tend to be deployed in preparation for, or subsequent to, a learning task or set of tasks, often at some distance removed from direct input and with the learner more in control of their learning. In this sense they are more consciously pro-active. Because they are more pro-active, they may well include some element of evaluation of the effectiveness of a number of more direct strategies being used. When asked, learners usually find these more indirect strategies easier to articulate than direct strategies.

Here are some strategies that learners (in the literature on learner strategies) have said they use that we would probably place at the more direct and subconscious end of the continuum:

1. *Linking* words or ideas to visual images as you see them or hear them.
2. *Inferring* what a phrase means from the immediate surrounding text.
3. *Grouping* certain lexical items under a mental category.
4. *Holding the sound of language just 'heard'* (the echo) in the working memory in order to begin doing something with it (e.g. making sense of it).
5. *Holding the 'gist'* of what some taped language means in your head as you try to work out details.

Here are some strategies more or less in the middle of the continuum:

1. *Deciding* if L2 words look like L1 words.
2. *Repeating* words to yourself in class (perhaps when you hear them for the first time).
3. *Memorizing* a list of vocabulary items by using some sort of system.
4. *Answering questions in your head* directed at other people (in the classroom).

Here are some strategies that learners have said they use (or have been recorded as using) at the more indirect end of the curriculum:

1. *Making mental associations* when trying to memorize difficult words by writing them on a piece of paper, sticking it on an object and then making an association between the word and the object.
2. *Asking the teacher for clarification* or to repeat something they didn't quite catch.

3. *Practising* a dialogue *with a friend* at home.
4. *Listening to a FL cassette* at home.
5. *Calming themselves down* when they are finding a task difficult (rather than giving up).

In addition, we could make a distinction between 'natural and taught' strategies and also strategies used both for L1 and L2 and those used exclusively for L2. A moment's reflection on the strategies that a 9 year old already has at their disposal will suffice to illustrate both these points. The 9 year old will have been engaging in first language learning for such a long time already that many strategies will already have become automatic. Deploying these strategies for the purpose of helping to learn the L2 may not need any prompting from the teacher – some students will be able to do this of their own accord. Some may need to go through a process of deconstructing what they already do in L1 before they can apply it to L2 learning. Others still may need substantial amounts of help, encouragement and monitoring simply to be able to apply them in the L2. We call the process of helping, encouraging and monitoring the application of strategies 'strategy training' and Chapter 6 looks at practical ways of doing this.

For now, let us return to the different authors' quotations for the last time. We should observe that in the quotations there is a link being made between strategy use and successful language learning: 'improve'; 'make more effective'.

PAUSE FOR THOUGHT

Are you convinced that there might be a need to make your students' language learning more effective?

Make a brief list of what you believe are the basic principles of Communicative Language Teaching. Are there any principles which might conflict with enabling students to use strategies effectively?

Making language learning more effective

An international interest in learner strategies appears to have grown concurrently with the widespread development of Communicative Language Teaching (CLT). Perhaps this is because CLT, with its emphasis on functional language use, on the importance of target language input and the much greater emphasis on oral activities, has given the impression that competence in learning will occur 'automatically' provided that the teacher adopts a sufficiently 'communicative' approach. In other words, the process we were examining above, of developing from controlled knowledge to automatic (sometimes called proceduralized) knowledge, occurs simply by interacting with the teacher or with other learners. In fact, CLT proponents have sometimes given the impression that we can skip the controlled stage altogether and just learn naturally and automatically. This may be true in learning contexts where there is high exposure to the L2. In the average foreign language classroom, however, not enough prominence has perhaps been given to the efforts that the learner has to put into the process of learning a foreign or second language. Teachers faced with a lack of complete success have, perhaps, begun to realize that it is not enough for learners to respond enthusiastically to their teaching requirements and tasks but that they need to be actively engaged in the process of learning. According to Neil Naiman and his co-authors (1996), successful learners describe themselves as being actively involved in the learning process. H. Stern claims that 'too little attention has been paid to the conscious efforts learners themselves make in mastering a foreign language' (1987: xi) and Suzanne Graham (1997) reports that, in her study of 16–17 year olds, unsuccessful learners viewed learning as an effortless process.

This interest in language learning strategies also reflects a more fundamental shift of interest from groups of learners (the class, for example) to the individual learner and their individual differences.[3] If learners have different learning styles or have strengths in different aspects of aptitude, then clearly a teaching method which relies on whole class teaching almost exclusively via L2 interaction will not be sufficient to cater for the diversity of the learners' needs. Thus, research has been centred on how better language learners use strategies appropriate to 'their own stage of learning, personality, age and purpose for learning the language and type of language' (Oxford and Nyikos 1989: 291). Research into learner strategies tends to be descriptive and centred on individual learners rather than methodologically prescriptive and aimed at whole classes. This book, while celebrating the advances made in language learning through an eclectic CLT approach, nevertheless acknowledges that the learner's role in the learning process has been neglected in many language classrooms.

PAUSE FOR THOUGHT

From what you have read so far, how would you define learner strategies?

Would you say that it is your most *motivated* learners that, to your knowledge, use these strategies?

Independent variables

Everybody uses strategies in order to learn a language and, as we have observed, they certainly use them to learn their first language. But a lot of interest has centred on particular groups or types of learners. What researchers wanted to discover was the way that certain groups of learners use strategies in order to learn because these had shown that they were either better learners or more effective strategy users. We can say that these 'groups' are the *independent variables*[4] in strategy use. But aren't these effective strategy users simply the more motivated ones?

Motivation

There is a strong link between extensive and appropriate use of strategies and the perceived or measured motivation of learners.[5] This is not surprising when we consider that strategy use is an effortful process. Thus it would seem intuitive that more motivated learners are likely to put in the time and effort required of consistent strategy application, especially when considering strategies which are more at the conscious and controlled end of the continuum. Conversely, it may take a great deal of conscious effort and motivation to deconstruct and modify the more automatic strategies which, when evaluated, prove to be ineffective.

There may be a problem in making too strong a link between strategy use and motivation without further research, particularly of a longitudinal kind. This is because we risk having an unclear construct. Is it, simply, the case that motivated learners use more strategies to the point where high strategy use and motivation become synonymous? That would be a fruitless quest to pursue. A more interesting question might be the following: do learners who have an intrinsic motivation to learn a language become high strategy users or is it the case that learners who use a wide range of strategies effectively become motivated by their own success? If the former is the case, then we have a dilemma. If we were to find that there was too strong a link in the direction: *motivation leads to strategy use*, then to attempt to bring about change in strategy use would be barking up the wrong tree – learners who are not motivated are those who refuse, and will probably always refuse, to use a range of effective strategies. The other conclusion is the much more optimistic one. That is, learners become demotivated when their lack of strategy use (or limited or misuse of strategies) blocks their progress. It would seem, then, that, in order for learner strategy training to be an acceptable part of the language learning programme, research needs to be able to demonstrate that successful strategy use leads to successful learning and therefore to motivation. Alternatively, and at the very least, it needs to demonstrate that unsuccessful strategy use is a contributory factor in demotivation. If you are planning to develop your own learners' strategies, then your investigation into strategy training in later chapters will need to suggest that better strategy use leads to more successful learning and that this, in turn, leads to greater motivation. That is why your investigation will have to be carefully evaluated.

PAUSE FOR THOUGHT

Do all my learners learn in the same way? Make a list of some individual learners or small groups of learners that you teach and try to think of how they are different from one another. What clues tell you that they are different? What is it about the way that they go about their learning that makes them different?

Do your learners change the way they learn over a period of time? Can you think of any of your learners (or perhaps even a whole class) who have changed the way that they learn since you have been teaching? How have they changed and why?

Sex

Research has suggested that females use more strategies and use them more effectively than males.[6] One of the motivating forces in setting up the Lingua project (see Introduction) was that I had carried out a pilot study in England which very strongly suggested that female learners used more strategies than male learners in the secondary sector. This appeared to resonate with the fact that, in England, girls are consistently outperforming boys in national foreign language exams at the age of 16. Moreover, girls seem to be motivated to continue studying a foreign language beyond the compulsory curriculum. It became apparent when discussing these themes with teachers in Italy that there could be a lot to learn from comparing the strategies used by learners in Italy with those used by learners in England to see if the same gender bias was in operation. We will therefore look at some of the results of this line of enquiry in later chapters.

Age

Age as a variable in use of strategies has not been researched extensively in its own right. A great deal of research has gone into comparing how younger and older learners make progress in their language learning but few studies have isolated strategy use as a focus of investigation. Suzanne Graham (1997) claims, therefore, that it is difficult to trace a clear-cut development in strategy use related to the age of learners. However, it would seem intuitive to suggest that older and more experienced (worldly wise?) learners would have, in general, a greater contextual knowledge than, say, 10-year-old learners. With this greater contextual knowledge they would be able to test their 'hypotheses' about, for example, what a word or an idiomatic phrase might mean. In addition, their much greater vocabulary store in L1 would help them to make links between words more readily than young learners. Finally, adults and older adolescents may use strategies much more flexibly and are able to employ many more of the support strategies (evaluating, monitoring, planning) that research suggests are key factors in rapid language learning development. This would account for the fact that reseach shows that older learners make much faster progress with their second language learning than very young learners although, in the end, young learners may end up with native speaker competence whereas adults very seldom do.

Background and cultural differences

Cultural differences have also been a 'variable' that researchers have explored. As a result, there is some evidence to suggest that the cultural background of the learner may affect the way they use strategies to help learn the language. Rebecca Oxford (1996)[7] in her review of language learning strategies around the world provides evidence that learners from Eastern countries are more reluctant to use clarification strategies (e.g. interrupt the teacher in order to ask for clarification) than western learners. Kate Parry (1991, 1993) explores the differences to be found in reading strategies used by learners from different cultural backgrounds and notices that these differences can be attributed to the way different cultural groups of people learn to read and this accounts for their dissimilar attitudes to written texts.

Aptitude, learning styles and beliefs about language learning

It is difficult to separate these three themes (see Ellis 1994: 541 for a concise discussion of this). If, as the literature suggests, aptitude and learning styles are 'fixed', then if we were to discover that effective strategy use was directly linked to either of these learner attributes, it would be fruitless to try to train students to use strategies. Fortunately, this does not seem to be the case. On the other hand, our beliefs about language learning will colour the way that we choose to learn a foreign language. Beliefs about language learning are likely to derive not only from aptitude but also from learning styles. Those who are analytical in nature may use more strategies involving explicit analysis. However, that may well be because they believe that language learning is about analysis. Learners who are very capable memorizers may not need to dissect language quite as much as the analytical learners and this is why they may hold different beliefs about how languages are best learnt.

Successful and advanced learners

This is the final group to be considered as an independent variable, and not surprisingly it is the more successful learners that appear to arrive at the most effective combination of strategy deployment. But we must take care not to confuse successful learners with advanced learners. While it is self-evident that the latter must have crossed a threshold of success, the advanced learning stage is not a necessary condition for effective strategy use. Many studies have demonstrated that advanced learners are using intricate combinations of strategies, far in excess of those used by beginner or intermediate learners. However, to infer causality between effective strategy use and arriving at a state of advanced learning would be a presupposition.

Differences in teaching approaches

One question that has not been explored to any great extent is: do the differences lie only with the learners? Earlier, we began to make connections between CLT and learner strategies. We asked ourselves if the way that CLT had been interpreted as a method left little room for developing a learner's own way of learning. Sometimes, however, there are constraints on the way we teach. Some national governments provide very strong guidelines on how teachers should go about their task. Moreover, the way that the teaching of a foreign language is structured (nationally or locally) sometimes provides less room for manoeuvre than we would wish.

PAUSE FOR THOUGHT:

How might the following aspects of your national education system have an effect on the attitudes and strategies that your secondary students bring to the process of learning a foreign language? It may be difficult to generalize at a national level, in which case think of your own local teaching context. Think about:

1. Whether they learn an L2 in primary school.
2. Whether the foreign language learnt is an international language such as English.
3. Whether there is some sort of change of school at a certain age which determines the way teachers teach (e.g. one teacher for all subjects; one teacher per subject).
4. Whether there is a prescribed national curriculum for learning an L2.
5. Whether the L1 is frowned upon in the foreign language classroom.
6. Whether the general teaching approach is more 'communicative' or more 'grammar-translation'.
7. Whether teachers generally use textbooks or rely more on their own materials.
8. Whether materials are on 'open access' to students.
9. Whether the L2 has equal amounts of teaching time as the 'first language'.
10. Whether a lot of importance is attributed to homework (or self-study).
11. Whether national exams figure early in the language learning curriculum.

Why should there be differences in the strategy use of learners from two different countries? For example, let us take the two countries used in the Lingua project: Italy and England. Do the cultural backgrounds provide potential differences, for example, their geographical location on the European continent, their history, their politics, attitudes to empire, attitudes to European integration, and so on? Or is it the case that Italian is not an international language and therefore Italian youngsters will have a more *instrumental* motivation (directly related to a material need) in wishing to learn a foreign language? Certainly both of these factors might have an influence on motivation and therefore potentially on strategy use. But should we not also consider the respective national teaching styles (if these exist) and consider whether these provide more or fewer opportunities for learners to develop effective learner strategies? In all the authors' quotations on p.17 there is an implication that learners are taking some measure of control over their learning process. But are the learners doing so no matter who the teacher is? Are Chamot's 'deliberate actions' being taken to compensate for what the learner sees as inadequacies in the teaching process or the language curriculum? Are Oxford's strategies 'making learning more effective' because it would otherwise be relatively ineffective, more 'self-directed' because it is relatively teacher-centred and more 'enjoyable' because it is relatively boring? Is it the case, in other words, that we can ignore the teaching approach that the teacher is adopting, or the educational or pedagogic environment in which that teacher is operating when we consider the frequency of use and the deployment of language learning strategies that learners are involving themselves in?

In this book we will at times refer to the differences in teaching styles and national contexts between England and Italy. In doing this, I am in no way passing judgement on which is the more effective style or context. Nor am I suggesting that all teachers in Italy and England teach like this. I am providing an overview of the situation as I see it which results from experience of both systems and long hours of discussions and observations. The intention is to raise the possibility that the educational context and the pedagogic approach should not be discounted. Moreover, in attempting, from time to time, a broad-brush description of these two national contexts I am limiting myself to the specific age group which was involved in the study, notably students aged 14–15 in year 10 (England) and the Prima Superiore (Italy). I will therefore start with a very brief comparison of these two countries.

PAUSE FOR THOUGHT

Look at Table 1.1 in which some differences in teaching styles and contexts between Italy and England are identified. In the right-hand column jot down a few key words as to how this might have an effect on the learners' approach and strategies for learning.

Table 1.1   *Educational differences between England and Italy*

Contextual difference for the learning	Possible effect on strategy use
In England the first foreign language learnt is French, in Italy the first foreign language learnt is English. Italian students of English will have been exposed to the L2 both before and outside their classroom encounters with foreign language learning.	
Whereas in England pupils would have been studying the foreign language in the same school and possibly with the same teacher, in Italy they would have done so in a middle school for three years and, consequently, this cohort would have just met their teacher for the first time.	
While the English National Curriculum is highly prescriptive in terms of teaching methods to be adopted, the Italian one lays down only a few fundamental principles related to learning to communicate in the target language.	
In England, since 1992, the National Curriculum has placed great emphasis on teaching entirely through the target language.[8] That is to say, teachers should consider the principle of excluding the L1 from the classroom as a major plank in their methodology. In Italy, while target language use is encouraged, it is not prescribed or controlled.	
In Italy, the Prima Superiore becomes, to a large extent, a 'language foundation course' for the study of literature and culture in the following three years. In England the objective is to be able to communicate to people, particularly young people, in the target countries (e.g. France, Italy, Spain).	
In Italy a great deal of emphasis will have been placed on the coursebook. In England teachers are much more eclectic about their choice of teaching materials and there is much wider use of worksheets. As a consequence, pupils do not always take coursebooks home.	
While both countries would claim to espouse a broad communicative approach in their teaching, English pupils will have been exposed more to a *presentation, practice and use* approach. Italian students are more likely to be expected to 'learn the chapter or unit', 'prepare exercises for individual interrogation', 'learn passages of text by heart' and 'understand grammatical concepts'.	
Italian students are, by and large, left much more to their own devices in their language learning. English students will have been much more 'spoon-fed'.	
In England the majority of students will have been grouped according to their perceived aptitude in the subject. In Italy, 14 year olds will find themselves learning languages in mixed ability classes and slower learners will be expected to catch up and/or keep up with the other students.	
In Italy school finishes at around 1.30 in the afternoon and students have many hours of homework to prepare. In England schools finish at approximately 3.30 p.m. and pupils have relatively few hours of homework to do.	

In later chapters we will compare what the students said about their use of strategies and you will be able to compare whether what you identified as a possible effect on strategy use was borne out by the research evidence. However, the data will certainly not be able to identify all the possible effects of teaching style and environment on strategy use. Apart from the two main studies reported in this book, little work has been carried out on the effect of different teachers' approaches on learners' use of strategies. Some work has been carried out by Kenton Harsch and Lesley Riley (1998) on comparing adult ESL and EFL learners in two different countries, Hawaii (USA) and Japan. In this work the teaching approaches are used as contexts to discuss the differences between the way that the learners in these two countries use strategies. In order to really understand if there is a link between strategy use and teaching approaches it is important to spend a great deal of time in the actual classroom where the learners are being researched.[9] That is why it is so important for the teacher to be actively involved in the research process. Both research projects described in this book involve teachers actively researching their own classrooms. But how does one go about finding out what strategies the learners are using and how they are using them? How do we get inside their heads?

Research methods in learner strategies

We will now look at how researchers have tried to find out how and which strategies are used by learners of a foreign language. The problem is, of course, that many of the strategies we have thought about or discussed so far are just not observable in the classroom. In any case we are also interested in the strategies learners use outside the classroom, given that time allocated to foreign language teaching is so limited. Even those that 'we can see' learners doing, we cannot be sure of exactly. We cannot be sure of how certain actions that we see are the results of certain mental processes. For example, we may regularly see a student writing down notes of new language as it comes up in our lessons. But how do we know that it is all new language to that particular student? If it is new language, how do we know on what basis that student has made the decision to write down the new word or phrase? Is it a language element that they intend to use later or is the strategy a more mechanical one perhaps not leading to the learning of the new word or phrase at all? What other, less observable, strategies might be associated with that action of noting down the new language element?

Thus, finding out how and which strategies our students are using is hard. But we shouldn't give up just because it is. We can at least try to discover the 'reality' of what is happening. Researchers have tried to do this by doing the following:

1. Learners have been *asked*, for example, in oral interviews, which strategies they use in general, or which strategies they use when attempting a particular task.
2. Learners have been *asked*, by using questionnaires, whether and to what extent they use particular strategies.
3. Learners have been *observed* while they work at their language learning tasks.
4. Learners have been *asked* to give *a retrospective commentary* of how they learn (e.g. through keeping diaries or through dialogue journals).
5. Learners have been *asked* to provide *a synchronic commentary* on how they accomplished a task (i.e. to talk about their thoughts to an interviewer while they were doing the task).
6. Learners' ways of tackling a language task have been *tracked* (for example, by using a computer to find out how often they looked up words in a dictionary or by using measurements of the lengths of pauses).

PAUSE FOR THOUGHT

What is your reaction to the ways that researchers have tried to elicit strategies from language learners? Particularly think about whether:

1. the information collected would be the truth;
2. how the process of collecting the data might influence the way the learners carry out what is being asked of them;
3. the time involved in collecting the data.

As a quick exercise, try to write a brief questionnaire (five questions only) which tries to find out from your learners what strategies they use for understanding you when you are giving them some oral instructions for an activity (procedural instructions). How hard was it to do? What were the problems?

In the two research projects described in this book a number of methods were used to discover the strategies the learners were using. The materials for most of these are given in later chapters. The idea is to use some of the materials (or adaptations of them) yourself to find out about whether and how often students use strategies and also to raise their awareness by discussing the results with them.

But is all this research into strategy use worthwhile? What have the above research techniques begun to unearth that we should put so much valuable time and effort into them?

What we know already about the way successful students learn to learn

In order to try to convince you that the effort is worthwhile, what follows is a brief summary about strategy use and strategy training for which there is a growing body of evidence. This evidence is supported by the two studies described in detail in this book. We will be examining these studies in Chapters 3, 4 and 5. We will also return to them in our concluding chapter.

Research suggests that the successful interpretation of written texts (reading comprehension) is dependent on a number of different strategies and the way these are combined to overcome difficulties in text.[10] Successful learners use a combination of *top-down processing* (thinking about the context of the text and the student's own 'world knowledge') and *bottom-up processing* (individual words and short phrases, analysed both for meaning and for clues in the syntax). Although individual readers have their own preferred strategies for understanding a written text, it is in the number, frequency, deployment and combination of strategies that success is to be found. Basically, good readers attack the text as a holistic problem to be solved by coming at it from different angles.

It is suggested that there are two approaches to a written composition task.[11] The first limits the learner to the L2 language they know, the other allows the learner to take risks with creating new sentences. In the first, the learner is able to use the L2 much more as the language of thought. In the second the learner uses the L1 as the language of thought and then 'translates'. More advanced learners use a combination of these strategies. It is believed that, in the skill of writing, some learners plan before they write, others plunge straight in. Again, the more successful learners are able to make effective decisions (perhaps based on knowledge about themselves and their current competence) about the amount of planning needed. Successful writers have a number of strategies for checking their written work. In addition, successful learners use teacher feedback effectively to redraft their work and to understand the workings of the language.

Effective listeners, it is believed, use a more top-down approach to decode the incoming text. That is, they use the context to make inferences of what bits of text they have selected to *sample* and check if their inference fits in with their world knowledge.[12] They also try to deal with whole blocks of information as it comes at them, predicting from what they already know what is likely to come next. Less effective learners focus on word-for-word decoding thereby running out of thinking time while the incoming text has moved on.

Effective speakers do not give up or hesitate for too long when they cannot think of how to say something. They find ways round the problem or ask the person they are speaking with to help them. In this way they are involved in much more exposure to and interaction with the L2.

Successful language learners seem to use strategies to help them stay focused in the classroom even when they are not directly involved in the L2 interaction. Some also use strategies to encourage the teacher to direct their attention on them. These latter strategies are not always welcomed by the teacher!

There is evidence to suggest that indirect, metacognitive strategies (see Figure 1.2) are used by successful students in order to make the right decisions on how to apply themselves to the task of learning. It looks as if it is more these types of strategies that are good predictors of the successful learner rather than the more direct ones. Perhaps it is because some of these indirect strategies *evaluate* the combined ways in which the direct ones are being used.

Strategies for acquiring vocabulary have to be quite numerous, varied and appropriate to the individual learner. Moreover, the learner needs to rely less on the teaching process and more on themselves and their own self-study practices in order to learn the large amounts of new vocabulary required for the compressed learning that occurs with adolescents or adults. Successful learners appear to have a hierarchy (or branching system) of strategies for learning vocabulary.

Successful language learners use a number of affective strategies which predispose them to language learning. They get themselves into the right frame of mind. This is where motivation and strategy use start to become inseparable again and the studies become less clear. Do these successful learners feel good about the target language or the target culture because they are making progress? Alternatively, does the fact that they are making progress make them feel good about the target language and target culture?

There is strong evidence to suggest that sex is a variable in strategy use with females showing greater strategy use. However, there is no evidence to suggest that females are inherently better at language learning. It is just that planning, revising and evaluating all aspects of language learning are features much more of female learners than male learners. Co-operation in language learning also features more among females. In certain contexts female learners tend to be the more successful language learners. In Chapters 3, 4 and 5 we will be looking in much greater detail at some of these variables and groups.

BEFORE WE MOVE ON

How much of what you have read and thought about in this chapter did you already know? If you already knew a lot, to what extent has thinking about it again helped to clarify your ideas and concepts?

If much of this chapter was new to you, try to summarize in a few sentences each of the following:

1. What are learner strategies and how do they differ from teaching strategies?
2. Why should you be interested in learner strategies?
3. How can learner strategies be categorized?
4. How might you or (an outside researcher) find out what strategies your students are using, how often and in what way?
5. What things might be restricting your students from using more strategies and more effectively?
6. In what areas does the literature on learner strategies feel reasonably confident?

If you found that learner strategies were something new to you, don't feel that you have in any way been at fault in not 'keeping up with the latest developments'. What follows are the reactions of some of the teachers on the writing project when asked at the outset if they had heard of the term *learner strategies*:

Yes I have ... but I don't know what it means. (Anna)

This year, just through working with the student teachers as a mentor (on the initial teacher training course) really. (Ben)

I came across it during my PGCE (initial teacher training course). On the course they tried to demonstrate to us that learners have different ways of learning. (Geneviève)

Not much, I think it's more come up through mentoring and working with student teachers. That's probably more where it has come up than on any particular in-service training course I've been on. (Joan)

Some teachers were only able to describe what strategies were in fairly limited ways:

Just helping the children to be independent really and discussing ways . . . I mean things like discussing the fact that a dictionary is not going to build a sentence for you and then looking at the dictionary to see what [it] can do for you. (Geneviève)

Mary [a student teacher] did a brilliant thing a few weeks ago . . . She introduced the seasons and she said in your mind you can put an S at the beginning [of printemps] then you get S-prin and then été . . . one of the kids came up with 'oh yeah, if you put an F at the beginning it looks like FETE, so then you would remember you have summer fetes' and automne looks like it anyway and hiver – she said think of hibernate – and I thought that was brilliant! (Ben)

Different ways of asking your pupils how they can learn. Just asking them when they're learning, for example, for the homework and for a test . . . I always try and give them some tips on how they learn as for instance when we're focusing on the spelling. (Clare)

As you can see, researchers and authors need to improve the way they communicate their findings to teachers as they have clearly failed to do so thus far with these teachers. Hopefully, this chapter has gone some way towards finding a remedy for that situation.

In the next chapter we will discuss what you would need to take into consideration if you wanted to find out about the strategies that your students are using. In order to do this we will look in some detail at the range of research techniques mentioned above.

Notes

1. To 'encode' simply means to convert some language information into another form. For example, you might convert what you hear in the foreign language into a visual image or vice versa.
2. For further reading on learner autonomy, see Holec (1988); Dickinson (1987); Gathercole (1990); Evans (1993); Little (1994); and Macaro (1997).
3. For further reading on individual differences see Skehan (1989).
4. A 'dependent variable' is what you are actually trying to research – in our case, use of strategies. The independent variables are all the variables that might affect the use of strategies, for example age, sex, nationality, how long they have been learning the L2, etc.
5. For further reading on the link between strategy use, motivation and personality, see Oxford and Nyikos (1989) and Ehrman (1990).
6. For further reading on gender as a variable in strategy use, see Ehrman and Oxford (1989); Bacon (1992); Bügel and Buunk (1996) and Macaro (1998).
7. In particular in the article by Bedell and Oxford (1996).
8. See Macaro (1997) for a full explanation of how the curriculum tries to influence teaching.
9. Parry (1993) calls for a more ethnographic approach to research into strategy use.
10. For further information on reading strategies, see Sarig (1987); Graham (1997) and Grenfell and Harris (1999).
11. See, for example, Cohen (1998) on 'the language of thought'.
12. See, for example, O'Malley and Chamot (1990).

CHAPTER 2

Investigating the Learners
in our Classrooms

Acquiring the tools of the trade

In the previous chapter we began to consider the ways in which it is possible to find out how some or all of our students are learning. You will remember that we cited (page 18) a distinction made by Steven McDonough (1995) between *skills, processes* and *strategies*. Let's just think of this distinction again in terms of you as a teacher and the way that you 'know' your students. Most teachers would claim, with some justification, that they know or can measure the skills that their students have. If a student is able to describe the town they live in or read and understand an extract from an article, a teacher can say that the student has the skills to do those things. The teacher may well also be able to claim that the student can trace the development of those skills over a period of time. Or, a teacher may be able to detect an improvement in the student's reading down to the level of being able to distinguish between skimming and scanning. Again these are recognizable skills that the student might be developing. The question the teacher may not be able to answer is *how* the student is now able to scan a text for detail better than before. This is because skimming for gist and scanning for detail are skills which can be measured through tasks that the teacher sets. By contrast, top-down and bottom-up processing (see Chapter 1) are strategies which the teacher rarely gets the opportunity to observe at first hand. Similarly, a teacher is well placed to measure to what extent a student is able to deploy the *process* of translating or interpreting or summarizing. Again, the teacher may be able to claim that the ability to process information, in one or all of these ways, has developed over time because of the visible output resulting from these processes. Both skills and processes are, by and large, observable phenomena. Strategies, on the other hand, are much more difficult to observe, record and measure because, by and large, they are happening inside the learners' heads and are not the visible signs of achievement but the actions that lead to achievement. This lack of accessibility can make it frustrating for teachers and researchers alike and may have led to strategies being ignored in the past. Yet, they are crucial. McDonough (1995: 5) categorizes them as the choices, compensations and plans which enable the development of skills and processes. Skills and processes are the surface manifestations of the strategies that learners use. Strategies are the network of thousands of *decisions put into action*, consciously or subconsciously, appropriately or inappropriately and with varying degrees of frequency and consistency, that form the underlying fabric of our foreign language learning.

Of course, given that no student is ever tested on how often or how well they use their strategies we may simply prefer to teach a language and expect that the skills and processes will develop. Indeed, some writers such as Janie Rees-Miller (1993) have claimed that there is little evidence that strategy training leads to improved language learning and have, as a consequence, argued that time spent on training students to use strategies is time that could have been put to better use just teaching the language, that is, just developing the skills and processes. Kellerman (1991) has denied the importance of strategy training because he believes that learners have already developed strategies from their experience of learning their first language.

If foreign language learning were almost always successful, perhaps many more teachers, researchers and writers would agree with the above criticisms. However, our experience shows that foreign language learning is far from being universally successful even within the same classroom and with the same teacher. What the teacher teaches is not automatically learnt by all of the learners. So, to restate the fundamental tenets of this book:

1. Learners will learn better if they are helped to identify the strategies they use, if they come into contact with other possible strategies and if ways of deploying them in combination are suggested.
2. Teachers need to know the strategies that their learners are using in order to better understand some of the problems they may be encountering with their language learning and in order to be able to adapt their teaching styles and materials to the learners' needs.

In this chapter, therefore, we will be looking in considerable detail at the ways in which we can investigate our learners' use of strategies. In doing so we will bear in mind the following things:

1. Not all teachers have time to investigate their learners in depth and therefore they will need to be selective about which methods of investigation they use and when.
2. No previous experience of research methods is assumed.
3. There is no suggestion that all aspects of a learner's learning need to be investigated.
4. The use of strategies can be considered by some to be a very personal matter and being questioned about it is somewhat intrusive. A system of discretion mixed with giving the learners the option of not divulging information should be employed at all times.

Finding out about strategy use

Basically, there are two ways in which we can find out what strategies our learners are using: we can ask them and we can observe them (with 'observe' being used in its broadest sense).

Asking the learners

The advantages of asking the learners are:

1. As teachers or researchers, we are not imposing our own understanding or misinterpreting what they do.
2. It is much less time-consuming to ask large groups of learners to tell us what they do than to try to observe what they do in any sort of systematic way.

The disadvantages are:

1. Some learners are not able to articulate the strategies they use.
2. What they say is affected by the fact that they have been asked. A particular kind of questioning may produce a particular kind of answer. Or, their answers might be affected by the fact that they have been asked at all. Perhaps they will provide an answer because they feel an answer is required. Or they may simply want to please their teacher or a researcher.

Nevertheless, a great many studies have used the method of asking the learners what strategies they use, how they use them and how often. I will therefore illustrate this approach with some examples and describe the tools (sometimes known as 'the data collection instruments') used.

PAUSE FOR THOUGHT

Learning how to research your own classrooms is one of the aims of this book. For each one of the studies described you may like to make a note of how this instrument might be applied to your own classroom using the following headings:

1. Data collection instrument.
2. The questions about my students' learning it may be able to answer.
3. How practicable is it in my current circumstances?
4. What would I need in order to be able to use and analyse an instrument such as this?

This is not the place to go into the finer detail of possible research instruments for gathering information on strategies but a few helpful hints are offered. Suggestions for further reading on research methods are made at the end of this chapter.

Diaries

For collecting data over a considerable period of time, diaries are a useful tool. Asking your learners to keep some kind of diary, that they are prepared to show you, of the way they learn will provide you with a broad picture of their development over time. Of course, not everything that they write in their diary will be of direct relevance to learner strategies and, conversely, there may be things which they forget to write, or choose not to write which would be a very valuable source of data in your attempt to investigate their learning. One way of overcoming this problem is to provide them with some broad headings under which to write their diary entries. An example of a learner diary is one given to 17-year-old advanced students of French and German by Suzanne Graham (1997: 195) in which she asked them to enter data under the following headings:

Date:
Activity and situation (in class/outside class):
Things I found easy/things I found difficult:
How I dealt with the task:
What have I learned/what have I achieved?:
How do I feel?:
What should I do now?:

As we can see, these are very broad headings, mostly reflecting aspects of metacognitive and affective strategies. This is because these types of strategies are easier to recall at a distance than the more immediate (direct) strategies involved in language processing itself.

Another way of ensuring that diaries provide slightly more structured data (but without restricting the student's potential to express other things that are important to him/her) is to involve the diary keeper in an ongoing dialogue with the teacher or a researcher. This allows the teacher or researcher to explore in greater depth any interesting data or patterns that are beginning to emerge.

Diaries can also be used for very specific aspects of the learning over a period of time. For example, you could ask your students to keep a diary of how they revise or recycle their language learning over, say, three months. The danger with this type of approach is that it risks being interventionist. The very fact that you have asked them to keep a track of their revision process suggests to them that this is precisely what they should be doing. Unless you are very careful in the way that you set up a diary activity, you will not be getting a true picture of what they do normally. Of course, this is a perfectly appropriate approach to take once you have decided to embark on a programme of strategy training.

Questionnaires

Questionnaires have been employed widely by researchers and teachers. They are extremely difficult to devise as you may have noticed when you tried to do a brief one in Chapter 1. Not only is it difficult to think of a question and phrase it in such a way that all learners will understand it perfectly, it is also difficult to make a decision as to whether to ask for an open-ended answer (e.g. 'please comment') or whether to provide more of a tick box approach. Obviously an open-ended question does not propel the respondent's thoughts through narrow channels and researchers may therefore gain insights which they would not have gained through providing the respondent with a range of options. On the other hand, since questionnaires tend to be anonymous, it is impossible to follow up something that a student has hinted at in an open-ended answer, or something they have said which is unclear. Even if you decided that your questionnaire should not be anonymous, you would have to take into account the fact that open-ended answers could well provide you with a deluge of information which you may not have the time or the inclination to analyse.

Questionnaires have often been used for broad areas of strategy use. Perhaps the most famous is Rebecca Oxford's Strategy Inventory for Language Learning (SILL) which runs to some 80 questions (Oxford 1990: 283). This questionnaire asks respondents to answer questions by using the categories:

Never or almost never true of me
Generally not true of me
Somewhat true of me
Generally true of me
Always or almost always true of me

The extent to which the statement is 'true' is related to a descriptor which in turn is related to frequency of use (e.g. more or less than half of the time). This works quite well with statements such as:

When learning a new word, I visualize the spelling of the new word in my mind. (statement 7)

However, it may become more difficult for a student to quantify a response to statement 61:

I actively look for people with whom I can speak the new language.

I don't know if I personally could answer this one. I probably would feel that this is generally true of me but, in that case, I would have to claim that I did this behaviour 'more than half the time'. More than half the time of what? More than half of my waking life? More than half of those periods of time when I am learning a foreign language?

In case readers are thinking I am smugly criticizing other researchers, let me provide a similar problem encountered with a simple question-naire used in the Lingua project (see Macaro 2000). This was with students in Italy and England who were about 14 years of age. Here the statement was:

When I don't understand I ask the teacher to clarify or repeat things.

And the response categories were:

Often
Sometimes
Not often
Rarely
Never

Apart from the difficulty of quantifying the difference between 'not often' and 'rarely', there was an added difficulty with this question which surfaced. We have hinted in Chapter 1 at the possible effect that different educational systems and practices might have on learners' use of strategies. Here is another aspect of educational practice: in Italy students have a classroom base and it is the teacher who moves around. Although this has a number of disadvantages, it does result in there being more time to consult the teacher and no pressure on students at the end of the lesson to get to the next lesson on time. In England, by contrast, students move around the school at the end of each lesson and the pressure is on them to leave the classroom quickly and arrive promptly at the next lesson. The opportunities for English students to seek individual clarification will be less. It is likely that English students will have imagined the question referring almost entirely to 'in the classroom during the lesson' whereas Italian students will have imagined it referred to both during the lesson and at the end of it. Comparing the frequency of strategy use is, therefore, problematic.

Therefore, questionnaires for discovering strategy use are not completely reliable. Yet frequency of strategy use is an important factor in trying to understand mental activity connected with language learning. If we think back to the distinction between controlled and automatized learning we encountered in Chapter 1 (page 24), the frequency of use of certain direct or cognitive strategies becomes very important. Automatization will only occur through repeated activation of controlled processing in the working memory.

PAUSE FOR THOUGHT

Can you think of ways of categorizing responses more effectively for the three statements, for example, by describing them much more specifically but still keeping some sort of categorization rather than open-ended questions?

A reminder that the three statements are:

1. When learning a new word, I visualize the spelling of the new word in my mind.

2. I actively look for people with whom I can speak the new language.
3. When I don't understand I ask the teacher to clarify or repeat things.

One solution to this problem might be to use just three clear categories of responses and reformulate the question as 'Do you do X?' rather than 'How often do you do X?':

1. Yes, I do.
2. No, I don't.
3. Not sure.

The problem with this approach is that it's so 'categorical' (i.e. it forces students to go through too few doors) that it may lead the majority of your students to opt for the 'not sure' category. This is fine if you were just using a questionnaire to raise awareness but not much use if you wanted to gather some statistical data in order to generate some sort of theory of strategy use from it.

The best we can ask of a questionnaire of this kind, therefore, is to provide us with a general tendency in very large samples. Despite problems with questionnaires, what the instrument does provide us with is an initial entry into the 'underworld' of strategy use. It also provides us with an impression of whether strategies are being used in rational combination. This may lead to further questions to be answered using different instruments and techniques. For example, the Lingua questionnaire provided a brief insight into how learners were going about coping with a written text by asking learners 'How often do you use the following ways to help you learn?' to this group of three statements:

I guess what words/phrases mean from context.

I start from the words or phrases I know and use these to help me make sense of the ones I don't know.

I think if words look like English (L1) words.

From this initial numerical data it was then possible to progress in a more informed way to the 'think-aloud' interviews described later in this chapter.

PAUSE FOR THOUGHT

If you were trying to find out what your learners were doing in order to learn new vocabulary, what sorts of questions would you ask them? Of course you could simply ask that very question: 'What do you do to learn new vocabulary?' and you would get a whole range of answers. One of these might be, 'I say them out loud to myself over and over'. That would be OK but it wouldn't give you an idea of the frequency – how often they used this strategy.

Try to come up with at least five statements that describe the strategies that you think your students might be using to learn new vocabulary. Don't worry about the response categories on this occasion, just the statements with a broad heading of 'How often do you . . ?'

Now think carefully about how you arrived at these statements. Was it:

1. Strategies you had read about?
2. Strategies that you use yourself?
3. Strategies that you have somehow noticed the students using?
4. Strategies that you have actually suggested they use?
5. Strategies that you have discovered from reading this book thus far?

If they are strategies that you use (or have used) yourself to learn a foreign language, but have not suggested these to your students, can you think of reasons why you have refrained from doing so?

Here are the five statements that were used in the Lingua project which relate to vocabulary acquisition. It was from the data from these statements that the idea of a learner training project in vocabulary acquisition came (described in the next chapter):

1. I practise saying new words out loud (at home).
2. I practise saying new words under my breath (at school).
3. I make a note of new words (at home or school).
4. I make a mental association when trying to memorize difficult new words (perhaps with something funny) (at home or school).

5. I learn new vocabulary through a system that suits me (e.g. look, hide, say, write, check) (at home or school).

These statements in the questionnaire have underpinning them the kinds of theories about cognition that were touched upon in the last chapter. The interest therefore was to find out what kind of a range of strategies the students were using, including visual/graphic; visual/ imaging; sound; keyword association in order to store language in long-term memory.

Questionnaires have been used in other studies to find how strategy use *varies* among different groups of learners. For example, 'independent variables' such as sex, age, level of language learning (or number of years of language study), ethnic or cultural background, social group – all these can be included in a questionnaire in order to see if they have an effect on the types and frequency of strategies used. An example of this type of study is the very large-scale one carried out by Oxford and Nyikos (1989) with university students.

Questionnaires can be used to make comparisons between different aspects of language learning, for example, reading and listening or indeed between L1 strategies and L2 strategies. Patricia Carrell (1989) used a questionnaire to ask students what their strategies were when they were doing silent reading, particularly their metacognitive strategies, in order to establish whether her readers read differently in their first and second languages.

Finally, questionnaires have been used to gauge whether strategy use has changed over a period of time, particularly if it changed due to a period of learner training in the use of strategies. In the writing strategies project I used such an approach where the 14–15-year-old students were given a 'pre-treatment' questionnaire (before strategy training) and a 'post-treatment' questionnaire (after strategy training). Here are some questions that were asked in the pre-treatment questionnaire (these are not necessarily in the order they were in).

Question 1

How often do you think that you look words up in *a dictionary* when doing a written composition (that is, looking up English words to find out what the French is)? This may not be easy to estimate but please have a go. (Please tick only one.)

☐   Nearly every word
☐   One word in every five
☐   One word in every ten
☐   Hardly any words
☐   I never look words up in a dictionary

PAUSE FOR THOUGHT

Do you think that different students might have interpreted the meaning of this question differently? In which way?

Could they have interpreted 'looking up words in a dictionary' to mean 'in order to check the spelling' of the word? Or does the phrase 'English words to find out what the French is' make it absolutely clear?

If they *could* have interpreted them differently, then we would say that the question lacked full *validity*. The idea that was in the researcher's head (the 'construct') was not the same as the construct that was in the respondents' heads. Hopefully, the question was a valid one because of the way it was formulated.

Question 2

This question is trying to find out *how you go about* doing a writing task. For each of the following statements try to estimate how much these strategies 'are like you' by ticking *one of the five* boxes.

(a) I think of a sentence in English and then try to translate it into French

A lot like me		←——→		Not at all like me
☐	☐	☐	☐	☐

(b) I think of a sentence in English and then, if I know the French for it, I will use it

A lot like me		←——→		Not at all like me
☐	☐	☐	☐	☐

(c)   I think of all the French sentences that I know and only use those

<table>
<tr><td>A lot
like me</td><td></td><td>←——→</td><td></td><td>Not at all
like me</td></tr>
<tr><td>☐</td><td>☐</td><td>☐</td><td>☐</td><td>☐</td></tr>
</table>

(d) I think of bits of language I know (e.g. short phrases) and try to put them together so that they make sense

<table>
<tr><td>A lot
like me</td><td></td><td>←——→</td><td></td><td>Not at all
like me</td></tr>
<tr><td>☐</td><td>☐</td><td>☐</td><td>☐</td><td>☐</td></tr>
</table>

(e) I use bits of language from the materials the teacher has given me and put them together so that they make sense

<table>
<tr><td>A lot
like me</td><td></td><td>←——→</td><td></td><td>Not at all
like me</td></tr>
<tr><td>☐</td><td>☐</td><td>☐</td><td>☐</td><td>☐</td></tr>
</table>

I do other things. Please describe . . . .

PAUSE FOR THOUGHT

Can you see why all these sub-questions were asked? Can you think of other ways they might compose L2 sentences?

(f) I use *a combination* of all the above ways

<table>
<tr><td>Always</td><td>Sometimes</td><td>Never</td></tr>
<tr><td>☐</td><td>☐</td><td>☐</td></tr>
</table>

Question 3

How do you check your written work? (Please tick one only from a–d.)

☐   (a) I mostly check my work as I write (e.g. sentence by sentence; word by word)

☐   (b) I write the whole thing without stopping to check and do most of my checking when I've finished writing

☐   (c) I don't really check my work

☐   (d) I leave the first draft for a while and come back to it later for checking (e.g. just before going to bed)

I have other ways of checking. Please give details . . . .

Question 4

If you have answered (a), (b) or (d) in question 3 please tell us what sorts of things you check. Please tick *only one box* from each one.

I check the spelling of words

☐   very often   ☐   fairly often   ☐   never

I check the word order

☐   very often   ☐   fairly often   ☐   never

I check the endings of words

☐   very often   ☐   fairly often   ☐   never

I check that it makes sense (e.g. by translating it back into English)

☐   very often   ☐   fairly often   ☐   never

I read the piece of writing out loud to see if it sounds right

☐   very often   ☐   fairly often   ☐   never

I look for mistakes I make all the time

☐   very often   ☐   fairly often   ☐   never

I do other things. Please give details . . . .

PAUSE FOR THOUGHT

When the researcher gathers all the open comments from the end of each question (the 'I do other things' comments, is there a danger that this data can be unreliable? Can you think of ways in which this could be the case?

If you and I separately collected all the 'other things' that the students said they did, is there a danger that we might interpret the data differently by attributing too much importance to, for example, what one student said he or she did? This is an issue of *reliability*.

Question 5

How do you rate yourself as a writer of French on a scale of 1–5? Please circle a number.

Very good   Poor

  1   2   3   4   5

Question 6

How much do you enjoy writing in French on a scale of 1–5? Please circle a number.

A lot   Not at all

  1   2   3   4   5

The issues of validity and reliability when carrying out research are thorny ones. This shouldn't stop you doing research on your own students but it should guard you against using questionnaires that haven't been properly thought through and from making hasty judgements from too little data (sometimes called 'high inference' analysis).

Let us return to the actual writing strategies project. After the questionnaire the students went through a period of learner training. This is described in Chapter 5. The questionnaire was also given to a non-treatment group or control group – one which did not receive the learner training.

PAUSE FOR THOUGHT

Look at the questions in the pre-treatment questionnaire. Imagine that your class had responded to these questions, then spent a few months discussing and experimenting with different strategies when preparing, composing and checking their writing. How would you at the end of that period try to find out if their strategy frequency or use had changed? Try to write out three or four questions that you would ask. You may also like to have a go at writing a series of questions that could be given to the control group. Don't forget that the control group would *not* have received any strategy training.

Interviews

Interviewing language learners about the way that they use strategies can be very productive and an excellent way of complementing a questionnaire. Of course it takes a long time to interview a whole class, let alone all your classes. But there are ways of reducing the onerous nature of this task. You can choose a selection of students to interview, perhaps two of those you consider most successful at language learning, two least successful and two in the middle. Or you can divide your class into groups of, say, six and carry out a more informal discussion with them about their strategy use. It is always useful to record the interviews or conversations even if you only have time to listen to them in a fleeting manner later. It is difficult to take notes when you are conducting an interview or chairing a discussion.

The advantage of group discussions is that you get a lot of interaction because they tend to feel more comfortable and they are more likely to react to each other's ideas. One of the disadvantages is that, particularly with adolescent learners, they may be pressurized by their peers into not telling you what they really do.

Interviews have been used in different ways in the quest for strategy use elicitation. Suzanne Graham used a 'semi-structured retrospective' interview technique (Graham 1997: 43) to elicit the strategies used by 17 year olds when carrying out a listening task. Semi-structured refers to the extent to which your interview questions are 'fixed' in your mind or on your interview prompt sheet and to what extent you allow your interviewee to diverge into other areas. A semi-structured list has a number of general questions you want answered but if the diverging route looks like a useful one to follow, you allow the respondent to proceed down it, perhaps bringing him/her back to your own line of questioning when the topic you have discussed feels as if it has been fully explored. Retrospective, here simply means that they were asked to *think back* to every time they did a listening task and try to articulate their strategies. One problem with this is that the more learners become distanced from the actual language learning task, the more they are likely to become inaccurate in reporting how they went about the task.

Fay Fleming and Geoff Walls (1998) used a post-task interview technique to elicit the strategies that 'successful' 14 year olds were using when organizing and conducting a paired dialogue. They were mainly interested in the metacognitive, social and affective strategies that the students were using. They wanted to know how they planned the task, monitored their progress with the task, and how they co-operated in the task. They also wanted to find out which language the students used to think in (the L1 or the L2), more of a cognitive strategy. The semi-structured interviews were conducted *immediately after* the students had done the task.

Another study using interviews has been carried out by Lynn Erler from the University of Oxford with 11 year olds who had been learning French for only one year (Erler in progress). One of the things she wanted to find out was what strategies they used when trying to read more difficult French words. Did they hear the word in their heads, did they sound out the word, did they just skip the word, etc.? Erler interviewed the students in pairs and, in addition, provided them with words on cards both as a way finding out if they found the word difficult and as a stimulus for strategy use elicitation. In a further session she timed the students to see how long it took them to start reading (out loud) each word. To put it another way, she tried to find out what the processing time was that it took each student, from the moment they saw the word to the moment they started to articulate the word. She then compared this to their ability to pronounce the word correctly as well as their *perception* of how difficult the word was to read out loud.

Using a stimulus as a way of improving strategy elicitation needs to be explored further. The stimulus helps to overcome the problem of recalling the strategies being used in a task done some time previously without, as we shall see, the incumbent problems of eliciting strategy use during an actual language task. For example, if you wanted to find answers to your questions in Chapter 1 about what strategies your students use to understand your 'procedural instructions', you could video-record yourself providing instructions for a task or activity and then play the recording back to groups or individuals at a later stage in order to stimulate their recollection of what they did. This would be a particularly useful piece of classroom research for pre-service or novice teachers as it would give a real indication of just how difficult it is for beginners in particular to understand complex procedural instructions.

In a similar vein, during a paired oral task, Mike Grenfell and Vee Harris used an audio recording as a stimulus. Specific stages in the oral task were envisaged as being worthy of strategy elicitation, the task being prompted by a series of photos followed by some general questions. When the conversations were played back to the learners, the latter were invited to pause the tape and comment on their performance and their feelings at the time or in retrospect (Grenfell and Harris 1999: 53).

PAUSE FOR THOUGHT

Of course to call this a pause for thought is daft! You have been thinking all the time as you have read this chapter, and it would be arrogant of me to suggest that you only 'think' when I use a stimulus such as 'pause for thought'. But in a sense this illustrates the distinction between controlled and automatized processes. To what extent were you aware of your thinking, about what you were reading, as you read this chapter? Some of the time (hopefully not too often) when I hadn't succeeded in making my meaning clear, you would have stopped reading and thought about it in a more *controlled* way. At other times the process by which the passage of the meaning from a specific sentence in the book to a 'proposition' lodged in a more abstract form in your long-term memory would have been in a less controlled way. Perhaps you would find it difficult to articulate what this more automatic strategy was or how it was being deployed.

Can you think of three strategies that your foreign language learners might be using 'automatically' which they would find very difficult to articulate in an interview without some sort of stimulus? They would have to be things that they did quite a lot. For example, when reading a sentence 'looking for clues in the words on either side of a word which is not familiar to them'.

Interviews are an attempt to get closer than questionnaires to what learners actually do. But they are still not inside the learners' heads. Let's see if we can get a little further in.

Task-based self-report

In a task-based self-report, the learners are still telling you what they do in order to carry out the task but this time it is temporally more directly linked to the strategies used, as they are being used. We are still not observing or hearing the strategies themselves but they are being reported sufficiently contemporaneously such that we are surer that these were the strategies that were actually being used. By way of illustration we could say that there is a difference between the three (hypothetical) self-reported strategies below. Imagine that you had asked a student to articulate the strategies that she was employing in order to understand a piece of (L2) French written text. These are three different things which she might have reported:

Report 1

I really only looked up words in the dictionary which I couldn't guess from the rest of the sentence or from the context.

or

Report 2

I'm really only looking up words in the dictionary which I can't guess from the rest of the sentence or the context.

or

Report 3

OK, I don't know what this word is, can't work it out from the words around it . . . title of the text . . . uh, pottery in 16th Century France . . . no . . . doesn't really help . . . gonna have to look it up in my dictionary (*picks up dictionary*) . . . OK 'moules' m, m, m, mo, mou . . . moule one mussel, two mould . . . which can it be?

What we have in each of these reports is, first of all, a cognitive strategy: looking around a difficult word in order to guess or infer meaning. We then have a metacognitive strategy: evaluating/deciding when to give up on strategy number 1 and use a dictionary. Then, in report 3 only, evidence of a *learnt* strategy in the self-questioning with regard to the dictionary.

In the first of the three hypothetical report extracts above the student is reporting her strategy/strategies after a certain time has elapsed and after an assessment is being made by her that this is a *repeated strategy*, sufficiently repeated that it becomes what she perceives as a routine. She could have been prompted to divulge this strategy immediately the task finished or even at a certain point during the reading task, for example, after each paragraph in the text. This is a technique that was used in the writing strategies project. Here, as they were carrying out a writing task, the students could see on the page opposite the kinds of questions that they were going to be asked to respond to regarding strategy use when they had completed the task (see Figure 2.1). So they could be thinking about their strategy use *while* writing but without the interrupting and possible distracting effect of *actually* writing about strategy use (in L1) while they were writing about their work experience (in L2).

In the second hypothetical report extract the student is still reporting strategy use after it has happened but reflecting on it as, almost, a contemporary event. Consequently, there is less of an assessment being made by her that this is routine and that, in fact, there is the possibility that this set of strategies will not be used later in the text. This was a technique used by Nyhus (1994) where the subjects being researched were given a text with red dots placed between sentences to encourage them and prompt them to articulate their thoughts. If we were to put a request for an explanation of strategy use, using some kind of symbol, in a reading comprehension text, say, every three sentences, we might well get this sort of response.

The third report extract would be almost impossible to carry out in written form. It would interfere too much with the reading task in hand. It therefore has to be *verbalized*. This is a process of articulating one's thoughts and actions as one is carrying them out. This is usually called a think-aloud verbal report (or think-aloud protocol). Here the subject is not so much reporting what she is doing as providing evidence of what she is doing. With this kind of technique the teacher or researcher begins to take over and begins to do the 'observing' and 'interpreting' of what is actually going on in terms of strategy use. However, this technique is not without its problems as we shall see when we look at some transcriptions of think-alouds in later chapters. Certainly, thinking aloud about a language-related issue is more complex than doing so, say, about an arithmetical problem. This may be because language has semantics whereas numbers do not. For example, the following is perfectly possible as 'real' thinking out loud and we can almost 'see the mind working' and using strategies to talk through the problem:

Seventy-two times five . . . seventy-two times five . . . OK . . . five times two is . . . two times five is ten . . . five times seven is thirty-five and one is thirty-six . . . three hundred and sixty.

Before we go on to observing and interpreting, there are some other

Instructions for the students

Pretend that you have just come back from your first day of work experience. You have been asked by your teacher to write a little report (80 to 100 words), which should include:

a. A brief description of the workplace (e.g. shop / office), of your boss, Mrs O'Neill, and of Mark, one of your colleagues in the office (in the present tense and no more than 30 words long).

b. An account, in the past tense, of what you did which should include the description of something that went wrong while you were working, e.g. a little accident/problem (about 70–80 words).

....
....
....
....
....
....
....
....
....
....
....
....
....
....
....
....

Name: _____

Date: _____

After you have done the task, answer the following questions:

Try to explain your thoughts and actions about the task <u>before you started writing</u>.

....
....
....

Try to explain what you did during the writing in order to compose the report. What was your thinking process?

....
....
....

In what ways did you check your writing? For example, one sentence at a time; couple of words at a time; at the end.

....
....
....

What did you find easy about composing the report?

....
....
....

What did you find difficult about composing the report?

....
....
....

Figure 2.1 *Writing task*

very simple and effective ways of collecting self-report data. These are usually linked to specific strategies or clusters of strategies. For example, in a written task we can ask learners to record all the words that they looked up in a dictionary to see the variance between the learners in the whole class. Or we could ask them to put a circle around all the phrases they were absolutely sure about and compare the number of 'recycled' perhaps 'formulaic' phrases they were using as compared to all the phases that they had to 'put together' in a creative ('generated') sentence sort of way. In classroom oral discussion we could ask learners to keep a tally of all the times they noticed something new about the language (we will return to this notion of noticing in later chapters).

An intermediate technique is possible between self-report and 'observing' the learners' strategies. This technique may be particularly effective in eliciting listening strategies where strategy elicitation can be highly intrusive to the activity of actually listening attentively and decoding the oral text. An intermediate technique was attempted, with evident success, by Susan Bacon with 50 first-year students at an American university who were studying Spanish as a foreign language (Bacon 1992). They were provided with two, short, authentic listening texts culturally accessible to them (one more narrative, the other more technical). In order to help them focus on strategies as well as comprehension of the text, they were instructed to nod or raise their finger whenever they caught themselves thinking about what they had heard, then to focus on understanding the spoken text. After listening they were asked first to report on the strategies they recalled having used and, second, to report what they had understood. A similar attempt at an intermediate technique was adopted by O'Malley *et al.* (1989) who inserted 'short pauses in taped texts during which the interviewer stopped the tape and asked students to relate as much as they could about their thoughts whilst listening' (ibid.: 131).

Observing the learners
Think-aloud protocols
Let us think about think-aloud protocols just a little more and in particular how we can ensure that we get the best information out of them. The normal procedure for eliciting the data from a think-aloud protocol is to take the following steps:

1. Provide a student with a task (usually a reading or writing task) and ensure that they understand what they have to do to accomplish it.

2. Find ways of making them feel at ease.
3. Explain that you want them to articulate their thought processes and the strategies that they use while they are actually carrying out the task.
4. Demonstrate how this thinking-aloud process can be done by doing some of it yourself (with a similar task).
5. Start recording.
6. Start the student off.
7. Prompt the student if they are not articulating their thoughts and actions sufficiently.
8. Prompt but avoid using phrases like 'Are you sure?' and 'That's good'. Instead, use only phrases like: 'What makes you say that?'; 'What made you do that?'; 'What are you thinking at this moment?'; 'Please keep talking'.
9. Listen to the recording of the think-aloud process (after the session) and make a list of all the strategies used by the student.
10. Look carefully through the results of the task (after the session). What features of it might have been improved by better (or more frequent) strategy use?

PAUSE FOR THOUGHT

Although think-aloud protocols have been very widely applied in the elicitation of strategy use, they are not without their problems. Make a list of all the problems that might be associated with each of the above ten steps in the procedure.

In Suzanne Graham's study of 17-year-old advanced level students, think-aloud protocols were used to elicit reading comprehension strategies. The data that she collected were, however, probably a mixture of reporting what they had just done as well as actually verbalizing what they were doing. According to Graham: 'They might begin by simply externalising thoughts going through their head, then make inferences about the processes involved and finally make an observation which would suggest an element of looking back on what they had done' (Graham 1997: 44).

In the study by Mike Grenfell and Vee Harris the three learners were also asked to carry out think-aloud protocols based on a reading comprehension task. Again, the authors indicate that this technique is not without its limitations: 'It is difficult to select a reading text that is sufficiently accessible but also offers opportunities for learners to deploy the full range of strategies they have at their disposal' (Grenfell and Harris 1999: 53).

Think-aloud protocols were used both in the Lingua study and the Oxford Writing Strategies project. In the Lingua study (in the reading comprehension part) a similar problem to the one above arose. As a comparison was being made between students from two cultures, two nationalities and with different L2s, equivalence in choice of text for the task was extremely difficult to decide on. Only the most 'central' strategies could be compared, those that appeared common to both sets of subjects and both sets of texts. However, it could be argued that those strategies which appeared central were in fact only so because of the matching process between the two different languages of the texts (L2), the different L1s and the different teaching and learning contexts which the subjects were operating in. If we compared strategies applied to two different L2 texts and with different L1 learners (e.g. Japanese learners of English compared to Turkish learners of German), we might even arrive at a different set of central strategies. In other words, we are still some way from establishing that strategies are universal to all second languages.

In the writing project protocols one of the most problematic of the limitations was the matching up of thought and action. Whereas in a reading comprehension think aloud (where the student is merely demonstrating understanding orally), there is very little action, in a writing task the student is writing, speaking, looking up words in a dictionary, crossing out, going back and checking, reading through in L2, reading through by back-translating. All these visible or audible actions may be only surface manifestations of more subtle, underlying strategies. The other problem was quite simply that some learners were just a lot better at the process of thinking aloud than others. We do not know for sure if the latter's lack of verbalized strategy use was due to poverty of strategy use or inability to verbalize.

We can now collect a number of disparate thoughts and observations on think-aloud protocols. First, despite their limitations, most authors look on them favourably as a means of discovering not so much the frequency and range of strategy use but when and in what way they are used and the effect they have on achieving a given language task. More importantly perhaps, they provide an insight into the decision-making that learners engage in – *the if X, then Y* process of cognition. Whether this is at a very conscious level or at a more subconscious level varies considerably according to the requirements of the task. Nevertheless, the problems and limitations of think-aloud protocols have to be recognized.

As I have already suggested, thinking aloud in an L2 task will not get as close to the real thought process as working through an arithmetical problem out loud. When you considered these limitations in the 10 steps above, you may have come up with some of the following ideas matched against the steps:

1. The type of task will have an effect on strategy use not only because of its intrinsic nature but also because of the language that is involved. In a reading comprehension task, very different strategies will be used by students who are familiar with the language of the task than by those who are not. Comparisons should therefore be made with care. Pitching a text or task just above the competence or performance level of the students is tricky.

2. In any interview situation students will not feel at ease. This factor is increased if they are being required not just to give their thoughts and opinions but also carry out a complex linguistic task. Anxiety is most likely to occur with adolescent learners.

3. The nature of what you want them to do may not be obvious to them without a demonstration, and, even then, thinking aloud may be an alien activity for learners who are normally introspective.

4. Your own demonstration of the thinking aloud process may produce preconceptions about the strategies that they should use in the task and therefore bias their responses.

5. Inevitably the point at which you start recording will be an arbitrary one. The student may well have started planning the task before you switch on the tape.

6. Ditto step 5.

7. How often should you prompt? Might the prompt interfere with an actual thought process about the language in the task or even the articulation of a strategy?

8. It is all too easy to sound like a teacher when prompting. Even phrases like 'What makes you say that?' may be interpreted as suggesting that the strategy just articulated was 'wrong'. 'What are you thinking at this moment?' needs just the right tone of voice so as not to sound intrusive or even 'bullying'.

9. Is each strategy discrete and definable? If it is, how do you know what sub-sets of strategies are lying below the articulated strategy? How has your own bias about important strategies affected which strategies you have been able to discern?

10. To what extent did the student not achieve the task simply because of the extra processing load on the working memory brought about by having to articulate strategies? To what extent did the process of articulating strategies already bring about a kind of initial awareness raising and therefore produce a better task result?

Think-aloud protocols are very time-consuming, perhaps the most time-consuming of all the strategy elicitation techniques. This is because there is no choice of cut-off point. The student really has to finish the task, otherwise comparisons between students is somewhat invalid. But there are other, less time-consuming ways of observing strategy use. We can 'look for traces' of strategy use.

Looking for traces
Although the following may not be as scientific and comprehensive as the above techniques, they do offer the busy teacher an opportunity to make a start with thinking about how their learners are learning. For each of the following it is advisable, at the very least, to take down some notes (field notes as they are sometimes called) during or after the lesson, about what the students appear to be doing to help themselves learn. In this way some sort of systematic pattern may start to emerge.

1. When engaged in questioning sequences we can observe which students are moving their lips which might be an indication that they are preparing themselves to speak by practising under their breath.
2. When engaged in questioning sequences we can observe to what extent and which students are 'buying processing time' by using such markers as 'uh' or 'well' or other discourse markers designed to show that they wish to keep their turn.
3. When engaged in any activity which involves students speaking we can observe to what extent they are employing the compensation strategy of circumlocution (finding alternative ways of saying something they don't know how to say) and the positive or negative effects that this has.
4. When presenting new language we can look around the class to see which students are taking notes of what is being said or written.
5. We can observe which students are asking a friend for help when they don't understand and in general which students like to collaborate in their language learning.

6. When speaking with written support (e.g. a dialogue, role-play or jigsaw activity), we can observe which students are sounding out words before saying them and to what extent this is helping or hindering their transition from graphic medium to oral medium.
7. When attempting a group reading comprehension (or collaborative reading task), we can observe which students are reasoning by deduction ('it must mean this because of this').
8. When attempting a listening comprehension 'feedback session'[1] we can identify which students are focusing on every word rather than the gist and the positive or negative effect that this is having. In addition we can, from time to time, enlist the help of a colleague or assistant by asking them to stand behind the students and note which sections of a recorded text they are having difficulty with.
9. When we have asked students to carry out a writing task, we can observe how many students plunge straight into the activity and which students spend some time planning their work.
10. In a reading or writing task we can observe which students use the dictionary and with what frequency.

One quite innovative form of 'looking for traces' in task-based learning is the use of computers. For example, Baily (1996) carried out a study of French learners and their frequency of use of resources while they were in the process of written composition using a computer. The computer was able to track how the students compensated, by using software resources, for deficiencies in vocabulary and sentence structure.

We started this chapter by bemoaning the fact that we couldn't get inside the students' heads in order to find out what strategies they use, i.e. how they go about learning. We have come a long way since then. It looks as if we can make the most of a frustrating situation by finding alternative ways: by asking and by observing or both. One thing we need to ask ourselves before we finish this chapter is, in which language are we going to carry out this strategy use elicitation? Are we going to use the students' L1 or the target language that they are studying?

Use of L1 in strategy elicitation

We will remember that one of the criticisms levelled at learner training is that it is time taken away from learners simply learning the language. In the next chapter I shall be arguing that investigating your students' current strategy use is an essential component of a training cycle. We therefore need to ask the question about how effective strategy elicitation will be in either the learner's L1 or L2.

Some authors have argued (e.g. Harbord 1992; Macaro 1997) that one of the drawbacks of excluding the L1 from the foreign language classroom is that it creates an obstacle in trying to establish close relationships with students. Getting to know them on a less formal level is impeded because of the lack of language that learners (particularly beginner learners) have at their disposal. Building social relationships, as opposed to the didactic aspects of teaching and learning, requires complex nuances of language. I have also argued elsewhere (ibid.) that those teachers who would like to take steps towards learner autonomy in general find their efforts blocked by the exclusion of L1 because of the amount of organizational language needed to set up more independent learning activities.

In the same vein, it became obvious to teachers on the two projects described in this book that at least some of the elicitation instruments have to be in L1. Beginners particularly would otherwise just not understand them. This does not mean that every favourable opportunity to produce a questionnaire in the L2 should not be taken up. Advanced students should be able to cope with most of the written questions that we have seen examples of in this chapter. If some of the questions are difficult, they can simply be expressed in both languages or a glossary of terms provided. Whether the students are to answer in L1 or L2 will depend on a number of factors, not least their own beliefs about which language they would feel happier to express themselves in.

The situation is more complex with interviews and think-aloud protocols because of the switching from one language to another (known as 'codeswitching') that would have to take place. What does the research tell us about this? First, there is nothing intrinsically unnatural about codeswitching. Advanced bilinguals do this all the time. But there do seem to be some natural rules involved in codeswitching. For example, bilinguals never switch in the middle of a sentence with a closed class of words. Closed classes of words are things like prepositions and pronouns – all the types of words that you can't add to the lexicon of a language without changing the language itself. But nouns and verbs and adjectives are all lexical elements which are constantly being added to a language and these, research suggests, are the elements which bilinguals codeswitch with both frequency and ease. In fact, codeswitching into your more familiar L1 word(s) is a compensation strategy often used when conversing with other bilinguals. In some cases, it can even be a kind of enrichment strategy because some words express a concept better in one language than in another.

If we accept the above arguments, then it is perfectly feasible to conduct parts of an interview in the foreign language and parts of it in the L1. The think-aloud protocols, on the other hand, may present a greater difficulty. It is one thing to codeswitch within the same communicative framework (sometimes called a 'language plane') but quite another to do so in vastly different ones: the plane of the task itself and the plane of verbalizing the strategies. Again, what can research tell us that might be of help? There is strong evidence to suggest that, even with advanced learners, the language of thought for some tasks (particularly where there is plenty of processing time, as in writing) is the L1. The switch from thinking in L1 to L2 may become increasingly fast so as to be almost imperceptible (or unreportable) but it is there none the less. Since most think-aloud protocols are conducted using tasks where there is an abundance of processing time, it would follow that there would be an element of L1 thought for both the language processing and the processing involved in verbalizing strategies. It would seem therefore advisable to conduct think-aloud interviews in the student's L1. The questions we always have to ask ourselves are: what will make the student feel more at ease and to what extent am I sacrificing a real in-depth understanding of how the student goes about learning for the sake of a few extra exchanges in the target language?

I have taken this brief digression into the theory behind the debate on the value of the L1 in the language classroom because it is a question that we need to ask ourselves not just in the elicitation stage of the strategy training cycle but also in later stages. We will thus have to return to this issue in later chapters. But before we do this we need to be convinced that strategy training can actually be beneficial. The purpose of the next three chapters is to examine the results of some of the studies described above as well as the results of other studies.

BEFORE WE MOVE ON

How much of what you have read and thought about in this chapter did you already know? If you already knew a lot, to what extent has *thinking about it again* helped to clarify your ideas and concepts? If much of this chapter was new to you, try to summarize in a few sentences each of the following:

1. What are some of the problems associated with strategies elicited via 'self-report'?

2. What are some of the problems associated with strategies elicited by 'observing' students while they are engaged in a language task of some kind?

Have you begun to formulate some of the over-arching questions about strategy use that you might like to investigate with your students? Are these related to more 'indirect' strategies or are you more interested in the 'direct' strategies they apply to a language task?

How do you react to the idea that strategy elicitation can be:

1. Carried out in L1?
2. Carried out with a mixture of L1 and L2?

How do you now feel about carrying out a strategy elicitation project with your students? Are you daunted? Confident? Sceptical?

For further reading on research methodology these works offer a wide range of experience and are generally fairly accessible. Cohen and Manion (1994) provides a comprehensive manual for consultation on appropriate techniques for carrying out research. Cohen (1998: 24–64) provides an overview of research methods specifically for the purposes of strategy elicitation. Ericsson and Simon (1987) and Anderson and Vandergrift (1996) provide a thorough discussion of think-aloud as a technique for strategy elicitation.

Note

1. By this I mean when the teacher goes back over the task with the students in order to gauge how much they have understood.

CHAPTER 3

Studies which Describe Strategy Use

In Chapter 1 we explored our own understanding of the way that our students learn and related this to our beliefs about language learning. We began to make a list of *primary* strategies that students use both in direct contact with the target language and those that they use as a *support* for their learning. We have noted that research suggests that there are some broad variations according to sex, age, beliefs and motivation in strategy frequency and strategy deployment. In Chapter 2 we explored the possible methods that we can use in order to investigate how our own students learn. In doing so we continued to build on the list of possible strategies that they might use. In the next three chapters we will focus on the findings of studies in order to see whether these can illuminate and inform solutions to the problems that we encountered in Chapter 1. Some studies will be described only briefly as they merely provide a background to the findings. Others we will look at in some detail because they would appear to have immediate applicability to teachers working in all types of L2 classrooms.

Studies in learner strategies fall into two basic types. The first is a broad clutch of *descriptive* studies. These have attempted to define:

1. the features of a good language learner;
2. the total number of strategies that learners (or groups of learners) use. This definitive list is sometimes referred to as a taxonomy.
3. comparisons of strategy use between one group of learners and another group of learners.

The second is a clutch of *intervention* studies. These have attempted to discover whether it is possible to bring about change in strategy use in learners through, in most cases, a process of learner training by the teacher or by researchers. In other words, they describe the process of teachers helping students to 'learn to learn'. The underlying aim with this type of study is that change in strategy use will bring about improved language competence. These will be discussed in the next two chapters.

What the research literature can tell us

The earlier studies of the 1970s and 1980s on learner strategies were essentially attempts to explore a broad range of strategies and they usually tried to relate this range to a concept of a good language learner. Later studies have narrowed down the focus to particular areas (such as memorization of vocabulary), and have explored learners performing specific tasks, or have made comparisons between groups.

Studies of good language learners

One of the seminal descriptive studies on good language learners is described in Naiman *et al.*'s book called, in fact, *The Good Language Learner* (new edition 1996) which was originally published in 1975. The first part of the study was of 34 adult learners who were selected on the basis of them being successful learners or 'highly proficient' (ibid.: 9), as rated by the interviewers themselves or 'through recommendation', coming as they did mostly 'from our immediate university circles, from departments such as curriculum, anthropology, linguistics and modern languages' (ibid.: 10). The interviews showed that these highly academic learners (but possibly varied in terms of learning styles) attributed their language learning success to the following strategies:

1. An active approach to tasks (by responding positively to learning opportunities and finding ways to exploit them).
2. By treating language as a system (e.g. by making effective comparisons with their L1; making inferences).
3. By (also) treating language as a means of communication (e.g. by emphasizing fluency over accuracy in the early stages of learning).
4. By managing the affective demands of language learning (e.g. by overcoming inhibitions to speak; laughing at their own mistakes).
5. By monitoring their performance (e.g. by testing their hypotheses; wanting to be corrected).

We can see that these learners had a tendency to describe their approach to language learning in broad terms, not necessarily those strategies directly applied to language learning or not in the explicit, 'pinpointed' fashion that we have been trying to achieve. Of course it may be that the way the researchers asked the questions was in very broad terms. Sometimes in research it's a question of 'don't ask don't get'.

It was only when researchers began to delve more deeply and tried to get somewhere near what we might call 'an irreducible strategy' (a mental or physical process related to language learning which cannot be further broken down) that taxonomies of strategy use began to emerge. A series of descriptive studies of this kind was carried out by Michael O'Malley and co-researchers (reported in O'Malley and Chamot 1990) who looked at strategies used both by ESL student and FL students. Although their prime concern was to arrive at a taxonomy, they too discovered that the most successful learners seemed to correlate with those who used meta-cognitive strategies. By using these support strategies they were more aware of the whole process of learning a second language. The meta-cognitive strategies identified by O'Malley and Chamot (1990: 119) were:

1. Advance organization (previewing the task in hand in order, for example, to look for an organizing principle).
2. Directed attention (deciding in advance to focus on the task and avoid distraction).
3. Selective attention (deciding in advance to focus on specific aspects of the language, for example, by scanning for key words, concepts, etc.).
4. Functional planning (planning and rehearsing linguistic elements necessary to carry out a language task).
5. Self-management (understanding the conditions that best suited their learning and ensuring that those conditions were in place when carrying out a language task).
6. Self-monitoring (for example, checking one's speech for accuracy or for appropriateness as one is speaking).
7. Delayed production (consciously deciding to postpone speaking to learn, initially through listening).

In addition, successful learners (as in the study by Naiman *et al.* 1996) used social/affective strategies to reduce their anxiety in order to make themselves feel able to do the learning task.

Chamot and Küpper (1989) went further than merely describing the strategies that good language learners used. They looked at how they used them *in combination*. They discovered that it was the flexibility of their subjects in adopting metacognitive strategy use which made cognitive and social-affective strategy use more effective. It was the evaluation and decision-making process (the effective deployment of strategies) rather than the activity of engaging in strategy use itself which was a feature of the good language learner.

As we have noted in Chapter 1, Suzanne Graham's contention resulting from her study (Graham 1997) is that good language learners consider language learning an effortful process. In her book she describes one particular successful 17-year-old learner of German. Student M devoted more energy to her language learning than most of her peers. But what was interesting was that her effort was channelled into two fairly distinct but evidently complementary directions. On the one hand, she was assiduous in devoting an enormous amount of time to vocabulary and grammar learning and varied in her list of strategies for memorization; she was also meticulous in looking up and re-using new language. On the other, she was able to stand back from the learning process and reflect on it: she considered that spending time in the foreign country lay behind successful language learning; she determined to build up her self-confidence by frequent contributions in class; and she evaluated ways of coping best with difficult listening comprehension tasks. In other words, high levels of self-direction meant that she 'seemed to have enough insight to have discovered independently a highly effective mode of learning at an early stage, a quality which may be an essential feature of what is commonly referred to as aptitude' (Graham 1997: 151).

In the Lingua study it was possible to compare not only the strategies used by adolescent boys and girls but also to compare strategies used by learners in England and learners in Italy. As we have noted in Chapter 1, this is useful in order to see if different learning environments give rise to different strategy use. We will therefore investigate this study in some detail.

The Lingua study

We should note that the list of strategies that the students were given was drawn up with 14 year olds in mind. It was not intended to be a comprehensive list of strategies used but as an initial entry into the way they worked. In fact, a selection of only 25 strategies was given to the students for them to answer.

First, let us see what strategies were being used most by all the respondents in the Lingua study. Table 3.1 provides an analysis of direct strategies used by learners. We will need to remember that if they said they used the strategy 'often' this was coded as '1'. Therefore the lower the mean score, the more frequently they reported the strategy being used.

Table 3.1   *Direct strategies*

Strategy	Mean in ascending order (i.e. most often used first) for both countries
start from known words	1.73
answer others' questions (in your head)	1.76
guess from context when reading	2.10
guess from context when listening	2.19
think if words look like L1 words	2.42
silent practice (thinking in your head)	2.49
learn vocabulary, etc. by a system	2.57
repeat words to self (in class)	2.68
make mental associations (of difficult words and phrases)	2.88
practise new words under breath (in class)	2.99
practise new words out loud (at home)	3.01
Total mean for both countries	2.43
Total mean for Italians only	2.49
Total mean for English only	2.38

Key (often = 1; sometimes = 2; not often = 3; rarely = 4; never = 5)
Note: N = 368

PAUSE FOR THOUGHT

Direct strategies, we should remind ourselves, are strategies that learners use to decode, make links, process, practise and store the foreign language. Look at the list of strategies in Table 3.1. Can you subdivide these direct strategies into the following?:

1. strategies used to make sense of or decode language;
2. strategies used to practise language;
3. strategies used to commit language to long-term memory.

Do any strategies serve more than one function? What other conclusions could we draw from analysing this table?

We note that 'answering other's questions in your head directed at other people' (a practising strategy) was the single most used strategy along with 'start from known words' (a decoding strategy).

The discovery that 'answering others' questions in your head' scores so highly is probably explained by the fact that questioning techniques are widespread in all types of classrooms in all types of cultural contexts. It is not surprising that this direct strategy should be recalled by learners as being highly used, given that the opportunities for using it are almost constantly present in foreign language classrooms. Of course, we can assume that it is a very effective learner strategy in ensuring maintenance of attention on the activity in hand and efficacious in getting the learner ready to speak should they be asked. However, we should note that it is ranked much higher than the other four strategies which are connected with getting ready for oral production: 'silent practice'; 'repeating words to self'; 'practising new words under breath'; and 'practising words out loud'. Why should these be used less? The answer probably lies in language teaching methods. The reason may be that opportunities for practice in which the student has a greater amount of control are fewer in classrooms than are opportunities for practice controlled by the teacher, as in the case of teacher questioning. Another possibility is that whereas in the 'teacher–students' questioning situation there is a high level of motivation for pre-production practice, in other situations involving talk (for example, role play) there is less motivation for pre-production practice. It may be that checking one's speech for correctness in terms of pronunciation, grammatical accuracy and tone of voice is less likely to occur in student-centred dialogue unless teachers take the time to show the importance of so doing through pre-task preparation.[1]

By analysing the data in Table 3.1 we can also infer that strategies deployed for developing *receptive* skills rank fairly high compared to strategies for developing *productive* skills. Four out of the five top ranking strategies would appear to be associated with receptive skills: 'start from known words'; 'guess from context when reading'; 'guess from context when listening'; 'think if words look like L1 words'. This clustering of frequently used strategies would suggest approaches to decoding of FL texts with an appropriate combination of top-down and bottom-up processing, a process observed as effective by a number of researchers.[2] Whether this effective use of strategies is confirmed via actual practice cannot be ascertained without other data. This will be examined below when we explore the strategies that learners used for reading comprehension using a think-aloud technique.

The three remaining cognitive strategies from Table 3.1 are: 'learning vocabulary, etc. by a system', 'repeating words to oneself' and 'making mental associations'. These are all memorization techniques which do not appear to have a high place in the ranking. The low-ranking place of the strategy, 'making mental associations' sometimes known as the 'keyword technique'[3] suggested that learners hadn't thought about it, or they found it laborious because of the sheer quantity of new items to process in this way and/or it was simply quite hard to do. Again, we shall return to this group of strategies below.

Table 3.1 also provides the total mean for both countries by way of a general comparison. As we can see, learners in England claimed to be deploying direct strategies slightly more than their Italian counterparts. In analysing Table 3.1 and particularly in making cross-national comparisons we should apply caution for two reasons. The first is the issue of the reliability of self-reported frequency in general and in different cultural or educational contexts in particular. We have discussed this aspect of reliability in a previous chapter. Second, the cultural/educational issue itself may be a factor here. Italian students simply are not asked by teachers to learn vocabulary as lists but rather to learn sentences and larger chunks of texts. If they learn vocabulary as a list, it is likely to be their own decision, their own support strategy.

We now come to the remaining strategies in the questionnaire. These have been combined into a table headed indirect strategies (see Table 3.2). These are strategies that are less directly linked to the language itself. Learners use these to overcome problems in their learning, to arrange and to plan their learning and to support the learning that they have done in the classroom.

Table 3.2   *Indirect strategies*

Strategy	Mean in ascending order (i.e. most often used first) for both countries
use a dictionary at home	1.89
make a note of new words (class or home)	2.30
ask teacher to clarify or repeat	2.30
go back and revise a topic after some time (without the teacher telling you to do so)	2.97
listen to FL songs at home	3.01
ask parents (or others) for help	3.13
use FL outside the classroom	3.13
practise with a friend at home	3.67
watch FL videos at home	3.77
listen to FL cassette at home	3.78
use a computer to help re-draft writing	3.88
act out language at home (for example, a scene in a restaurant)	4.13
turn language into songs, rhymes, etc.	4.18
Total mean for both countries	3.24
Total mean for Italians only	2.97
Total mean for English only	3.51

PAUSE FOR THOUGHT

What do you note about the scores in Table 3.2 as compared to Table 3.1? Don't forget that the lower the score, the higher the frequency of use.

Which of these frequencies of strategy use might be affected by a national characteristic or a cultural characteristic? You do not need to limit yourself to the countries or cultures involved in the project.

To what extent does the educational context in which they are learning facilitate the adoption of metacognitive/support strategies? Is there anything in the cultural make-up of your learners that could account for wide differences?

Why should it be that learners report using direct strategies 'often' and 'sometimes' whereas indirect strategies 'not often'?

Which of these indirect strategies are more 'run of the mill' strategies and which require a special or unusual effort by the learners?

Do you have any other reactions to these results?

As we can see, the situation is quite different in the case of the more indirect strategies. Here, the overall mean was 3.24 and 9 out of the 13 strategies fell into the clines 'not often' and 'rarely'. From the overall sample of learners, then, we can infer that these strategies are less used than the direct strategies. When we compare the types of strategies in Table 3.2 with those in Table 3.1 we should bear in mind how difficult it is to compare strategy types. These strategies require much more conscious effort than the direct ones. In addition, the frequency of, for example, listening to a FL cassette at home, is going to be dependent not only on whether this material is available but also on the sheer amount of time that it takes to do it once compared to how long it takes to deploy once a strategy such as 'think if words look like L1 words'. Nevertheless, it is useful to remember that writers like O'Malley *et al.* (1985) note a tendency for intermediate level students to use a greater proportion of metacognitive strategies than beginner level students. This, Peter Skehan observes, would suggest that they are becoming more aware of themselves as learners and invest greater efforts in controlling and directing what they do (1989: 89), very similar to student M in Suzanne Graham's study. In other words, research suggests that having *executive control* through selection and monitoring of strategy use is of critical importance to the individual learner. Thus, it may be that frequency of direct strategy use is a useful but not essential research question to answer unless we are able to *cluster* direct strategy use frequency such that it begins to build up a picture of what the students are doing *in combination*. This picture is beginning to appear in the case of the decoding strategies above.

If these more indirect strategies (and others like them) have been shown elsewhere to be effective indicators of successful learners, was there any further pattern revealed when comparing the learning environments of the two nationalities of learners? Table 3.3 demonstrates those strategies for which there was statistically significant differences ($p = < 0.5$)[4] between the two nationalities. By 'statistically significant' is meant that the difference was large enough that, even with this size of sample, it couldn't have happened purely by chance. The right-hand column compares by nationality the percentage of students who said they *never* deployed that particular strategy (only the high scores are noted). It therefore provides what we might call the 'cause for concern' data if it were established that those students who were generally unsuccessful at language learning also never used a range of strategies such as these.

We have already discussed why it may be that Italian students reported asking the teacher to clarify more than English students. They simply may have had more opportunities to do so. But the Italians also reported using five other support strategies more than the English students:

1. Practising with a friend.
2. Listening to L2 songs at home.
3. Using the L2 outside the classroom.
4. Listening to L2 cassettes at home.
5. Watch L2 videos at home.

Through discussions with teachers in Italy and though my own knowledge of the English system I would like to discuss how it is that these strategies might be influenced by the cultural and educational environment and hopefully these will complement what you hypothesized the effects might be in Chapter 1.

In England most of the students were studying French whereas in Italy most of the students were studying English. Listening to songs and watching videos at home would have been greatly facilitated by the accessibility of English as an international language. This may not be the whole story, however. Those Italian students who were studying French appeared to be able to access and willing to listen to target language

Table 3.3 *Significant differences in frequency of strategy use between students in Italy and England*

Strategy	National trend overall	'Never used' comparative high scores (%)
asking the teacher to clarify	Italians used this strategy more	no high score registered
think if words look like L1 words	English used this strategy more	Italians 13.8 English 3.9
used a computer to re-draft written work	English used this strategy more	Italians 67.0 English 33.5
used the context to help them guess	Italians used this strategy more	no high score registered
practised with a friend	Italians used this strategy more	Italians 25.4 English 41.3
listen to L2 songs at home	Italians used this strategy more	Italians 3.7 English 79.9
noted down new words	Italians used this strategy more	no high score registered
used L2 outside the classroom	Italians used this strategy more	Italians 15.4 English 26.8
asked parents or siblings for help	English used this strategy more	Italians 31.6 English 16.2
answered questions directed at others (in head)	Italians used this strategy more	no high score registered
did silent practice in their heads	English used this strategy more	no high score registered
learn vocabulary by a system	English used this strategy more	Italians 20.0 English 6.7
listen to L2 cassettes at home	Italians used this strategy more	Italians 25.5 English 80.4
start from words you know and work up	English used this strategy more	no high score registered
watch L2 videos at home	Italians used this strategy more	Italians 30.2 English 82.7

Note: $p = < 0.5$

songs as were the Italian students of English. Similarly, there were no significant differences in the Italian sample in terms of listening to either French or English foreign language cassettes at home. This coupled with 'practising with a friend' may indicate a greater motivation to find alternative, collaborative and self-directed ways of learning a language than did those students living in England. You may well have noted that if school finishes early in Italy (at around 1.30), then afternoons and evenings can be devoted to large amounts of self-directed learning as well as the considerably more heavy burden of homework. With greater amounts of self-directed learning, students are more likely to resort to working collaboratively. However, working collaboratively and tuition from older learners have always been important features of Italian students. In other words, both the culture and the educational system may have been contributing to Italian students using more of these support strategies.

We will note that at this stage I have not made a claim for either of the two nationalities being in any way 'better language learners'. It would be highly spurious to do so on the basis of such superficial evidence. We will return to some comparisons, however, in some of the remaining chapters. One further comparison which I wish to make is in terms of the sex of the students in the project. Table 3.4 confirms earlier studies that females report much more frequent strategy use than boys.[5] In the Lingua study, the only strategy that boys reported using more than girls was 'using a computer to re-draft' ($p = 0.00$) and this was in the Italian sample only.

PAUSE FOR THOUGHT

Look at the results of Table 3.4. Of the fifteen strategies which females reported using more than males, is there anything that strikes you as important? How many are direct strategies and how many are indirect/support strategies? What do you notice about the gender differences in each of the countries?

So far we have examined the strategies that students have reported as using in their language learning in general. The studies we have looked at usually collected data either from semi-structured interviews or from questionnaires. Many studies have, in some way, made a link between frequency or type of strategy used and measures of general language learning success. We will now examine some findings related more directly to particular skills and processes in language learning.

Table 3.4   *Gender differences*

Italian only gender differences	Gender differences common to both countries	English only gender differences
learn vocabulary using a system	practising out loud	asked teacher to clarify
use of the L2 outside the classroom	listen to cassettes at home	made mental associations
	act out language at home	used dictionary at home
		used dictionary at school
		practise with a friend
		listened to foreign language songs
		guessed from context when listening
		made a note of new words
		turned language into songs, raps, etc.

Reading strategies

I have already (suggested that strategies associated with reading comprehension can be clustered into what are known as 'top-down' strategies (e.g. guessing from the context while reading) and 'bottom-up' (e.g. starting from known words or phrases you know and use these to help you make sense of the ones you don't know). The terms top-down and bottom-up strategies are used in the considerable body of literature reporting studies into reading comprehension) but there is a remarkable lack of depth of definition. In order to remedy this we will try to provide concrete examples when we examine the transcripts of the think-aloud tasks in the Lingua project. However, first let us look at a few other studies of reading comprehension strategies.

Sarig (1987) observed reading strategy use in four broad categories which she called:

- technical aids (e.g. skimming, scanning, skipping, marking, writing key elements in margins);
- clarification and simplification (e.g. being able to select appropriate units of language to be simplified in order that they can be examined and understood; recognizing utterances in a text by their lexical, morphemic or syntactic clues);
- coherence detection (e.g. identifying the overall framework of the text; using prior knowledge of the topic or information outside the text);
- monitoring (e.g. self-evaluating effectiveness of an action; changing tack when a particular course of action is not going well).

PAUSE FOR THOUGHT

When we talk of reading skills such as scanning, skimming and reading for gist, what do we mean? What are the actual *underlying* cognitive strategies that are going on that attempt to bring about these processes?

Which of Sarig's strategies are top-down approaches to a text, and which are bottom-up?

A lot of research has gone into trying to ascertain whether the strategies we use in our L1 reading are simply transferred to our L2 reading. Carrell's (1989) study showed that very few of the subjects in the study were reporting using a matched set of strategies for L1 and L2. Kate Parry confirms this view. She argues that we are unsure about the way reading skills are transferred, if at all, from L1 to L2 although it is possible that they are transferred after a high level of proficiency in L2 is reached. In addition, she proposes that the ease with which people may transfer strategies from their L1 to their L2 will be determined by how important the L2 in question is to them and the educational context in which the literacy of L1 was learnt. For example, Japanese students have a highly analytical literacy because of their writing system. By contrast she quotes a study of Nigerian learners of English who had little need to prioritize precision and a great need to prioritize communication. Hence they had never been encouraged to isolate words and build up meaning. Yet varied strategy use and in the right combination would seem to be good predictors of being able to decipher a written text. Marilda Cavalcanti (1987) evaluated strategy use of Brazilian students of English and matched this to success of interpretation of the text. This is what we will now do.

In the Lingua project sixteen students were asked to take part in think-aloud tasks, individually, which asked them to attempt to translate an L2 text and to try to articulate their thinking processes as they did so. The texts were selected, after consultation with the national co-ordinators, as being a little above the normal ability level of the learners. In other words, the students should find them challenging but not impossible to do. A similar technique was used by Anderson and Vandergrift (1996). In the Lingua study the following were the characteristics of the less successful readers, those who had a great deal of difficulty in decoding the text:

1. They made wild guesses not corroborated by other semantic information in the text.
2. They stuck to a guess regardless of conflicting evidence: context; syntax.
3. They didn't use world knowledge (their general knowledge and common sense).
4. They didn't use prior knowledge of lexical items and idiom (they didn't focus on words they could have retrieved with minimum effort).
5. They overused cognates; cognates overrode everything else.
6. They constantly focused on nouns; they neglected verbs or other syntactic features.
7. When verbs were tackled, 'meaning attack' was superficial or formulaic.
8. They lacked textual awareness and awareness of writing conventions.
9. They gave up easily and lost confidence.

As we can see from the above list, the poorer readers were rarely able to combine the top-down and bottom-up strategies. The top-down strategies they failed to employ were all that conglomeration of knowledge (sometimes known as *schemata*) that they could bring to bear on the surface language of the text. That is, the context as given away by a title or the shape of the text or their knowledge of the world in terms of what the topic might predict about the finer details of content. Poorer readers lacked the strategy of making links between early parts of the text and later in-text evidence and seemed oblivious to writing conventions. But they also failed to scan for the important words and phrases (that they knew or half-knew) which they could have had confirmed by the schemata. But it was the bottom-up level which surprised us most by its ineffectiveness and this can be divided into two features or trends. The first was their enormous reliance on L1–L2 cognates. The transcripts of the think-aloud protocols revealed that they were scanning for cognates for as much as five or six lines of text before coming across a cognate they recognized, stopping and making an attempt at meaning. This was to the detriment of any attempt at retrieving words which they should really have known. It may be that scanning for cognates wiped out any desire to look for words they actually knew. It is not suggested here that looking for cognates is not a useful strategy, merely that it needs to be combined with and supported by other strategies. In later chapters we will therefore question whether emphasizing this strategy in class is not having an inhibitory effect on all the mental processes that could be going on when learners try to decode a written text. The second was the attention that these learners paid to nouns to the neglect of verbs. It was almost as if the verbs were getting in the way of the process of comprehension.

What were the successful readers doing in order to overcome the barriers to the comprehension of a text? Obviously we could say that they did all the things that the less successful readers did not do and they did it in much better combination. Specifically, they did one or more of the following:

1. They read ahead silently; they read under their breath; they read out loud.
2. They didn't get anxious when they didn't understand.
3. They made inferences about the meaning of words based on the 'data' that they had worked out so far.
4. They had doubts about their interpretation.
5. They used awareness of syntax to check interpretation.
6. They divided text up into chunks.
7. They attacked the text holistically as a problem-solving exercise.

We will be looking at these data in greater detail in a moment. First, though, what do we mean by guessing from the context? To what extent is the act of guessing an inference and on what is that inference based – what do we mean by the context? Similarly, what do we mean by 'knowing a word'[6] and what is the process of using this to 'help you make sense of other words'? There is no space in this book to go into these questions in any detail. However, I would like to propose that the top-down–bottom up categorization is convenient but simplistic and that we may need a further intermediate category which I shall call *intermediary reading strategies* and to explain this I will need to make a brief detour.

If we think about this general distinction of top-down, intermediary and bottom-up strategies applied to the skills involved in reading comprehension, we might consider the reader, metaphorically, as either a migratory bird, a deer or a vole. The bird passes over a wood (our metaphorical text) and sees the general blotch of colour which is the trees. It sees the surrounding countryside which throws the wood itself into sharp relief while simultaneously placing it in a geographical context of sea and mountains which it has seen and 'recorded' in the past. But it has no knowledge of what a wood actually is. The deer, as it runs through the forest, may allow trees and undergrowth to flash by or it may choose to select, look more closely and then sample a particular leaf. In order to do this, it uses its highly developed 'instinct' to decide which juicy leaves to feast on. It may have only a limited knowledge of the confines of the wood, no knowledge of how the wood is affected by, for example, the mountains or the shoreline that surrounds it. The vole only sees the forest undergrowth. It has detailed knowledge of insects, nuts and grasses but probably has no mental concept of either a tree and certainly not a wood.

An effective reader, the research seems to tell us, is a combination of the bird and the vole. They use top-down and bottom-up strategies in combination. I would like to argue, however, that the reader also has to operate at the level of the deer and that all three levels have to be used for effective textual interpretation. I will therefore propose the following hypothesis.

To use top-down and bottom-up processing strategies effectively a reader has to use a number of intermediary strategies which link the two levels of cognitive processing. If effective readers (unlike ineffective readers) do not spend all their time thinking about individual words and how they link to the next word, and if effective readers do not over-use contextual information to make inferences in a text (for fear of being sent in completely the wrong direction), they must be using a number of intermediary strategies which allow them to make judgements about, at the very least, the following:

1. The pace at which to read and how to vary this.
2. Which key words or chunks of language in a text they should select and pause over.

3. What words or language chunks to ignore (perhaps temporarily) in a text.
4. When L1 knowledge should be subordinated to L2 knowledge (and vice versa).
5. When the context provided by the text might be called upon to assist with a decoding problem.
6. When world knowledge and common sense might be called upon to assist with a decoding problem.

They must be using these intermediary strategies because we know that the working memory's capacity to hold and process information is limited. The working memory is too limited for the reader to be a bird, a deer and a vole *at the same time*. However, the automatization of strategy use makes it appear 'as if' they are operating all three levels concurrently. These intermediary strategies would tend to fall into the general metacognitive category because of their evaluative and decision-making nature but, in highly successful readers, they may be being deployed at such speed that they resemble and are sometimes described as cognitive strategies.

Let us now look in some detail at the way certain students tackle a foreign language text. We will start off with James, Adrian and Amanda. The first two were judged from the think-aloud task to be rather poor readers. For a reminder of how this data was collected refer back to Chapter 2. No dictionary was allowed during the think-aloud, unlike in the study by Suzanne Graham (1997). James, Adrian and Amanda were given the following French text (see Figure 3.1).

Below is the typed format version of Figure 3.1. Words in italics were those *non-cognate words* which their teacher felt they should have known or had certainly been taught at some stage. Underlined tenses had *not* been taught at that stage. Also provided are the typed transcriptions of extracts of think-aloud sessions with the three students: James, Amanda and Adrian.

Chers Amis

Nous vous *envoyons cette* brochure *parce que l'an dernier nous avons passé* de merveilleuses *vacances dans la* région. *Nous avons* loué *un gîte tout* à fait *bien* aménagé: *un petit* appartement *très* agréable. *Les enfants ont* adoré *parce qu'ils* pouvaient *faire de la natation* tous *les jours*; c'était *gratuit*, ce qui était *bien et* en plus, il y avait un maître nageur de service, *donc* j'étais tranquille. Ils auraient *pu aussi pratiquer d'autres* activités sportives, *mais* c'était *un peu difficile* car

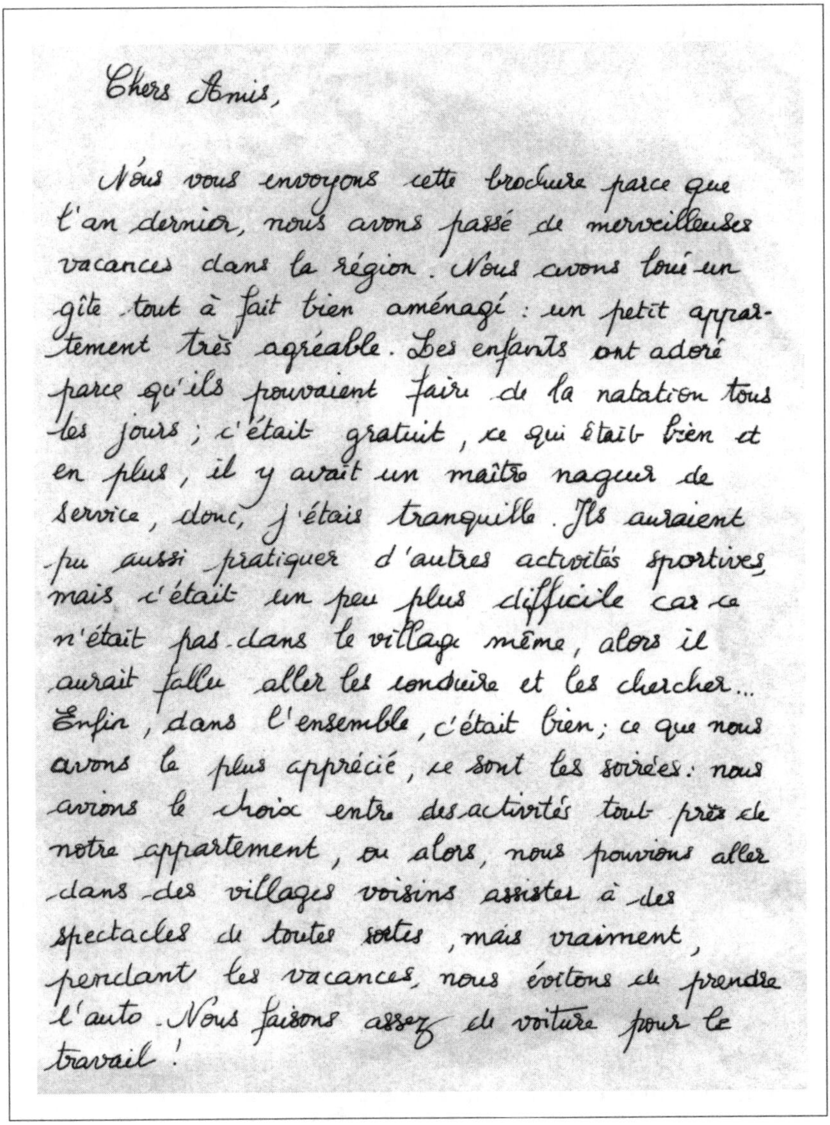

Figure 3.1 *Handwritten French letter*

ce n'était *pas dans le* village même, *alors* il aurait fallu *aller* les *conduire* et les chercher . . . Enfin, *dans* l'ensemble, c'était *bien*; ce que *nous avons* le plus apprecié, *ce sont les soirées: nous* avions *le choix entre* des activités *tout près de notre* appartement, ou *alors, nous* pouvions *aller dans les* villages voisins assister *à des* spectacles *de toutes* sortes, *mais* vraiment, *pendant les vacances, nous* évitons *de prendre l'auto. Nous* faisons assez *de voiture pour le travail!*

PAUSE FOR THOUGHT

Before looking at the transcription of the think aloud, look carefully at the typed text in conjunction with the handwritten text. To what extent is the handwritten text an additional obstacle to comprehension? If it is, what additional strategies will the reader have to deploy?

In the text, according to the pupils' teacher, there are roughly the following proportions of known words to unknown words:

(a) 57 per cent (should have been) known words;
(b) 10 per cent cognates or near cognates;
(c) 33 per cent probably unknown words.

Given the proportion of known words and cognates to unknown words, would you consider this text to be hard, fairly easy or easy for the reader? Are the unknown words mostly nouns, adjectives, verbs, prepositions, other? Now look first at the think-aloud transcriptions of James and Amanda. In what way do they differ in the strategies that they are using?

Transcription of extract from think aloud by James:

James: Er, it's Dear Thomas, (*he reads*) Dear Thomas . . . he likes going to the er . . . *parce que* means because, er, not quite sure, (*reads*) he wants to go to the . . . holidays in the region

Teacher: What makes you say that?

James: Because *vacances* means holidays and *région* looks the same as region...it just looks the same, er (*reads from Nous avons . . . aménagé*) er, it's hot in *amenage*

Teacher: What makes you say that?

James: I think *fait* means hot and *amenage*, I think, is like a country, or something like that (*reads: un petit appartement très agréable*), a small apartment, very, er, not quite sure . . .

Teacher: What makes you say that?

James: Apartment looks like the same word, *petit* means small, *très* means very and I'm not quite sure about the *agréable* (*pronounced agreeable*) . . . the infants all adore (*reads parce qu'ils . . . tous les jours*) infants adore it because he can play around there.

Teacher: What makes you think that?

James: *Jours* (*pronounced jeus*) means play, *parce que* means because and *enfants* means, er, children . . . not quite sure about *nation*, just took a guess from the sentence (*reads: c'était . . . en plus*) . . . it's good and plus, er (*reads: il y avait . . . service*), er, it's good and plus there's snow, no, there's a service station near it.

Teacher: What makes you say that?

James: Er, it says service, not quite sure about the *nageur* (*pronounced negout*) I think that might be snow, I'm not quite sure of that (*reads: Ils auraient . . . sportives*) it's practical with other activities and sports.

Transcription of extract from think aloud by Adrian:

Adrian: Er, it's to James, er . . . something about going somewhere . . . some region.

Teacher: What makes you say that?

Adrian: Cos it's got the end *dans la région* so that means region . . . the region . . . holiday somewhere, cos it's *vacances* . . . er I think it's in Germany . . .

Teacher: Why do you think that?

Adrian: It's got a man . . . er, *tement* (*reads: un petit appar . . . tement tres agréable*), it's with little kids . . . should be good, er, at the end . . . it's tranquil, practical activities, sports.

Teacher: Why do you come to that conclusion?

Adrian: It's *sportives, activités sportives* . . . it's got something about the apartment . . ., it's in the village, the apartment.

Teacher: Why?

Adrian: It says *dans le village* . . . should be a good holiday.

Teacher: Why do you say that?

Adrian: Er, no, they're going by car on the holiday, cos it says *voiture pour le travail* . . . don't know anything else.

Transcription of extract from think aloud by Amanda:

Amanda: It's to, er . . . that's their name, I'm not quite sure what it is . . . is that a brochure someone's sent them? Or it could be something to do with a letter.

Amanda: *Vacances* . . . that's holiday to a region somewhere and that could be the region or the name of the town.

Teacher: What makes you say that?

Amanda: Er, cos the French have things backwards usually and they say that (*pointing to text*) in front of that, so he's been on holiday to a region, so that region there, that looks like a town . . .

Amanda: It's a small apartment but it's ok . . .

Teacher: What makes you think that?

Amanda: *Agréable* (*pronounced the French way*), it's alright . . . is that children adore? . . . children like . . .

Amanda: There's practical activities and sports but some of them are difficult *aller dans les villages* . . . they go to the village . . .

Amanda: . . . that could be glasses, maybe, spectacles, or something nice to see

Analysis of James' think aloud:

1. Mistakes Thomas for *Amis* (lack of care with regard to handwritten text but also no confirmation of Thomas anywhere else in the text).
2. Takes a huge gamble with gist of first sentence with 'likes to'.

No 'attack' on any of the pronouns or verbs. Does not attempt to retrieve prior knowledge (*an, dernier*). Goes straight for the first cognate, *région* although does make the link with a prior knowledge word *vacances* and with prior knowledge *parce que*.

3. Again, in next sentence, completely ignores pronouns and verbs. Relates *fait* immediately to a formulaic expression 'il fait chaud' – no transference of chunks or verbs.

4. Thinks *aménagé* is a place or country (*Allemagne?*) even though it does not have a capital letter.

5. At this stage James has not made any attempt at top-down processing (relating to context or world knowledge), it's all bottom-up (individual words spotted and deciphered at random).

6. The cognate *appartement* is latched onto and prior knowledge words *petit* and *très* are attached to it. This might have been an opportunity to try and sum up so far or go back to the beginning and start again with what he's got so far.

7. He doesn't attempt a better pronunciation of *agréable* (although this doesn't matter, it might do in different circumstances).

8. He misreads *jours* for play *jouer*, a poor grapheme to phoneme link – doesn't link it to any grammatical pattern – i.e. there is no pronoun so it's unlikely to be a verb.

9. He doesn't spot a known word *natation*, possibly because he misreads it as 'nation' which is a wild guess anyway. His later translation of sports activities does not lead him to cast doubt on this earlier attempt at understanding

10. *Service* becomes a service station – wild guess not corroborated by any other in-text evidence especially so closely situated to his guess of *nageur* as snow.

Analysis of Amanda's think aloud:

First of all, it looks as if Amanda is actually able to recall known words better than James. In which case, it is possible that she has used better strategies for storing language in the past. Cognitive theory would suggest that the strategies and pathways through which lexical items are retrieved will be the same as the pathways and strategies with which they were stored. If this is so, James may have the more fundamental problem of how he learns lexical items in the first place. But of course we don't know this for sure. Perhaps he stores and retrieves them in the same way as Amanda but in this task simply does not activate the retrieval strategies.

Or, in this task he allows other strategies to dominate. The following analyses *infer* a number of strategies missing from James's repertoire and present in that of Amanda:

1. She has doubts about her interpretation ('I'm not quite sure') and she asks questions ('is that a brochure?') which later she may be able to confirm or discard.
2. She thinks about the overall look of the text in terms of writing conventions.
3. She too looks for cognates but, again, she asks questions about the text, casts doubts on her interpretation ('that could be the region').
4. She is aware of aspects of French grammar and word order ('the French have things backwards'), this may be a bit of a generalization on her part but she's right and she's using what she's learnt about the language to help her make sense of it.
5. She focuses both on the cognate (*appartement*) and prior knowledge (*agréable*) but she also makes links according to what might make sense ('it's small but ok').
6. From the transcription one also gets the impression that she is hopping backwards and forwards in the text to check that things make sense by in-text evidence elsewhere.
7. She decides to skip the difficult phrase '*il y avait un maître nageur de service*' and samples the next string of words that make sense at the gist level 'practical activities and sports but difficult' . . .
8. 'They go to the village' – although she hasn't quite got the first person plural right, she has got the sense that it's 'they' from the rest of the text.
9. 'That could be glasses' – she is tempted by the cognate but holds on to a doubt long enough to make her come up with a more plausible (from the context) possibility.

We should note here that I have chosen Amanda's transcript not because she has high aptitude in language learning and has no difficulty in understanding the whole text, but because of the way she tries to understand the text. We could hope that if James used the same strategies as Amanda he would be able to understand the text at least as well.

Combinations of reading strategies

We will now look at some learners who use a number of strategies in particularly good combination with one another. The text, according to the teacher who used it in the think aloud, is a fair way above the expected level of the students.

Pietro (Italian L1 English L2) is attempting to understand a text on the use of English in the world. For readers of this book who are non-speakers of Italian, the right-hand box provides a translation of what Pietro said (published text spoken or read by Pietro is in italics).

this will be no doubt continued . . . eh questo sarà . . . non continuerà per sempre! . . . e questo che vuol dire? *Doubt* . . . non so che vuol dire . . . *continues the.(inaudible word)* la preposizione è simile all'italiano ma non so . . . però bene . . . eh . . . è questa che riferisce a questo? . . . tutte le lingue saranno . . . forse vuol dire che tutte le altre lingue non rimarranno fuori . . . che è assurdo	*this will be no doubt continued*, well, this must be . . . it won't go on for ever! . . . what does this mean? *Doubt* . . . I don't know what *doubt* means . . . *continues the (inaudible word)* . . . the preposition is similar in Italian but I don't know exactly . . . is this referring to this? . . . all languages will one day be . . . perhaps it means that all the other languages will not be excluded which is absurd

Comment on Pietro's strategy use

1. Pietro constantly asks questions about his interpretation.
2. He always doubts an interpretation if there is not sufficient evidence to back it up.
3. He holds the 'doubted element' in the working memory while he searches for other clues.
4. He looks for grammatical links and clues within a sentence.

Later in the text Pietro sometimes encounters problems with a number of other words.

Il 75 per cento delle poste del mondo e il 60 per cento dei telefoni del mondo e all . . . adesso non lo so che vuol dire cosi . . . continuo? . . . *The future of English* . . . il futuro dell'inglese . . . e qui già capisco di quello che dovrebbe parlare . . . *geographically English is the most widespread language on earth second only to Mandarin Chinese in the number of people who speak it* . . . geograficamente è il più . . . *widespread?* . . . parlato? la più parlata lingua del mondo . . . della terra? Secondo solo . . . in che senso? Solo in Cina? . . . i numeri delle persone che parlano esso . . . anche loro rientrano? . . . cioè che loro . . . come secondo? . . . o secondo loro . . . secondo essi solo i cinesi . . .

75 per cent of postal systems in the world and 60 per cent of telephones in the world and . . . now I don't know what it's saying . . . shall I go on? . . . *The future of English* . . . the future of English . . . well, here I can already understand what it's likely to be talking about . . . *geographically English is the most widespread language on earth second only to Mandarin Chinese in the number of people who speak it* . . . geographically it's the most . . . *widespread?* . . . spoken? the language which is most spoken in the world? Second only . . . in what sense? . . . Only in China? . . . the number of people who speak it . . . they too are among its number . . . in other words they . . . how can it be 'second' or does it mean 'according to' . . . according to them only the Chinese? . . .

As we can see, Pietro has a problem with two parts of the text. The first is the word 'widespread'. This he makes an informed guess at. His *parlata* (spoken) makes perfectly good sense in the context and puts across the author's meaning even though *diffusa* would be more accurate.

The other problem is the English phrase 'second only to Mandarin Chinese'. This is because in Italian the cognate of 'second' (*secondo*) has also the meaning of 'according to' – this creates confusion in his mind. But he does not allow the false cognate to establish itself so strongly that it dominates every other possible interpretation. Rather, he keeps asking himself the right questions, evaluating his interpretations in terms of whether it makes sense.

Sometimes, in the think aloud, a teacher asks one of the students (in this case, Alessandro) to summarize how they have understood a whole section of the text:

Alessandro: Ho cercato di collegare una frase con l'altra e con quello che riuscivo a capire . . . forse per fare le frasi che non riuscivo a capire mi ha aiutato anche il fatto della cronologia . . .

Teacher: Cioè le date che ci sono?

Alessandro: No, praticamente so che una cosa viene dopo l'altra e quindi riesco a . . . mi ha aiutato a capire di più di ogni frase perché non potevo dire prima che l'inglese era parlato nel diciassettesimo secolo dopo che mi ha detto prima che . . . non so spiegarmi pero . . . qui parla di dopo la scoperta dell'America . . . che si è insiediata la lingua inglese . . .

Alessandro: I tried to relate one phrase with the other and with what I was managing to understand . . . maybe with the phrases I couldn't understand what helped me was also the chronology of the thing . . .

Teacher: You mean the dates that are there?

Alessandro: No, I mean I know that one thing follows on from another and therefore I manage to . . . it helped me to understand more than any single phrase because I couldn't say that English was spoken in the seventeenth century after it has just told me that . . . I can't explain what I mean . . . here it's talking about after the discovery of America . . . that the English language established itself . . .

Comment on Alessandro's strategy use

1. He makes sure that the interpretation of the phrases in the text demonstrate the necessary coherence that a text written by a native speaker would have.
2. He uses the chronology of events to help him make sense of the text.
3. He uses his world knowledge to help provide a back-up to his interpretation of the text.
4. He attacks the text as a problem-solving activity.

Here too the teacher asks Alessandro to summarize his strategy use:

Teacher: Try to recap what helped you, what are the things that you thought of, what was of use to you in trying to understand?

Alessandro: Uh, in the first part it's talking about when the language was not yet famous . . . in the second it's talking about the spreading of the language . . . in the third part it's talking about who speaks English and in the fourth part it's talking about the future of English and the other languages . . .

Teacher: And what allowed you to understand these things? From what did you understand them?

Alessandro: This I understood from the construction of the phrase because . . . *belongs* . . . I don't know what that means . . . but then after it says that it's incredible that 75 per cent of postal systems in the world and 60 per cent of telephone systems in the world are in English . . . so it allowed me to understand that, I mean, initially it's not talking about the future of English but then it says that in the future . . . certainly it won't be the case that English only is left . . . the other languages will be left too because it would be absurd for them to disappear.

Teacher: And so the words you knew in this phrase?

Alessandro: Well . . . *will* helped me because it's in the future . . . *all languages will* . . .

1. He breaks up the text into 'meaning sections'. He then sees if
    the evidence of each section confirms the meaning 'label' that
    he has attributed to it.
2. He tries to follow the author's intentions in dividing up the
    text (whether Alessandro is using this strategy only
    retrospectively we cannot tell from the transcript).
3. He uses an awareness of the tenses being used in the text to
    help him come to informed interpretations of the text at key
    points in the text. He looks out for key syntactic clues in order
    to do this.

We again note the use of metacognitive strategies such as monitoring
being more used by the more successful learners.

We have looked in some detail at reading strategies not only because
I have personally been involved with researching them but also because
there has been considerable interest in them in relation to a key skill.
At high intermediate and at advanced levels (and certainly in courses
of language for academic purposes) reading is the skill through which
most language is encountered. In addition, written text is often a
springboard to task-based activities involving other language skills at
these levels. Successful students' strategies which make authentic and
difficult texts accessible are, as a consequence, of great interest to
researchers and teachers alike. We will now go on to consider studies
which have endeavoured to describe strategies used with other skills.

Strategies for listening
Listening strategies have mostly been studied in tasks where the listener
was not involved in interaction. This is because of the inherent difficulty
with eliciting listening strategies while doing the task itself which would
be compounded by the listener also being involved in speaking.
Awareness of strategy use can only reside in the working memory and
the capacity of this is being virtually exhausted by the processing of the
listening task itself. Nevertheless, as was suggested in Chapter 1, it is
important not to assume that listening will automatically lead to
acquisition of language and that no active involvement by the learner
is necessary. As O'Malley and Chamot point out: 'The exclusive focus
on teacher behaviours fails to take into consideration deliberate learner
strategies for comprehending language texts, for processing new
information and for learning and retaining concepts related to academic
language and content' (1990: 129).

PAUSE FOR THOUGHT

What stages do you go through when you listen to a text? Find, if possible, a foreign language taped text which is likely to be quite challenging for you. Listen to it and while trying to comprehend, try to identify what happens to the language as it 'invades your brain' and when and if any different stages appear to be taking place.

What strategies did you use when you tried to understand the spoken text? In other words, try to identify the things that you did in order to facilitate the processes at the various stages. Compare the stages, processes and strategies that you have identified with some of the research below.

A number of fundamental stages have been identified in the process of listening.[7] In the first stage, the language is *perceived* by listeners by them focusing on the sounds of the language and storing them in working memory as a kind of echo. Because of all the other demands on the working memory they almost invariably begin some processing of the language, looking for ways of breaking it up into likely manageable segments. Alternatively or in addition, listeners will scan the incoming text for the right strings of words to sample. By sampling is simply meant the bits of language they want to focus on because they think they will hold the key to the meaning of the text. Some initial comprehension of meaning will inevitably occur at this stage. Simultaneously listeners may refer to contextual information in order build up hypotheses of the meaning of what they have sampled and what they are likely to hear next. The second stage has been described as the *parsing* stage where words and phrases (perhaps some of them formulaic language chunks) begin to be matched with representations already stored in the long-term memory. The information is reorganized here into a meaningful unit which can be stored again, temporarily in the working memory. In the final stage, listeners use or *elaborate* the decoded text so far by relating it to their conscious knowledge which the working memory retrieves from long-term memory. They do this by activating more and more parts of the brain which have a connection with what has been processed in stage 2.

A major study of listening strategies was carried out O'Malley *et al.* (1989) with ESL students in high schools (upper secondary schools) in America using think-aloud techniques. The students were from Spanish-speaking backgrounds and they were identified by their teachers as effective listeners and ineffective listeners. The researchers discovered significant differences in strategy use between the effective and ineffective listeners. The effective listeners reported using more strategies that maintained their concentration on the task during the perception stage. Poorer listeners were distracted by single words they couldn't recognize. Effective listeners reported focusing on larger chunks of language during the parsing stage than did their less effective counterparts, shifting their attention to individual words only when their comprehension failed altogether thus using both a top-down and a bottom-up approach. In the final stage (utilization/elaboration) the effective listeners used world knowledge, personal experiences, self-questioning and inferencing in order to consolidate their understanding of the meaning of the text.

Susan Bacon (1992), it will be remembered from Chapter 2, interviewed 50 university students of Spanish using a compromise between a think aloud and a post-task self-report. She wanted to find out how strategy use, level of comprehension, confidence and affective response were influenced by the following independent variables:

- the type of passage (more narrative or more technical);
- the order in which subjects listened to the passages;
- whether the subjects were male or female.

She found that:

1. The more narrative passage was more accessible and produced better comprehension and students were therefore able and willing to report a greater number of strategies.
2. Women used more metacognitive strategies than men (planning their listening, monitoring their comprehension and evaluating their strategy use) and were more likely to use metacognitive strategies when faced with the difficulties of the more technical passage.
3. Women were more consistent in their use of cognitive strategies than men. It was as if they had got into a routine of strategy use.
4. Men were more likely to adopt a transactional approach with the passage they found difficult – women kept reminding themselves to 'think in Spanish'.
5. Men were more consistent in expressing their feelings – expressing higher levels of confidence overall.

However, despite these differences in strategy use, there was no significant difference in the level of comprehension between males and females. We should therefore remind ourselves that we should not impose strategy use on learners but make learners aware of the range of strategies available and that a different response may be needed according to the type of passage they are listening to. Finally, we should remind ourselves that strategy use needs to be evaluated for its effectiveness. A number of strategies which are specific to listening (or particularly relevant to listening) were identified by Bacon's study. They are shown below.

Metacognitive strategies

Prior to listening
- Focus attention: concentrate; clear mind.
- Apply an advance organizer: 'You told me it was (about) a product so . . .'
- Go in with a plan: 'I listen for words I know, key words, cognates.'

While listening
- Self-management: get used to speed, keep up with speed. 'I've got to listen to this. Try to keep up.'
- Aware of loss of attention. Refocus: 'Well, I said, I've got to concentrate.'

Cognitive strategies

Bottom-up processing
- Hear a word and repeat it. 'I'll hear a word and repeat it over and over.'
- Use intonation and pausing to segment words and phrases. 'I listened to an entire phrase until there was a pause, then tried to understand that before it went on to the next phrase.'
- Listen for all the words. 'I try to hear every word.'
- Listen for each word one at a time. 'Wait for the first word I know, then another one. See if I can put them together.'
- Listen to sounds rather than meaning. 'I kept hearing the "r" word, remarkable?, the accent is throwing me.'

Top-down processing
- Infer; guess from context, intonation. 'It sounds like a commercial with the music.'
- Visualize: 'I've got a picture in my mind as if I were really in it.'
- Reference to English, translate: 'I have a dictionary in my head. When I hear a word, I leaf through my head really fast to see if I can find out what it means in English.'

- Transfer: use previous linguistic or discourse knowledge.
  'I went for the topic sentence.'

(Adapted from Bacon 1992)

> ### PAUSE FOR THOUGHT
>
> Are you surprised by some of the strategies for listening that Susan Bacon discovered university students were using? Why? Can you recognize any of your own students in them? If so, do they match your more effective listeners or your less effective listeners?

The target language and the language of thought

In Chapter 2 we finished by considering which language should be used for the elicitation of strategies. We will end this chapter by considering what language the learners are likely to be using when they are actually carrying out many of the language tasks that we have referred to above and the implications that this is likely to have for their strategy use in connection with those language tasks. In other words, what is the language of thought that is employed when the learner is involved in a language process and what is the language of thought that the learner uses in order to apply, monitor and evaluate strategies? As Andrew Cohen speculates: 'The very choice of language of thought may have significant implications for ultimate success at learning, using as well as forgetting a language' (1998: 157). We will therefore examine three studies in which the language of thought has been analysed.

The first study is by Richard Kern (1994) and involves strategies used when reading. He used interviews and think-aloud protocols on 51 intermediate level (university) students of French. This led him to identify a number of disadvantages and advantages of making L1/L2 connections when reading.

To start with, let us look at the disadvantages of thinking in L1 when attempting a reading task. First, Kern concludes, mental translation may lead to inaccuracies and miscomprehension if the lexical item is wrongly connected to the L1 equivalent. This is likely to happen particularly with 'false friends'. Second, bottom-up de-coding (word-by-word translation) may not assist with the integration of meaning. The learner cannot see the wood for the undergrowth, let alone the trees. Third, the comprehension activity may actually stop at comprehension. Once the meaning has been identified by the learner, they will move on quickly thereby focusing attention for too short a time on the L2 forms on the page and reducing the possibility of *noticing* something new. In other words, comprehension may not lead to the *intake* of new language. Now let us consider the advantages of thinking in L1 when attempting a reading task. It is likely, concludes Kern, that use of the L1 helps with semantic processing (with the storage of meaning) and permits consolidation of meaning. The L1 helps with chunking (grouping) L2 lexical items into semantic clusters, a way of attempting to reduce memory constraints. The L1 helps with thought processes (the train of thought), and avoids losing track of the meaning as the reader works through a text because the L1 logically puts less processing load on the working memory. The reader's network of associations can be made richer with L1 use simply because activation of connected ideas will have been going on for many more years. In this way, therefore, the L2 meaning will be better integrated and assimilated. The input is converted into more familiar terms, thus enhancing the reader's confidence and lowering affective barriers. Mental translation may help in clarifying the syntactic roles played by lexical items (by contrasting the L1 with the L2 to verify a verb tense or checking for comprehension).

These advantages are taken up by other authors. For example, Ian Campbell (1997) sees value in teachers encouraging learners to make L1 comparisons and contrasts as learning strategies. Particularly in cognate languages like English and German, features of the two languages such as liaison, emphasis, stress, weak and strong verbs, idiomatic expressions, all can help the acquisition of the language rather than hinder it. In other words, Campbell would advocate the strategy of 'proceeding from the known to the unknown', that is, from the L1 to the L2. A study of 11 year olds by Nina Spada and Patsy Lightbown (1999) would tend to support Campbell's view. It suggested that learners need to be shown explicitly that structures in L1 do not transfer to structures in L2, the implication being that this can later be retrieved as a strategy when the occasion arises.

Andrew Cohen, a multi-linguist, carried out a study of his own language learning and also a mini-survey of university students with mixed L1s. He concludes that there would appear to be definite benefits from, at times, making an effort to think in the L2. But what, he asks, is this 'thinking'? What learners plan and rehearse sub-vocally may not really constitute thinking in the L2. It may be more like 'thinking about the L2 in L1'. It is possible that learners do not think complex metalinguistic thoughts at all through the L2 but rather make passing reference to the L2 in the form of fleeting or limited thoughts. Multilinguals may choose to think in one of their 'non L1s' in order to help the other 'non L1'.

Hawras' (1996) study seemed to suggest that advanced students used less translation than beginner and intermediate students. However, the more advanced students, when they actually used translation, benefited more from this process Perhaps the more proficient you are, the more you know when it is appropriate to use translation. The challenge for a learner is to distinguish a genuine need to translate from a perceived need.

All these studies point to the fact that we are not in a position to be able to exclude aspects of the L1 as a strategy contributing to language processing. However, it may be that some individuals or groups find it more helpful as a strategy than others. Susan Bacon, as we have seen above, provided some distinctions in strategy use between male and females with regard to use of L1 translation as a strategy. First, men used this strategy more. Second, this strategy was used more in the technical information text than in the narrative text. Yet Bacon found no difference in proficiency in comprehension of a spoken text.

There are clearly some benefits in not putting too many obstacles in the way of the L1 as the language of thought. It is used both for semantic comparison, for storage of lexical items and for some aspects of syntax. However, there is clearly a danger that either learners or teachers might opt for the soft option of only using the L1 to think in. Perhaps there is a threshold of L1 use which, once crossed, the L2 is no longer involved in thought. Up until then the L2 is involved in the thinking process alongside the L1.

BEFORE WE MOVE ON

To what extent do you understand better the mental activity which lies beneath the surface of reading and listening?

Are you clearer now about the processes of top-down and bottom-up processing?

Have you begun to think of ways, other than by using think aloud, that you could find out what strategies your students are using when reading? Could you now do this in a systematic way?

If you were going to ask your students how they go about a listening task, what do you predict they would say? What specific questions could you ask to prompt them to think about their listening strategies?

In this chapter we have examined in some detail studies which have sought to describe the strategies used by students. As well as comprehensive (cross-skill) lists of strategies, we have focused specifically on strategies for reading and listening.[8] It is now time to look at studies whose primary aim is to train students to use strategies more often and more effectively.

Notes

1. For a discussion of task-based learning and particularly pre-, during and post-task processing, see Skehan (1998).
2. For a further discussion on top-down and bottom-up processing, see Bernhardt (1991), Block (1992) and Parry (1993).
3. For further reading on keyword technique, see Carter and McCarthy (1988) and Beaton *et al.* (1995).
4. 'Significance' in statistics means that, despite the size of the sample (which in some cases may appear small), what you seem to have found out didn't happen by chance. This is because the statistical calculation takes the size of the sample into account. If the p figure is less than 0.05, then the finding is said to be 'significant'.
5. For further reading on gender differences, see Oxford and Nyikos (1989); for articles dealing with the under-achievement of boys in language learning, see Harris (1998) and Clarke and Trafford (1996).
6. For a discussion of what it is to actually 'know a word', see Nick Ellis (1995).
7. For further reading on this, try Anderson (1985).
8. For further reading on listening strategies, you might like to try Thompson and Rubin (1996) where the results of an intervention study involving students of Russian are reported.

CHAPTER 4

Intervention Studies

In the last chapter we gained an overview of studies of learner strategies whose main objective was to describe the type of strategy use and the frequency of use. That is, they were exploring the range of strategies that good language learners seem to use and comparing them to those used by less successful learners. These studies provide us with a greater understanding of the ways learners learn. Some of the studies described strategies that learners used to support specific skills and processes in language learning such as reading and listening. Others compared strategies used by groups such as males and females. However, simply to have a greater understanding of how learners learn is not enough. We also have to explore whether, through pedagogic action, we can bring about better strategy use and better language learning.

In the next two chapters we will be doing two things. We will be focusing on the skills and processes involved in oral interaction, memorization and writing. At the same time, our selection of studies which will inform our discussion will be weighted towards those which have attempted to bring about change in strategy use. That is they are, by and large, intervention studies, intervening usually through a process of raising the awareness of the learners and/or submitting them to a programme of strategy training. These types of studies have either measured a change in the use of strategies, measured a change in language competence or both.

One thing I cannot do because of lack of space is provide a summary of how some of these studies went about eliciting strategies in the first place. Nevertheless the initial elicitation process is indispensable. This is because it is my belief that intervention without a prior stage of strategy elicitation of those particular learners (and therefore description) is invalid. Let me try to explain why.

Let us say that we want to improve our students' ability to listen to our procedural instructions for tasks in the classroom because we wish to avoid simply telling them in L1 how to do a task. We could set up an experiment using two classes, class A and class B. In both classes we could, over a period of two weeks, only deliver our procedural instructions in the target language regardless of whether we felt the students had fully understood the task. We could then observe them doing the task to see if they were performing it correctly (correctly in terms of what they had to do, not the language). We could, in addition, provide them with a short list of questions relating to their understanding of the task. For example: did you find my instructions easy? Were you able to get on with the task straightaway? Would you have preferred it if I had given you the instructions in your L1? This would be our *baseline* assessment of how they coped with our instructions.

We could then proceed with a short period of strategy training with class A, the experimental group (sometimes referred to as the *treatment* group). For example, over a period of three months, every time we provided L2 procedural instructions we would give them a sheet of paper which guided their thoughts and actions as they listened. This might contain hints like:

- What is the overall message that I'm trying to put across?
- What things do you already know are likely to be in my message (predict from previous experience)?
- Try to hold these things in your head as you try to understand the remainder of the message.
- If you don't understand, put up your hand and ask me an 'either/or' question.
- Jot down one or two words you don't understand as they sound to you (phonetically) and then ask me to explain at an opportune moment.

We could then hope that some of these strategies became more automatic and natural to our students. Of course with class B (the *control* group or *comparison* group)[1] we would carry on as normal, without the training. At the end of the three months we would determine whether class A had improved over class B on their understanding of oral instructions by measuring whether they performed the mechanics of the task better than class B or had, at least, made more progress with understanding the instructions than class B (because, of course, class B may have been better or worse than class A at the beginning). We could additionally ask them the same questions as in the baseline assessment.

If class A had made more progress than class B, we could get very excited and say that our treatment had worked. But did it? Well, it may have done but we can't be sure. What our baseline assessment measured was only their ability to cope with the task, their surface skills and feelings. It did not describe or measure the underlying strategies that they were using. They may have already been using many of the strategies suggested in the training and therefore their improvement may have been due to other factors, for example, that they simply felt more motivated because the teacher was doing something different in the classroom and they were therefore paying more attention. If class A had made equal or less progress, we could get very depressed and say that the treatment was a waste of time. But was it? The treatment group may have been starting from such a low baseline of strategy use that the treatment was not sufficient to make an impact on their surface skills. Alternatively they found the strategy training confusing, unpalatable or just plain hard. In other words, we need to describe and measure strategy use (and the students' attitudes) before and after treatment prior to: (a) making claims that it did or did not improve performance; and (b) making claims that it did or did not increase the frequency of strategy use and, most importantly, improve the deployment of strategy use.

PAUSE FOR THOUGHT

We have taken this detour into the principles behind intervention studies in learner training not only to explain some of the issues and pitfalls connected to them (and the wrong assumptions that can be made) but also to introduce you to some of the terminology that you will encounter as we work through the studies in this chapter and the next.

Can you now describe briefly:

1. What an intervention study is?
2. What a baseline assessment is?
3. What a control group is and how this differs from a comparison group?
4. What a treatment group is?

Strategies for interaction

This section is about certain things that learners do when attempting to have a conversation in a foreign language. We began to think about this in Chapter 1 when we considered whether communication strategies should be included in our general list of learner strategies. I suggested that learning strategies (strategies which learners use to assist them in the process of learning) could not easily encompass communication strategies except in a very broad and indirect sense. Let us explore this idea a little further. In order to do this we need to remind ourselves briefly of the distinction between the concepts of *competence* and *performance.*

The distinction, as Ferdinand de Saussure originally made it in 1916, was one where a learner's competence was their knowledge of the language. For example, I know that, in Italian, the perfect tense (*passato prossimo*) takes an auxiliary verb which is sometimes *essere* and sometimes *avere* according to a rule about verbs that, I have to admit, I have never fully understood. The fact that I don't fully understand the rule does not mean that I do not have knowledge of the language. I can, at any time, tell you how to formulate a perfect tense in Italian or how to translate a past tense from English. This is an aspect of my competence in Italian. But I also never make a mistake or (as far as I know) hesitate with the perfect tense when I'm speaking Italian. This is my performance, my use of the language. On the other hand, while my competence with regard to the *passé composé* in French is also 'perfect', I have been known occasionally to hesitate in my performance of it. I know how it works but my *neural networks* sometimes get a bit mixed up when attempting to perform the phrase *j'ai été* (I have been). This is, I think, because of the influence of Italian whose equivalent is *sono stato*, taking a different auxiliary. It's only a split second's hesitation and it only occurs very occasionally when I'm switching to French after long periods of time speaking Italian, but it's there nevertheless. Thus my performance in French doesn't always quite match my competence. But this isn't the whole story because I can sometimes compensate for my lack of competence in French (perhaps a complex tense structure) while I'm *performing*, by avoiding it altogether and using a different construction. In this way it appears as if my fluency isn't impaired and I don't make any errors. However, this 'formal reduction strategy' (Faerch and Kasper 1983) or 'achievement strategy' (Faerch and Kasper 1986) which I use to compensate for my lack of competence in no way helps me to increase my language competence in the future. Successfully avoiding the area of uncertainty in the 'performance' does not help to increase my knowledge of the language even though it might be demonstrating some pretty nifty advanced metacognitive strategies. De Saussure's distinction is less used nowadays because of a preference for the theoretical concept of interlanguage[2] but it is useful here for the purposes of our discussion.

Let us look, therefore, at other communication strategies. The early work on communication strategies (strategies which compensate for lack of competence) were very general.[3] These have been refined by authors such as Rebecca Oxford who classifies them under 'overcoming limitations in speaking and writing'. These are:

1. Switching to the mother tongue (e.g. one word in L1 in the middle of an L2 sentence) (sometimes called 'codeswitching').
2. Getting help (e.g. asking the person you are talking with to provide you with the L2 word or phrase you don't know or can't remember).
3. Using mime, gesture, or non-verbal noise such as a sigh (as a substitute for the word/phrase you don't know or can't remember).
4. Avoiding communication partially or totally (e.g. avoiding certain parts of a topic or a message when you're not sure of the relevant vocabulary).
5. Adjusting or approximating the message (making ideas simpler, less precise, or slightly different).
6. Coining words (e.g. paper holder for notebook; teachers' room for staff room). Alternatively you could attempt to make an L1 word sound like an L2 word, e.g. 'you need to revise' becomes *devi revisere* in Italian).
7. Using circumlocution or a synonym (getting around the problem word or phrase by describing it or paraphrasing it or simply providing a close equivalent).

(adapted from Oxford 1990: 50)

Let's add a few more:

8. Syntax avoidance (using a different grammatical construction to avoid one we are unsure of).
9. Functional reduction (requiring the interlocutor to use context to fill in the gaps in what would be a longer and more difficult utterance, for example, 'the door!' instead of 'it's very draughty in here, I wish you'd always shut the door when you come in!').
10. Discourse avoidance (omitting aspects of a target language's social discourse because of the linguistic demands this would

make on the speaker, for example, avoiding the formal *vous* in French).

11. Using the tone of voice to communicate meaning (for example, changing to a high tone for the words in bold as a substitute for the phrase *j'ai eu peur!* (I got scared) as in: *'Je n'ai pas fait les devoirs de maths et . . . **monsieur Baker dans le couloir!***) (I haven't done my maths homework and . . . Mr Baker in the corridor!).

PAUSE FOR THOUGHT

Of all these communication strategies which compensate for inadequate language proficiency, try to identify any which contribute to improving language learning. In doing so think about the distinction above between competence and performance. Try to think about it in terms of:

- improving the vocabulary store;
- improving the internalization of the rule system of the target language.

Also try to think which of the above strategies 'give up' on the intended communicative objective (the message someone wanted to put across) and which try to achieve the same objective but by a different means.

You may have come to the same conclusion as I have that, apart from '2', none of them help much to improve directly the language competence. We could say that numbers 5, 7, 8 and 10 reinforce aspects of language already learnt. For example, in 8, avoiding the French subjunctive by using a modal verb plus an infinitive (*je dois prendre* instead of *il faut que je prenne*) would help us to consolidate the former construction. But it won't improve our knowledge or use of the subjunctive.

On the other hand, all the above strategies are used by learners and they are used because they greatly improve the quality of a conversation even if they don't improve the quality of the speaker's L2. In improving the quality of the conversation, the speaker/learner improves language competence and performance indirectly. This is because:

1. Native speakers (and near native speakers) are more likely to want to talk to a learner who keeps the conversation going and puts across a message than to someone who stops to ponder over every other word.
2. Conversations which flow are likely to generate higher-order ideas and therefore richer vocabulary and more complex sentences such that the input the learner receives will be of a better quality.
3. The use of strategies which try to achieve the same objective but by a different means may lead learners to test hypotheses about the language (for example, codeswitching or word coinage) by 'forcing' a reaction from the person they are talking to.

PAUSE FOR THOUGHT

Can you think of any other benefits which might accrue to language competence indirectly from learners using these communication strategies?

We seem to be working towards a conclusion that we cannot regard communication strategies which compensate, as they do, for lack of proficiency, in isolation. We have to treat them as part of a set of strategies which involve both participants in the discourse. Communication strategies cannot operate without an interlocutor and without rules of discourse and interaction. That is why I have chosen to call this section *strategies for interaction*. If this is an appropriate way to consider them, then we need to take into account not only strategies used when speaking in a conversation but also strategies used when listening in a conversation and to see the interplay of the two sets. Laurens Vandergrift has studied the *reception strategies* used by learners in interactive listening (that is, listening as part of a conversation rather than listening to a tape or a lecture). Building on work carried out by Rost and Ross (1991) and by Lynch (1995), his study of 16-17 year olds learning French (English L1) identifies the following reception strategies (adapted from Vandergrift 1997):

- *Global reprise* (either in L1 and L2) – the listener asks for outright repetition, rephrasing or simplification.
- *Specific reprise* (either in L1 or L2) – the listener asks a question which refers to a specific word or phrase that was not understood.

- *Hypothesis testing* (either in L1 or L2) – the listener asks specific questions about a specific piece of information but by giving a prompt or an alternative (e.g. '<u>after</u> *les devoirs?*').
- *Kinesics* – the listener indicates a need for clarification through use of his/her body language.
- *Uptaking* – the listener uses kinesics and verbal or other non-verbal signals to indicate to the interlocutor to continue, that they understand.
- *Faking* – the listener sends *uptaking* signals or non-committal responses in order to avoid seeking clarification and admitting to the interlocutor that they have not understood.

Vandergrift found that novice learners of L2 used more kinesics and global reprises and hypothesis testing in L1 than did intermediate learners who used less of these strategies anyway. Of course this is not surprising. The more proficient you are, the less likely you are to need clarification of the message (provided that the topic of the conversation is at the same level of difficulty). But what was interesting was that Vandergrift was able to detect more qualitative differences in the patterns of strategy use. The more advanced learners were able to do the following:

> process groups of words leaving attentional energy for giving feedback to the speaker, continually advancing the conversation. They no longer needed the more rudimentary strategies to signal lack of comprehension . . . they could pin-point more precisely where they needed help . . . furthermore they could do this in the target language.

This idea of pinpointing where help is needed would seem to be a crucially important strategy for learners to employ. Furthermore (although Vandergrift does not discuss the point), it would seem to me that *faking* could well be used by advanced learners in a positive manner. It is perfectly reasonable to fake understanding if the listener has understood the gist of the message but considers it not worth stopping the flow of the conversation in order to understand every detail.

In reading the work of Vandergrift you may have been struck by the parallels with the discussion at the beginning of this chapter about descriptive and interventionist studies when I outlined a possible study for improving learner's understanding of procedural instructions. I developed this idea by building on an experiment by Mary Haynes, one of the teachers involved in the Lingua project. Mary selected a number of 'learner-centred' lessons[4] in which she knew the procedural instructions to set them up would be very complex. She then used the instructions as a listening comprehension exercise with typical exploitation activities (some materials for experimenting with this are offered in Chapter 6). She found that not only did the learners understand better what they had to do but they also began to interact with her more in order to ensure that they had understood. In a limited form, this piece of action research is an interventionist study. It sought to develop better reception strategies by making the 'listening to the teacher' more interactive.

Of course it is not always possible to interact with speakers. There are times when the oral message is coming at us in a way which we cannot control. This does not mean that we have no control over our reaction to it. There are strategies we can use in order to compensate for that lack of control. We will return briefly to listening strategies by reading what some Italian learners of English said they do in order to cope with an incoming recorded text with which they were having difficulty. The following are snippets of interviews recorded during an earlier study (reported in Macaro 1998) and which are translated here:

> I try to identify the words I already know and from these I can usually understand the gist of the text . . . other times I use the tone of voice. (Anna)

> First of all, to get a general feeling of what's going on, I identify the subject of what I guess is being talked about and I link to this all the characteristics that I would associate with it. (Lorella)

> In that listening exercise there weren't lots of sounds and so I couldn't use them, there weren't even any feelings expressed [in the tone of voice] and so I just had to rely on the words. (Massimo)

> To understand a dialogue in English I really concentrate on all the phrases as they are pronounced so that I can then re-order them into a longer phrase . . . thanks to recognizing a few of the words I manage to get hold of (afferro, literally 'grab') the meaning of the phrase. (Chiara)

PAUSE FOR THOUGHT

What do you notice about the variety of strategies that these students are using in order to understand an oral text over which they have no control?

Can you detect the same type of bottom-up and top-down processing that we came across in Chapter 3?

Do you use the tape recorder a lot in your teaching? If you do, then do you think that it is important to counterbalance this 'lack of control' over incoming input by giving learners the opportunity to exercise some control as in the experiment that Mary Haynes carried out above?

We can now posit in diagrammatic form what we mean by interaction strategies (Figure 4.1). Faerch and Kasper (1986: 189) report the findings of another study where an attempt was made to train learners to use interaction strategies. They were adolescent Danish learners of English. An oral communicative task was video-recorded and learners were then asked, immediately on completion, to self-report on problems they had encountered and how they had tried to solve them. The recording and the self-report provided the researchers with a list of interaction strategies that the class used as a group. The training for strategy use then lasted three months. Following the three months period, a post-treatment recording was made. The findings were that:

- Middle proficiency level learners made considerable progress in using interaction strategies.
- Low and high proficiency learners made less progress.
- The general attitude in the class towards errors and towards risk-taking had changed. More learners accepted the need to make an attempt even if they did not know the right word.

Faerch and Kasper do not speculate as to why the intermediate learners were the group that made most progress but this finding is not unique in the literature on learner training. Moreover, there is no mention of a control group (which would not have received the training) with which to compare the effect of the training.

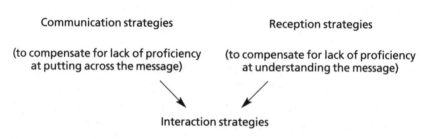

Figure 4.1 *Interaction strategies*

Perhaps one of the most successful studies of training for interaction strategies, and one which did use a control group, was that of Dadour and Robbins (1996). Here, Egyptian university students of English received strategy training for three hours per week over more than a three-month period. The treatment group was found to have made significant improvements in their speaking over the control group, specifically in fluency, range of vocabulary and grammar. Interestingly, the effect of the training seemed to permeate all types of strategy use, not only interaction strategies.

To summarize this section, then, we could restate the claim that communication strategies are learner strategies that do not, in themselves, provide direct evidence of improving language competence. However, their spin-off effects may lead indirectly to improved language competence because of their involvement in the more complex set of interaction strategies. In addition, the beginner student is provided with

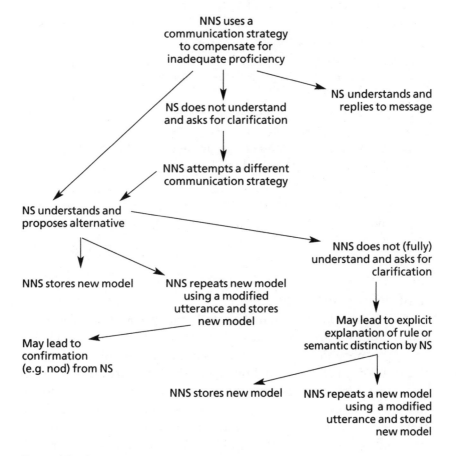

Figure 4.2 *Learning opportunities in interaction*

Note: NNS= non-native speaker; NS= native speaker

the evidence that communication can take place despite gaps in their language competence. Communication strategies, in this sense, are surface manifestations of social and affective strategies. Training for communication strategies, like other strategies, may need substantial amounts of time before significant results begin to show. Figure 4.2 demonstrates the sorts of opportunities for learning which derive from communicative strategies. In order to simplify matters we will suppose that in Figure 4.2 we have a conversation between a native speaker and a non-native speaker.

PAUSE FOR THOUGHT

In which of your teaching strategies might you find out about strategies for interaction being used by learners in your classroom? To what extent and how might the following factors impede or promote the use of interaction strategies?:

(a) size of class
(b) motivation of learners
(c) current language proficiency of learners
(d) age of learners
(e) cultural background of the learners.

You might also like to consolidate your understanding by providing a real L2 example of Figure 4.2. That is:

NNS says: 'XXXX'
NS says: 'XXXX'

and so on.

Memorizing language

It will be remembered that in Chapter 3 there was a cluster of learning strategies whose frequency was elicited from learners on the Lingua project as possible ways in which they might commit language to memory. We need to remind ourselves that memorization involves processing language in the working memory such that it can be stored, and later retrieved from the long-term memory. It has also been suggested that the strategies and pathways by which language is retrieved will be similar if not identical to the way it was stored. However, it is unclear from the literature on cognition which strategy is used for retrieval if a whole network of strategies has been used for storing the language items. The following cluster of five strategies (from the Lingua project) could be said to consist of strategies which are a definite conscious effort to commit language to memory:

1. Practise saying new words out loud at home.
2. Learn vocabulary by a system which suits you (e.g. look, hide, say, write, check).
3. Make mental associations when trying to memorize difficult words (perhaps with something funny).
4. Turn language into songs, rhymes, raps or mnemonics.
5. Act out language at home (for example, a scene in a restaurant).

In addition, we could say that the following strategies may be used by learners both to practise in preparation for immediate production and (probably but not inevitably) for committal to long-term memory:

6. Repeat words to yourself when you hear them in class.
7. Do silent practice, thinking in your head.
8. Make a note of new words.

Classifying strategies according to whether they serve a single direct purpose or whether they serve multiple purposes is one useful way for learners to consider their effectiveness. Language learning requires effort but that effort will only be exerted by the learner if the results appear encouraging and if they can have a number of positive effects.

Another way of classifying memorization strategies is offered by Rod Ellis. He draws a distinction between those strategies 'used to memorize isolated lexical items and those strategies used to learn new words from context' (Ellis 1994: 553).

Two further distinctions might be drawn:

1. Between those memorization strategies which use the L1 (or even the L3) as a vehicle for storage and recall and those that use only the L2 (however, we should bear in mind our discussion about the language of thought at the end of Chapter 3).
2. Between strategies for learning grammar (for example, mnemonics of groups of verbs) and those for learning vocabulary. This is because vocabulary is more likely to be linked to semantic fields – networks of meaning connections. Mnemonics, on the other hand, will use connections which are not necessarily linked semantically but between idea and idea.

Later in this book we will be looking in some detail at how memorization strategies are used by learners, how you can make them aware of these strategies and how to train learners to use these strategies. For the moment we will look at the results of three intervention studies.

The first is by Cohen and Aphek (1981). This study was essentially concerned with whether strategy training improved Hebrew vocabulary acquisition. Students were shown how making mental associations could assist in vocabulary recall. This is sometimes called keyword technique and is explained more fully later. They then selected their own words from a reading text and made their own associations. A variety of other activities were used in order to practise this strategy. The initial association led to better performance at retrieving vocabulary.

The second is by Chamot, Barnhardt, El Dinary and Robbins (1996) in which strategy training included strategies for learning vocabulary. In this study no pre- and post-test analysis seems to have been carried out or improvement in competence measured, but the students did self-report that they had found the strategies useful.

Third, there is the study by Brown and Perry (1991). Here the research into vocabulary acquisition investigated whether learners retained vocabulary better if they tried to make semantic associations (for example, linking words to other similar words) or keyword associations (linking words to visual or auditory images which had no semantic connection but which, usually, involved a combination of L1 and L2). The results showed that the semantic associations helped more than the keyword associations but the students who were asked to store language *both with semantic and keyword associations* actually retained the vocabulary best. Again, it is a combination of strategies that seems to be the most effective.

The Lingua project on memorization

The fourth study was carried out as part of the Lingua project but only by the English group of learners (13-14 year olds). That is to say that only the English group of learners went beyond strategy elicitation to an intervention which attempted to find out if training could help them memorize vocabulary better. These were matched against a comparison group. Four 'experimental' classes and two comparison classes were used. Most researchers would argue for an equal number to be in the comparison group as the experimental group but unfortunately ideal conditions are not always possible. On this occasion the enthusiasm of the teachers led them to want to train more classes than not. Moreover, because of absence, not all students who did the initial baseline test completed the Stage 3 test, see Table 4.1. Numbers which matched both tests were therefore reduced and this should be borne in mind in terms of size of sample. Table 4.1 provides a detailed procedure that the teachers agreed upon in order to standardize the process by which the study was to be carried out. The protocol is slightly adapted for the purposes of this book. We should not forget that prior to the procedure the students had filled in a general questionnaire about strategy use which contained questions about techniques for memorizing.

In order to generate awareness during the strategy training period a list of strategies which had been collected during the project as a whole was discussed with the learners. This included the original items relating to memorization on the questionnaire but also the additional strategies suggested by individuals in the open-ended section of the questionnaire which simply asked 'Can you describe any other things you do which help you to: understand, memorize or study the foreign language?'. These are the memorization strategies they said they used:

1. When there is a test coming up I make notes on paper of the very important or difficult words and then I make check cards which I can look through and come back to.
2. I record my voice on a cassette and listen to it in order to help me memorize the words.
3. To memorize a text, first I try to understand what it's about, and then I repeat it out loud a short piece at a time until by the end I can say it all and I've learnt it off by heart.
4. I make up phrases or dialogues from words I've learnt on a particular day (even if I don't have to).

During early discussions about memorization strategies a very interesting technique was proposed by one learner. She was a very able learner, according to her teacher. She said she wrote words or phrases on Post-It stickers and left them stuck on to items in her bedroom one or two days before the test. She then made mental associations (created a mental picture) between what was on the sticker and the item it was stuck to (e.g. *un séjour* stuck to a portable stereo, and she pictured herself *staying* in France and carrying the portable stereo around her penpal's house). What is particularly interesting about this self-reported account is that there is a combination of two strategies going on here. The first is to have continuous exposure to language elements in comfortable and often-visited surroundings (her bedroom). The second is to make mental associations which is sometimes known as the keyword technique. This double approach, perhaps with particularly difficult words or phrases, was providing sufficient in-depth processing of the language such that it lodged in her long-term memory.

Table 4.1   *Procedure for Lingua memorization study*

Experimental group	Comparison group
Stage 1. Pre-treatment test 1 (November)	
Teachers prepare list of 25 items of vocabulary or short formulaic phrases *in L2* (not verbs and including genders), (maximum of 5 cognates) which are a mixture of 2 topics which have been completed but not tested for at least 2 weeks (preferably not tested as specific vocabulary items at all). For example: 'parts of the body' and 'restaurant food'. The vocabulary should be the result of work done on written and aural texts.	Same procedure
Students are given list and told they have 15 minutes to memorize in class. Teachers don't give any instructions or suggestions or hints. However, teachers offer the use of a dictionary during the 15 minutes memorization stage.	Same procedure
Students tested on the 25 items using a list with the L1 equivalent.	Same procedure
Immediately after the memorization session, students have approximately 15 minutes to complete the test (no dictionary of course). At end of test students are asked to write down what strategy they used to memorize the words during the 15 minutes given for memorization.	Same procedure but students are not asked to write down what strategy they used to memorize the words (in order not to raise awareness of strategy use)
Teachers mark the test: 0 = incomprehensible or wrong; 1 = minor spelling mistake but not affecting communication; 2 = completely correct. Marks out of 50	Same procedure
Stage 2 Treatment (Between January and March)	Group receives no training
(Learner Strategy training)	
Students undergo programme of awareness of memorization strategies (class discussion, referring back to questionnaire); plus some system of recording their use of strategies, modelling of strategy use – anything which will encourage students to use memorization strategies when learning at home (see below). Plus a series of tests during these three months to give them opportunities to deploy strategies. This could be any sort of test involving memorization: verbs; phrases; vocabulary.	
Stage 3 Post-treatment test 1 (early April)	Same procedure but no 'advice on strategy use' given
Students given 25 different items of vocabulary in L2 only. Procedure as for stage 1. Students given 15 minutes to memorize. This time teachers give instructions: 'Please make sure that you use one or more strategies for memorizing that you have tried out in the past three months.'	
Test list given to students using L1 equivalent	Same procedure
Students have approximately 15 minutes to complete the test. At end of test students asked to write down what strategy they used to memorize the words during the 15 minutes given for memorization.	Same procedure but students are not asked to which strategies they used.
Same marking scheme as in stage 1.	Same procedure

Finally, one of the teachers in Italy asked a number of her best students (14 year olds) in her class to write down what they did to memorize English irregular verbs before a test. Here are two particularly interesting accounts.

Student 1	Student 2

I read and repeat all the verbs starting with a 'B'. After having done that about ten times I write them down, just as I remember them maybe three or four times. After having checked them . . . .if they're wrong I repeat them and rewrite them until there are no more mistakes.
 	
    Those which are impossible to remember I write on a small sheet of paper which I put in my pocket and every now and then I read it. At night before going to bed I say them to someone.
 	
    Early in the morning I go through them again for the last time.
	I read and repeat orally and at random the verbs to my mother. Then I try to repeat them in order and write them down on some rough paper. I repeat the irregular verbs in my head, on and off and then I check my answers.

Evidently this amount of effort was paying off. If it is true, as Brown and Perry (1991) claim, that vocabulary acquisition is dependent on 'depth of processing' (i.e. the amount and different ways in which we process and store language), then Student 1 and some of the other successful vocabulary learners in the study were 'doing the right thing'. But what is particularly interesting is that both these successful students were using their own personal strategies and, furthermore, it appears that strategy deployment is more successful in clusters of strategies. Finally, a noticeable feature is that they had evidently monitored and evaluated what worked best for them.

As we can see from Tables 4.2, 4.3 and 4.4 the average (mean) scores in the baseline test for the comparison group suggest slightly higher achievement levels. In other words, at the beginning of the study, the comparison group, by chance, scored higher. After the strategy training period both groups score higher in their tests. There are two probable explanations for this. First, the test might have been easier and, second, both groups might have improved their techniques for committing language to memory – some of the learners in the comparison group may have developed some successful strategies themselves, without being trained in strategy use. The important thing,

Table 4.2   *Results of test 1 using memorization strategies*

Test 1 (baseline) 25 vocabulary items: 1 point communication 1 point accuracy	Number of students	Average score out of 50	SD
experimental group	76	22.8	9.7
comparison group	51	25.0	9.1

Table 4.3   *Results of test 2*

Test 2 (after memorization training) 25 vocabulary items: 1 point communication 1 point accuracy	Number of students	Average score out of 50	SD
experimental	83	34.6	9.4
comparison	43	31.0	9.7

Table 4.4   *Comparison of results of tests 1 and 2*

	Number of students	Average gain for each group	SD
experimental	70	12.35	8.5
comparison	41	5.41	10.6
2-tail significance:			
equal: 0.000			
unequal: 0.001		Mean difference: 6.94	

however, is that the scores are reversed – *the experimental group scored higher*. Statistically, the gain is significant ($p = 0.001$).

The results of the above experiment suggested to both teachers and researcher that some adolescent learners when told to learn language or revise for a test normally go home without much idea of how to go about the task of learning and that they do need to be trained to use more strategies and more effectively.

PAUSE FOR THOUGHT

How is your list of strategies progressing? Which of the above categorizations of memorization strategies do you find most helpful for your own teaching context? Rebecca Oxford has one further way of dividing them up, see Table 4.5.

Table 4.5 *Oxford's categorizations of memorization strategies*

Category of memorization strategy	Example
creating mental linkages	classifying language into meaningful units
applying images and sounds	associating an abstract word with a visual symbol
reviewing well	revising language in carefully spaced intervals, at first close together and then more widely spaced apart
employing action	writing words on cards and moving cards from one stack to another when a word is learned

Adapted from Oxford (1990: 43)

Does your list of strategies fit better into Oxford's classification?

Use of the target language

In our strategy training should we be encouraging the learner to avoid reference to L1 for specific tasks or use the L1 in a positive and effective way? We can do this by looking at the two areas we have explored in this chapter: interaction strategies and memorization strategies.

Interaction strategies

In this aspect of language learning it would make sense to suggest that the learner should be avoiding conscious thinking in L1. Or, at least, they should be making strategic decisions about when to rush ahead with the L2 spoken communication and when to slow down and/or use linguistic devices in order to 'buy time' in which to monitor (probably with some L1 involvement) the output. We have catalogued above all the benefits of deploying a number of strategies in order to keep the interaction going. However, we have also noted that the good L2 learner will be studying the feedback from the native speaker interlocutor for elements which they can add to their repertoire in the future. This *noticing* of new language will be operating concurrently with the oral output in L2. Given our discussion on the limits of working memory processing capacity, it is not an unwise conjecture that the noticing will be mediated by the L1.

Memorization strategies

It would seem appropriate to conclude that a balance needs to be struck between strategies that use the L1 to aid memorization and strategies which use only the L2. Strategies that involve sub-vocalization of the target language are clearly attempting to by-pass the L1 in their efforts to achieve deep processing into LTM. Strategies which involve putting language to music or go about linking an L2 item with a visual image also would seem to be by-passing the L1 and our teaching strategies should attempt to exclude the L1 in these situations. This is all well and good and in a way, this was what the audio-lingual method of language learning was also trying to do. The problem is that there is a limit to how much language can be stored in this way. Just how many visual images does the teacher (or the learner for that matter) have to create in order to help the beginner and intermediate student store large quantities of language? In any case, the visual approach is likely to limit storage to individual lexical items or short phrases. To effect the kind of increase to the vocabulary store that adolescent and adult learners need to make in order to make satisfactory progress (1,000 words a year?), they will need more than just this limited range of strategies. It is here that the L1 can offer support by providing the L2 with the highly developed storage system that is the long-term memory and through its interaction with the working memory. Further research may be able to provide answers of when some kind of threshold is reached. When do learners become sufficiently advanced that new vocabulary and idiomatic phrases are stored, apparently, in an effortless manner and one which appears to exclude the L1?

BEFORE WE MOVE ON

What strategies are used by learners when they are engaged in a conversation with a native speaker of the foreign language? To what extent do you already encourage your learners to use these strategic interaction strategies?

If and when you ask your students to 'learn' some language, do you share an understanding of how they might go about this?

In what way could you help your students take on more responsibility for the way they revise and consolidate new language that they have learnt in the classroom?

Notes

1. Strictly speaking, a control group has to be assigned at random. In our example we would have to toss a coin to see which group we wanted to experiment with and which group we wanted to 'control' in the experiment. If they are not assigned at random they are 'matched' with a comparison group.

2. The theory of interlanguage goes something like this: learners who make mistakes when speaking or writing do not do so (necessarily) because they are lazy, inattentive, careless or have a low aptitude for the language. Their 'interlanguage', their current competence in the language, is quite systematic. Errors, compared to the native speaker model, are the result of systematic hypothesizing about the target language. These hypotheses may be influenced by transfer from their L1 or by over-generalizing from what they already know (or have noticed) about the L2.

3. For further reading on earlier work, see Tarone (1981).

4. For example, carousels where groups of learners move around to perform a variety of tasks.

CHAPTER 5

An Intervention Study in Detail

Having explored in the previous chapter intervention studies which looked at oral interaction and memorization, it is now time to describe and look in detail at the findings of the Oxford Writing Strategies Project. This project endeavoured to help 14–15-year-old learners of French to learn more about themselves as writers and thereby improve their writing potential. First, a little contextual background to the process of writing in the foreign language.

Throughout the 1970s and early 1980s a great deal of attention was dedicated to L2 writing and many teaching materials were produced which tried to focus on writing *as a process*, an approach which, according to Silva, provided:

> A positive, encouraging, and collaborative working environment within which students, with ample time and minimal interference, can work through their composing processes. The teacher's role is to help students develop viable strategies for getting started (finding topics, generating ideas and information, focusing, and planning structure and procedure), for drafting (encouraging multiple drafts), for revising (adding, deleting, modifying and rearranging ideas); and for editing (attending to vocabulary, sentence structure, grammar and mechanics). (1990: 15)

However, as Krapels (1990: 37) observes, few of the proposed principles were based on empirical research. In particular, few of the proponents of a process approach had explored the underlying processes used by the learners as they prepared themselves to write and as they wrote. This began to change in the late 1980s and 1990s as teaching strategies began to be based on a more thorough understanding of learner strategies. This shift towards the learner also revealed that, contrary to what had originally been thought, the strategies used for L2 writing were not always the same as those used for L1 writing.

PAUSE FOR THOUGHT

In Chapter 1 we paused to think about what sorts of strategies your learners might adopt when they are sitting at home attempting a written task. In Chapter 2 we looked at some questions which tried to elicit strategy use from learners while doing a writing task. You may need to remind yourself of these, they are on pp. 51–5. Let's now take this a stage further. Imagine your students are about to do a writing task, this time in your classroom. Think about your teaching strategies. For example:

1. Have you decided that the writing task should come at the beginning, middle or end of a series of lessons on the same topic?
2. Does the writing task have a direct link or indirect link with the vocabulary and phrases that you have been working with recently?
3. What have been your criteria for choosing the writing task topic? For example, is it something 'about the target country' or something 'personal to the learners'?

What advice do you give them?

1. Only use the L2 when planning? That is, only use the foreign language that they already know?
2. Use a mixture of language they already know and language they have to make up?
3. Use only the phrases that you have provided for them and rearrange these, perhaps adding a few new words here and there?
4. Do you tell them that the content (what they manage to express) is more important than the accuracy of what they write or vice versa?
5. Do you tell them to write a draft first and then re-draft?
6. Do you allow them to use a monolingual dictionary?
7. Do you allow them to use a bilingual dictionary?

Elsewhere in this book I have suggested that learner strategies cannot be divorced completely from teaching strategies. Although there is evidence that some learners go about it their own way, whatever the teacher asks them to do, my contention has been that the range of possible strategies is reduced by our teaching approaches. In order to demonstrate this let us look at one piece of writing strategy research. Alexander Friedlander (1990) was particularly interested in how the first language of Chinese (L1) students of English (L2) at university had an effect on their preparation for writing (planning) and on writing itself (composing). The students were asked to perform two written tasks. In the first task they were to plan in their L1. In the second they were to plan in the L2. Planning consisted of brainstorming ideas on the topic and organizing these ideas in preparation for the composing part of the task. In order to explore one further aspect, Friedlander made the two topics different by asking the students to write about a Chinese festival (thus a topic the students had definitely only experienced in their L1) and about life at the American university (thus a topic that the students had essentially experienced in the L2). This provided a matrix as shown in Figure 5.1.

He then called AX and BY the 'matched conditions' and AY and BX the 'mismatched conditions' for planning. Friedlander found that the students demonstrated much higher quality of planning in the matched condition than in the mismatched condition. Students produced more details, richer ideas and wrote longer and better plans. Moreover, the essays themselves (which of course were in L2), resulting from the planning in the matched condition, were longer and of superior quality than those used in the mismatched condition. Friedlander concluded that when writers

> use their second language to write on a topic related to their first language, and when they plan in their second language, they are constrained in terms of the amount of material retrieved; in contrast, translation does not appear to hinder writers in their text production by causing them to take more time over their texts.

A Task planned in L1		X Task related to previous (L1) cultural experience
B Task planned in L2		Y Task related to target country experience

Figure 5.1 *Matrix of tasks*
Source: Adapted from Friedlander (1990: 114)

We can see how these findings relate to the questions you were asking about your teaching strategies above. It would seem that planning in the L2 is limited in that it is only beneficial in those topic areas which students have actually experienced in L2. As soon as they want to put in something of themselves, they become constrained.

A similar study was carried out by Hiroe Kobayashi and Carol Rinnert (1992). Here the comparison between translation versus direct composition was even simpler in that the nature of the topics was not compared. Some forty-eight Japanese university students of English were able to produce compositions with greater syntactic complexity when they translated what they wanted to say from L1 than when they wrote directly in L2. The other variable was in the perceived level of the students. For students with less competence in writing the advantage of translating over direct composition in L2 was even more marked than for students with higher writing competence. Higher-level students, when translating, also made a greater number of errors which might interfere with communication than did the lower-level students when they were translating.

These two studies provide us with two diverging avenues to explore. First, are the teacher's teaching strategies running contrary to what at least some students find a facilitating strategy? That is, if we force students to plan in the L2 for a topic that is personal to them, the experience of which was acquired in L1, we may be inhibiting their preferred (and possibly successful) writing strategy. Second, it is quite possible that, despite the teaching strategy that we adopt, the students will be thinking and planning in L1 anyway. If this is so, should we fight against it or find ways of patching up the negative effects of planning in L1 and thus turn it into a successful strategy? It is these two avenues that we will explore now in relating in detail the Oxford Writing Strategies project. In doing so we must bear in mind that we will be talking about low to intermediate learners. It is likely that very advanced learners are able to plan effectively and compose entirely in the L2. In any case, if they're that advanced, they have probably worked out their whole panoply of effective strategies and therefore don't need our help anywhere near as much.

The Oxford Writing Strategies Project

Six classes of 14–15 year olds, in six different schools took part in the writing strategies project. All had been studying French for three and a half years when the project started, averaging about 2.5 hours per week. The classes were randomly assigned thus providing three experimental (treatment groups) and three as control groups as is shown in Table 5.1.

Table 5.1 *Allocation of groups in the Oxford Writing Strategies project*

School	Allocation	Description
A	experimental	13–18 mixed comprehensive[1]
B	experimental	11–18 mixed comprehensive
C	experimental	11–18 mixed comprehensive
D	control	13–18 mixed comprehensive
E	control	11–18 mixed comprehensive
F	control	11–18 mixed comprehensive

Table 5.2 provides a description of the instruments of data collection used in the project. In addition, interviews were carried out with all six teachers at the beginning of the project and with the three 'treatment group' teachers at the end of the project. The project lasted approximately five months from the end of February to July. However, it should be noted that a number of school holidays and calendar events greatly reduced the amount of time available for learner training of the experimental group. It will be observed from Table 5.2 that the various instruments used to collect data had the dual purpose of finding out what strategies the students were using and what level of writing performance they were at.

It will also be observed that a number of instruments are designated as '1'. These were the baseline data collection instruments – the ones that tried to find out where we starting from. After these were administered, a programme of strategy training was carried out with the experimental group only. Because of the large quantity of data collected in the study it is impossible here to provide anything but an overview of how the researchers and teachers went about their work and a summary of the findings.

In the interviews the six teachers were asked what the learners found most difficult about writing and below are some of the things that they came up with.

Recognizing the different types of words . . . what is a verb . . . gender . . . they find very difficult . . . adjectival endings . . . uhm, the partitive . . . linking words . . . they never remember the linking words to join two clauses in a sentence. (Ben)

Table 5.2   *Instruments used for data collection and their purposes*

Purpose: writing strategy elicitation	Instrument of data collection administered to both experimental and control groups	Purpose: to gauge level of language proficiency
consisting of 3 biographical questions, 9 strategy use questions, 5 attitude questions plus one final open-ended question	questionnaire 1: beginning of project (see Chapter 2)	no
no	series of previously attempted or completed writing tasks from students' exercise books or folders	estimate approximate levels of writing proficiency; types of language tasks offered; frequency of written tasks
students asked to identify which words they looked up in a dictionary; students asked to self-report what approaches/strategies they had used in order to complete task	writing task 1 (see Chapter 2)	error analysis carried out on task according to proportion of errors to number of noun phrases and verb phrases
students asked to self-report on whether they had used a rule or whether they knew the structure/ morpheme 'off by heart'	structures and morphemes test 1	gauge competence in: perfect tense; agreement of adjectives
on-task observation/ elicitation of strategy use	think-aloud task (18 students)**	error analysis carried out on task according to ratio of errors to number of noun phrases and verb phrases
strategy use questions and attitude questions. Some necessary variability between experimental and control questionnaires	questionnaire 2: end of project	no
students asked to identify which words they looked up in a dictionary	writing task 2	error analysis carried out on task according to proportion of errors to number of noun phrases and verb phrases
students asked to self-report what approaches/strategies they had used in order to complete task		
students asked to self-report on whether they had used a rule or whether they knew the structure/morpheme off by heart	structures and morphemes test 2	gauge competence in: perfect tense; agreement of adjectives
on-task observation/ elicitation of strategy use	think-aloud task (18 students)**	error analysis carried out on task according to proportion of errors to number of noun phrases and verb phrases

Note: ** In these cases, the instrument of data collection was administered to only the experimental group.

I guess vocabulary to start with. They haven't got enough vocabulary to be writing about the topic. (Clare)

They get the ideas in their heads in English and their own use of English can affect how they want to translate things into French and they say to you: how do I say 'I've got' and they can't see that that is I 'have' . . . that their own use of English restricts what they can write in French. (Ben)

I guess the first thing is certainly just to understand the way the grammar is working because they are thinking too much in English. (Anna)

They tend to try to say things which they don't know how to say. (Daniel)

They find verbs very difficult – it's the verbs outside the set phrase (formulaic expression or chunk) where they do have to know the verbs themselves. (Geneviève)

We will now focus on two aspects which involved intervention:

1. In what way did the learners say that their writing strategies had changed over the period of five months? That is, via the questionnaires, did the treatment group feel they had changed as a result of the learner training and did the control group feel they had changed simply because of the passage of time and normal teacher input?
2. In what ways had the learners' writing process (planning, composing, checking) changed over the period of the project? That is, what evidence was there that strategy training had affected the treatment group and what evidence was there that the passage of time and normal teacher input had affected the control group?

Let us start, therefore, with the questionnaires. In questionnaire 1 (the baseline questionnaire) a number of themes emerged which proved very useful in designing the kind of strategy training that followed. This confirmed the view that researchers have to find out from the particular groups being researched their current strategy rather than relying on previous research and then embarking on some form of learner training. Learners' strategy use will depend on a number of factors, of which the most important are just as likely to be age and educational context as they are to be related to sex. In fact, the most striking finding about this initial questionnaire was the lack of significant sex differences found in the sample in favour of females. Only four significant differences were found and these were that females were more likely to:

- use a wider range of resources (e.g. teaching materials $p = 0.00$);
- were more likely to check the spelling of words ($p = 0.05$);
- read what they had written out loud ($p = 0.00$);
- describe themselves as 'less sloppy' than males ($p = 0.05$).

Males, however, rated themselves higher as 'writers of French' than females and this over-confidence in their abilities is a feature to be found elsewhere in the research literature.

Differences in approaches to writing at the beginning of the study (baseline)

We will be looking at these different approaches under five headings:

1. Strategies for checking written work
2. Help from others
3. Thinking in English and translating into French
4. Using a combination of composing strategies
5. Careful students and sloppy students

Strategies for checking written work

There were significant differences ($p = < 0.05$) to be found between those learners who reported that they checked their work as they wrote and those who checked their work at the end of the composition process. I shall call the former the *As I Writers*. These had been given the examples of 'sentence by sentence or word by word'. The *As I Writers* had a number of significant characteristics. They were:

- much more likely to check the spelling of words;
- much more likely to check the word order;
- much more likely to check the endings of words;
- much more likely to check that it actually made sense by using back-translation;
- much more likely to read the writing out loud to see if it sounded right;
- much more likely to look for mistakes that they made all the time.

As well as this, the *As I Writers* were more likely to describe themselves as very careful or fairly careful and they were more likely to rate themselves as good or very good writers of French. However, these last two features, while being significant, suffered from not having the benefit of a larger sample.

Now, what can we deduce or infer from this initial data? First, I should try to dispel one or two objections. You may have reacted by saying, 'Well, it's obvious, the *As I Writers* are bound to check more and be more vigilant about their work.' But is it so obvious? As teachers have we ever given the advice: 'Get it all down quick and check your work afterwards'? Has this not been further compounded by the use of computers to re-draft our work where the assumption is that they will brainstorm the whole of the piece of writing onto the screen and then meticulously check each word and sentence? I was certainly surprised by this result. I thought that learners just had a different approach (*as you write* or *check at the end*) and that either was effective. The think-aloud transcripts, as we shall see later in more detail, do not support this view. The students who left most of their checking to the end simply read it through out loud to see if it (vaguely) sounded right to them. They neither checked word endings nor back-translated sentences to see if they made any sense. Consequently most errors went unnoticed. A second objection might be that those who check at the end just haven't been taught properly. They haven't been made sufficiently aware of writing as a process, that re-drafting is as important a part of writing as the initial composition. This may be true. In which case the answer may lie in cognitive theory again. So, let's go back to this.

PAUSE FOR THOUGHT

How do *you* write in the foreign language? You may well have a second foreign language in which you are not very confident. Do you check as you write? What produces the greatest processing load on your working memory? Try both approaches out if you wish. Let's take both scenarios.

Scenario 1

You check as you write – you check every sentence and you selectively check words within that sentence. You are involved in dual processes. You are composing language (retrieving propositions/ideas from long-term memory and coding them in language). At the same time you are monitoring the language against declarative knowledge (explicit knowledge you have of the rule system) before writing or while writing. You may either hold the sentence/phrase in your head and monitor or write and then monitor. All the time you may be thinking of what ideas you are going to write down next.

Scenario 2

You check at the end – no dual endeavour here. You are simply monitoring what has already been written. However, the amount of monitoring you have to now do is huge. It probably takes a great deal of will power.

What do you think? Do you think scenario 1 has the highest processing load? Probably yes. Perhaps that's why 49 per cent of the sample said they were not *As You Writers*. If it's true that *As You Writers* are the more successful writers in this age group then it may be that they have a greater working memory capacity. Perhaps this is an interesting avenue for research. Of course there is also the possibility that they felt that they had too little time to check as they wrote.

Of course, psycholinguistic processes are not the only ones to have an effect on the way that we write in a foreign language. There are also social factors and affective factors.

Help from others

There were significant differences in those students who reported that they enlisted the help of parents or friends when writing. These students were:

- more likely to check the endings of words;
- more likely to enjoy writing French;
- more likely to check that it made sense;
- more likely to read the writing out loud to see if it sounded right;
- more likely to look for mistakes that they made all the time.

In other words, the profile of the successful writer for this age group and context may well be one where the written work is checked sentence by sentence and one who considers writing sufficiently important to want to involve others in helping him/her to achieve success.

Thinking in English and translating into French

The pre-treatment questionnaire revealed a few differences in the planning process. Those students who thought in L1 and translated into L2, at least sometimes, were more likely to look for mistakes they made all the time. On the other hand, those who didn't use a translation strategy were less likely to check the spellings of words. This would make sense. Students who checked more were also likely to use a translation approach more because the very process of translating caused them to stop and think analytically (but not necessarily correctly) about what they were writing.

Using a combination of composing strategies

The questionnaire wanted to find out whether the hypothesis was sustained that the more confident learners used a combination of composing strategies. Cross-referencing this question with others produced the following findings. Those who used a combination of composing strategies were:

- more likely to check spelling of words;
- more likely to check endings of words;
- more likely to describe themselves as careful;
- more likely to rate writing French as important.

Those that reported *not* using a combination were also most likely to be the ones who did *not* enjoy writing French although here too the statistics could be taken with greater confidence if there had been a bigger sample. There was no link between combination of composition strategies and actually rating themselves as 'good writers'. The hypothesis was thus confirmed only in part and additional data may provide a clearer picture.

Careful students and sloppy students

Finally, a question was put in the questionnaire which was a form of validation of the questionnaire as an instrument itself. Respondents were asked to describe themselves in terms of careful or sloppy in their approach to checking writing. Those who described themselves as careful were:

- more likely to look for mistakes they made all the time;
- more likely to read it out loud to see if it sounded right;
- more likely to describe themselves as good writers of French.

Differences between treatment and control group at baseline

A comparison of the strategies used between the *control* and *treatment* groups at this stage showed a few significant (or near significant) differences:

1. The experimental groups claimed to have had many different teachers over the five years that they had been studying French.
2. The experimental group was more likely to rely on teacher materials than the control group.
3. The experimental group reported being 'higher dictionary users' than the control group.
4. The experimental group described itself as less careful when it came to checking their written work.
5. The experimental group reported enjoying writing French less than the control group.

With some of these early results in mind, learners were provided with the first written task. The task was to write between 100 and 120 words. The first written task had the following guidelines:

Your French friend has just let you know that he or she will be coming to your house in April. Tell him/her you are pleased. Describe your house and garden and particularly the guest room. Also tell him/her about a weekend (in the past) when you did something particularly interesting. Ask if he or she has done anything particularly interesting recently.

The task was designed to establish levels of competence in both the present and past tenses, in the agreement of adjectives and in asking questions. In addition, task 1 aimed to elicit how often the students were resorting to the dictionary. They did this by circling the words they looked up. Thus certain features of written task 1 could be ascertained, namely, the amount of dictionary use, evidence of wrong dictionary use and the reported strategy use and areas of difficulty on this particular task.

This description of the project provides us with an overall picture of where the students were prior to the strategy training process. At this point, rather than describe the qualitative data in its entirety, I have chosen to provide the reader with case studies of two individual students. We will thus explore the qualitative data collection through the experience of two students chosen from the eighteen students who did the think-aloud protocols. They are chosen because they are interesting cases, not necessarily for their typicality.

Two case studies of students in the experimental group

Laura and Katie were in school B. Both are successful students for their year cohort. That is to say, they have been placed in a 'high ability set'. Katie is described by their teacher as being of average ability and Laura as above average ability *within that group*. As the questionnaires were anonymous we cannot consider their individual self-reported strategies for writing nor their attitudes to writing. However, we do have other sources of data. First, let us look at their test and task results (Tables 5.3 and 5.4).

In both the perfect tense structures and the agreement of adjectives Katie claims that she arrives at her answers by thinking about a rule. She describes the rule for the perfect tense as: 'depending on the ending of the word in the vocabulary column (i.e. the infinitive) I would change it to the past tense by crossing off the "r" and adding an accent'. This is only a partial explanation of the rule with no reference to the two-verb nature of the perfect tense in French and to the need to select one of two possible auxiliaries, even though she provides auxiliaries in virtually all her answers. Katie's explanation of the rule for agreement of adjectives is nearer the mark: 'change endings according to gender'.

Laura, on the other hand, claims to use a mixture of formulaic knowledge and rule application for the past perfect structures. She describes the rule for the past perfect as: 'you take off the "r" at the end of the word and put an accent (if there's an "e" before the "r") in the e (é)'. In other words, it seems that she too is unable to articulate the rule about the need for one of two auxiliaries even though she provides auxiliaries in virtually all her answers. Of course she may not have thought it important to explain about the auxiliary verb. Even if this were the case, it would suggest that her focus was on the past participle rather than on the auxiliary and, as we shall see, this was something that was tackled later in the strategy training. Laura's explanation of the rule for agreement of adjectives is also nearer the mark: 'if the subject is masculine the vocab stays the same, feminine adds an "e".'

It looks as if the adjectival agreement rule is an easy rule to remember. The rule for the perfect, on the other hand, is quite complex. If we take a phrase like *nous sommes allées* there are more than *twelve permutations* of mistakes that could be made. We will return to the implications of this later.

Table 5.3   *Test results before strategy training*

	Katie	Laura
aspect of test		
perfect tense structures	69%	57%
use of rule or 'off by heart'	rule	mixture
agreement of adjectives	97%	86%
use of rule or 'off by heart'	rule	rule

Table 5.4   *Error analysis of task before strategy training (%)*

Katie	Laura	Average for class	Average for class
NP error 58	NP error 25	NP error 31	NP error 38.1
VP error 15	VP error 33	VP error 28	VP error 34.6

Note: NP = noun phrase; VP = verb phrase

Table 5.5   *Results after the strategy training*

Aspect of test	Katie	Laura
perfect tense structures	89%	85%
use of rule or 'off by heart'	rule	guessed most
agreement of adjectives	92%	97%
use of rule or 'off by heart'	rule	rule

Table 5.6   *Writing task error analysis (%)*

Katie	Laura	Average for class	Average for class
NP error 33.3	NP error 5.5	NP error 29.8	NP error 33.6
VP error 15.4	VP error 10	VP error 27.3	VP error 35.7

The task analysis gives us a fairly complex picture. While, of the two students, Katie scored a much higher noun-related error rating (NP = noun phrase), Laura scores a somewhat higher verb-related error rating (VP = verb phrase). This is, in part , because Laura attempts some more complex sentences in trying to answer the task requirements. Now let us look at the test and task results, this time after the strategy training (see Tables 5.5 and 5.6).

By the end of the training cycle there have been some notable changes in these two students. Both their test scores for the perfect tense have gone up considerably. Laura's score for agreement of adjectives has also gone up. Katie's score on agreement, interestingly, has (slightly) suffered from a transference of an L2 rule: *j'ai une voiture rapidée* (instead of *rapide*). The two students' explanations of the perfect tense rule both show evidence of an awareness of the auxiliary:

> Whether it was *être* or *avoir* changes the beginning depending on above.
> Change the ending of the word wanted: *er = é, re = u, ir = i.* (Katie)

> I used the Mr Vanderstramp[2] (*être*) rule, where if it . . . (unfinished). (Laura)

The task analysis also shows considerable improvement although in the case of Laura we need to treat the improvement with some caution as she claims, in her self-report, that she has done a task like this before (it would appear) of her own volition. The tasks attempted for the think alouds also show a marked improvement (as we shall see in a moment). What has brought about this improvement? Is it simply that these pupils were taught how to formulate the perfect tense and taught how to make adjectives agree? The answer is no. There was no attempt to change the teaching of the language nor the programme. In fact, the teacher of these two students did not revise the perfect tense with her class during the period from the end of February to July. The strategy training focused entirely on decision-making during composition and checking after each sentence. In other words, Katie and Laura did not learn anything new about the target language structures nor did they practise the structures in any controlled way. They were merely encouraged through the strategy training to try starting with some *advance preparation*, to think more carefully when making composition decisions and to check more carefully as they went along.

Before going on to describe the strategy training we need to look in greater detail at these two students' thinking and checking processes.

First, we can look at the amount of dictionary use that they demonstrated and whether they were using this correctly. In task 1 they were asked to identify which words they had looked up in the dictionary. Let us start with Katie. Highlighted words are those Katie reports looking up in the dictionary. Translation available in Appendix.

KATIE'S PRE-TREATMENT TASK

Bonjour! Je suis très joyeux `cette` *vous* `pouvez` *visiter dans Avril.*

Ma maison est dans en ville s'appelle Thame, c'est pres d'Oxford, et une heure `de Londres` *. Ma maison est assez grande. Au* `rez-de-chaussée` *il y a un cuisine, un salon et une sale a manger. En bas il y a mes parents chambre, ma chambre et* `chambre d'amis` *. Ma chambre est assez grande mais j'ai beaucoup de* `meubles` *. Je suis fille unique. Le chambre d'amis est assez petit et est un bearo(??) aussi avec un l'ordinetuer. Ma jardin est très grande il y a un* `étang` *. Dans la vacance je visite ma tante dan Lincolnshire. Je suis allés cyclisme et natation. C'était fatigant mais très amusement. Et toi? As-tu un vacance amusement.*

Grossess bissess

Katie

As we can see from this task, Katie uses the dictionary rarely, relying very much on formulaic language she already knows. Generally, she uses the dictionary with some success when checking the spelling of words she already knows (*Londres, rez-de-chaussée*) or if they are new words but nouns (*chambre d'amis, meubles, étang*). When they are new words, she appears to make typical dictionary errors. In fact, as soon as she tries to go beyond the formulaic language that she has learnt she makes serious mistakes which could affect communication. It looks as if she is hamstrung by her inability to generate sentences and to say what she wants to say in order to complete the task. We will note that the description of the house (already known chunks, *re-formulated*) dominates the other part of the task which was about describing a weekend in the past. In her self-report on this task she writes:

> I always try to use sentences I know and link them together. I use different techniques when approaching different subjects (i.e. topics). I often had to look up words in the dictionary or textbook and see if they fitted into a sentence but I added my own

> descriptive words . . . I will often write a sentence down and then have to check in the dictionary . . . tenses and adjectives often confuse me, especially the endings of words.

In her pre-treatment think aloud Katie produced the following piece of work:

KATIE'S WRITING FOR PRE-TREATMENT THINK ALOUD

Task rubric: You are in France. You have been asked by staff in a supermarket to write a description of a thief you have just seen running out of the shop. Give as much information (in the present tense) as you can (eye/hair colour, height, approximate weight, clothes he was wearing). For reference they also ask you to give information about yourself: when you left England, when you arrived in the town, where you are staying, when you intend to leave.

N.B. the crossings out are Katie's corrections. A translation is provided in the Appendix.

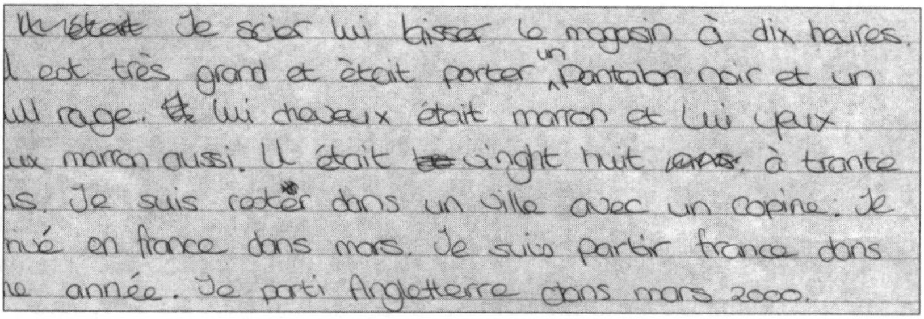
Il était Je scier lui laisser le magasin à dix haures.
l est très grand et était porter un pantalon noir et un
ull rage. Et lui chevaux était marron et lui yeux
ux marron aussi. Il était vinght huit ans. à trante
ns. Je suis rester dans un ville avec un copine. Je
rivé en france dans mars. Je suis partir france dans
ne année. Je parti Angletterre dans mars 2000.

Figure 5.2 *Katie's pre-treatment writing for think aloud*

Again, what we notice about Katie's work is that she finds it extremely difficult to generate a correct sentence when she is forced to write something specific. In the description of the thief she is able to rely to some extent on formulaic language she has learnt, but even here she displays considerable inaccuracies. Let us now look at brief extracts from this think aloud. In order to get the most understanding out of this you will need to refer simultaneously to Katie's writing, the transcription, my commentary and the strategy use summary on p.171.

Transcription extracts	Commentary
Katie: He was seen running away – *il était* Researcher: What are you thinking about? Katie: He was, the word for was . . . Huh, seen.	As we can see from this extract Katie makes a number of decisions. Some of these are right for her and some wrong.
Researcher: So is there a problem here? Katie: I don't know the word for seen. Researcher: What are you looking up?	She wants to generate the sentence 'he was seen leaving the shop' but quite rightly senses a problem with the passive and opts for the easier (canonical) 'I saw him leaving the shop'. However, she immediately falls for the L1–L2 transfer trap where in English the past tense needs only one verb.
Katie: Saw or seen . . . saw – I'm gonna change it to I saw him – *j'ai* (writes *scier lui* having crossed out *il était*). Researcher: Why did you change it? What made you make that decision? Katie: I dunno, to change it from present to past. Researcher: OK . . . What are you thinking about? Katie: The word for leaving, I know it (looks in dictionary).	She then proceeds to fall into the next trap which is to look up the past form of the English verb 'to see' instead of the infinitive. She additionally chooses the wrong item from the list of verbs offered for 'leave' (i.e. *laisser* instead of *quitter*).
Researcher: What have you found? Katie: I saw him leave the shop (writes *laisser le magasin*). Researcher: How did you know the word *le magasin*? Katie: Used it before in other writing . . . At ten o'clock – *à dix heures*.	
Researcher: Could you hear the words *à dix heures* in your head as you did it or did you just . . . can you see it visually or in your head? Katie: It's in my head.	The two chunks *le magasin* and *à dix heures* pose her no problems.

Transcription extracts	Commentary
Katie: Uh was . . . was wearing . . . I'm going to look it up.	Katie decides to look up 'was wearing' even though she already knows the verb *porter*. She doesn't trust her ability to generate a sentence. Unfortunately the dictionary doesn't help her and she is forced back onto her own resources which produce the L1–L2 transfer problem *il était porter*.
Researcher: What are you going to look up?	
Katie: To wear . . . It doesn't make sense he was wear, I'll have to change it to he was wearing . . . I know the word *porter* and . . . He was wearing trousers – *pantalon*.	
Researcher: Word you already knew?	The already known *pantalon noir* and *pull rouge* pose no problems. There is no transfer of the English plural (trousers) to the French singular. This is clearly a thoroughly learnt lexical item.
Katie: Yeah, *noir et un pull, et un pull rouge* and I need the *un* before *pantalon*.	
Researcher: Right, so you remembered that – how did you do that, did you check that as you were going through, how did it come into your head?	She is able to spot the missing *un* in front of *pantalon* and puts it in.
Katie: I read the sentence through and noticed it was missing – *pull rouge*, uhm. He had – I don't know how to say he had brown hair.	
Researcher: Which bit don't you know how to say?	Again, it is the verbs which cause her the problems, in this case 'he *had* brown hair'. Something tells her not to go with her first (correct) hunch of using *il* which may well have triggered *avait* if she had pursued it a little longer. Or it may simply not be a phrase which is sufficiently learnt to jostle forward for prominence in front of the word-for-word translation. She therefore opts for the L2 translation of 'his hair was brown'. This almost definitely then triggers the subsequent L2 translation for 'his eyes were brown too' but (presumably) the *était* this time is pushed out of the way by *aux*. Is there a distant trace here of '*someone aux yeux marron*'?
Katie: Had.	
Researcher: Right, try and talk your way through the problem so that I understand how you resolve the problem.	
Katie: Had – *il* . . . the word I know the way of saying it . . . his hair *lui cheveux* was *était marron*.	
Researcher: Where does *marron* come from?	
Katie: Word I knew.	
Katie: That sentence I knew – *Il est très grand* – that we've done all together and that (his hair was) and that's word for word.	She then starts reading through from the beginning of that sentence and self-reports how she did it (i.e. some chunks and some word for word).
Researcher: Good, you're getting the idea of talking it through – where does that word *lui* come from – do you remember?	She is unaware of why *lui* has come to her rather than the correct possessive adjective *ses*.
Katie: No.	

Figure 5.3   *Strategies for a composing problem*

Although Katie is certainly using some strategies, she is not doing so in the right combination. She uses *resourcing* (consults a dictionary) but does not *self-monitor* at the same time (she knows that dictionaries have v for verb and n for noun). Similarly, she uses a *translating* strategy when forced by the task to do so (i.e. the L1 to *generate* an L2 sentence) but does not combine it with any form of *advance preparation* (what chunks do I already know that might help me?) nor with *self-monitoring* (what do I know about French patterns which might tell me if this is correct?). We can see, even from this short first extract, that the difference between an incorrect and correct decision is the application of a single strategy instead of a combination of strategies. She uses *recombination* (constructing sentences by transferring to new contexts already learnt chunks) effectively. The data here suggest that recombination may not need to be combined with other strategies to be an effective strategy.

We can see from both these extracts how difficult it is to get the student to think aloud and the researcher is constantly having to intervene in order to ask questions, otherwise the student would be writing without virtually saying anything.

As in the previous extract Katie's problems appear to lie with her L1–L2 transfer or word-for-word translation. Either she does not have at her disposal certain phrases as learnt chunks needed for the task or she is unable to recombine them to achieve her ends. In this situation, other than avoid the sentence altogether, thus not fulfilling the task, it is difficult to see what else she could do. The problem is that she deploys no self-monitoring strategies which lead her to doubt the results of her word-for-word translation. We can show how a student, at this level, might solve this composing problem graphically as in Figure 5.3.

The other lack of strategy we notice is any sort of auditory or visual monitoring as she writes. She does not ask herself, does this sound right? Is this how I have heard it before? Does it look right? Have I seen it like this before? Of course, the think aloud may not be revealing these inner thoughts but certainly one doesn't get the impression that the sort of monitoring which might have led to (for example) *ses* instead of *lui* is going on. The text reveals few crossings out, corrections and redrafting of phrases. In fact, she does do some reading aloud at the end of the task but, because there is now so much to monitor for errors or wrong decisions, it becomes an entirely perfunctory exercise and does not lead to any redrafting of the text.

Throughout the think aloud we have no evidence of strategy *evaluation*. In fact, one thing we notice in Katie's think aloud and recollections is that she never refers to herself as a learner. Of course it may be that the conditions of the think aloud don't encourage her to externalize her evaluation. Nevertheless she never refers to herself in terms of 'got to watch out for a problem here' or 'this is where I often go wrong'. Past strategies, like re-formulation and word-for-word translation have not, it appears, been evaluated for their effectiveness. This could be a metacognitive strategy that might benefit Katie if she employed it more. It might lead her to a sub-strategy of self-monitoring which would encourage her to be on the look-out for mistakes or wrong decisions she makes all the time. Of course, if the corrective feedback from the teacher is about the language, then it is unlikely that she will focus on the strategies associated with (in this case wrong) decision-making.

At the end of the think aloud the students were asked a general question about whether they normally went about checking their work once they had finished the initial draft. We have noted above Katie's ineffective reading aloud. She also adds:

> I usually prefer not to go and keep checking it because every time I check it I would find something . . . I would keep doubting myself but I'd rather not muddle myself up and when the teacher then takes it in to mark it when I get it back I have a good look through it and see why she's changed it – when I write I prefer to use phrases that we've already learnt at school and we usually have worksheets and a page in the textbook to help us or you make up a paragraph using the sentences we've already been given.

PAUSE FOR THOUGHT

Having examined some of Katie's thinking and decision-making and the way it leads to her written output, try to summarize the strategies that she appears to be using and why they are sometimes ineffective. Do you think it is a good thing that Katie relies on the teacher's corrective feedback rather than self-monitoring? What implications does this have for her teacher's workload?

If you were her teacher, what advice or 'targets' would you give Katie at this stage? What, as a teacher, would you consider doing now in order to help Katie's *interlanguage* move on?

We will now look more closely at Laura's thinking and decision-making and how this contributes to the quality of her written output. Highlighted words are those looked up in the dictionary by Laura. A translation is provided in the Appendix.

LAURA'S PRE-TREATMENT TASK

Bonjour

J'ai **recévé** ton lettre et ~~j'e~~ je suis trés **excité** tu est visité ~~Englan~~ Angleterre. Je n'**attend** pas de regarder tu.

J'habite à la campagne dans une grande maison. Il ~~ya q cin y~~ il y a cinq chambres et tu **droit être** resté en arr dans **la chambre d'amis**. La chambre est assez grande et trés mode. Il y a un lit, ~~une~~ un bureau, une amoire et une commode et une chaise et deux **miroirs**. Il est comfortable. La jardin est assez petit, mais il y a un tres grand jarden public prés de chez moi. Il y a aussi ~~une~~ un magazin et une piscine prés de chez moi. J'ai un chien qui s'appelle Pidgeon et elle très sympa. Tu-es un animal?

Semaine dernier ~~j'aller au~~ j'allé au cinema et allé au restaurant. C'etait trés sympa. **Voulez-vous** aller au cinema avec moi en Angleterre.

Like Katie, Laura appears to use the dictionary sparingly, turning to it only when her formulaic language does not provide her with the language she needs to complete the task. Laura appears to have a greater store and more consolidated knowledge of formulaic language and this may well be the reason why she is judged to be the more successful learner by the teacher. Whether she is a better learner because she is a better writer or simply because she is able to commit large chunks of language to memory is still unclear at this stage. If we consider what she writes in her self-report on the task we note that she also appears to have a clearer set of strategies for the writing process than Katie (or at least she articulates them better).

At first I thought it was alright but then got very stuck because it was a lot of revision work. Gradually I remembered words and became more relaxed.

I thought about how I would structure a letter in English then thought about any relevant French phrases I already knew. I put phrases and words I knew together and then looked at them to see if they were structured properly and looked right. Words I didn't know I looked up in a dictionary.

[I checked] a sentence at a time then at the end. I am also going to now use a dictionary for anything I am unsure of + masculine and feminine.

I found describing the rooms and garden easy and saying what I did at the weekend. I found telling her I was pleased about seeing her and beginning the letter very hard.

So, Laura uses the *advance preparation* strategies of overcoming feelings of anxiety by pausing and allowing her working memory to start retrieving a whole host of known language items, what we might call *brainstorming*. As well as her advance preparation and composition strategies, Laura's *monitoring* strategies also seem to be paying off. She not only monitors as she writes one sentence at a time but she also monitors that they are following a French pattern she recognizes ('structured right and looked right'). However, what the data so far on Laura also seem to tell us is that she too is hamstrung by an inability to generate sentences. An example of this is when she attempts to complete the second half of the task about something interesting in the past tense. The output and the self-report suggest that she uses avoidance strategies (of content) in order not to run into difficulties. She allows the part of the task that she can address via formulaic phrases and language she already knows to dominate the part of the task which requires *generated* language from her. This avoidance strategy provides better quality language but limits her powers of self-expression. As a consequence, it allows her only to make progress with the interlanguage at the speed which the teacher dictates. She cannot forge ahead by experimenting with new language. Let us now see if this analysis is confirmed by the think-aloud task, see Figure 5.4. A translation is provided in the Appendix.

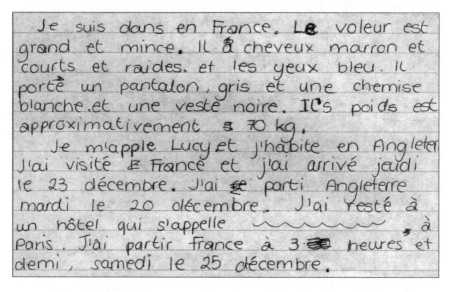

Je suis dans en France. Le voleur est grand et mince. Il à cheveux marron et courts et raides. et les yeux bleu. Il porte un pantalon, gris et une chemise blanche.et une veste noire. Il's poids est approximativement à 70 kg.

Je m'apple Lucy et j'habite en Angleter J'ai visité E France et j'ai arrivé jeudi le 23 décembre. J'ai et parti Angleterre mardi le 20 décembre. J'ai resté à un hôtel qui s'appelle ～～～～, à Paris. J'ai partir France à 3 æ heures et demi, samedi le 25 décembre.

Figure 5.4   *Laura's pre-treatment writing for think aloud*

Transcription extracts	Commentary
Laura: So I've got to start with 'I'm in France' . . .	
Researcher: So what are you thinking about?	Here Laura is thrown by the rubrics which provide the context but she doesn't need to give the context as in this situation everyone would know she was in France. She is forced to generate a sentence because she realizes her formulaic '*j'ai visité*' will not fit the situation.
Laura: How to say I'm in France	
Researcher: Which bit is giving you problems?	
Laura: Can I say . . . can I start *j'ai visité*?	
Researcher: You can write anything you like – don't worry about it (Laura writes)	
Researcher: So you've made a start – *je suis dans en France* – so you're looking at that sentence – how did you come to that sentence? Did you already know it or?	
Laura: No. I thought *dans* means in and *en France* means France and *je suis* is I am.	
Laura: Don't know what the thief is so . . .	
Researcher: So you're going to look it up – what have you found?	Makes the common sense if somewhat sexist decision that all thieves are male.
Laura: Ve . . . voleur and it's got the feminine and masculine and I'd say it's masculine and that means that has to change (changes *la voleur* to *le voleur*).	
Researcher: So now you have to describe him . . . what are you thinking about?	
Laura: Word for is . . . I'll say he's tall.	
Researcher: Why did you decide to do that?	

Laura: Because if I wanted to say about his eyes I'd have to say he has and not he is

Researcher: OK so you made that decision after you'd written the *est*

Laura: Yeah – he's tall and . . . Size and thin (writes *mince*)

Researcher: And where has that come from, that word?

Laura: Just from what we'd done before – describing people . . . we've already described people before so you'd say I am tall and thin . . .

Researcher: And you switched it round . . . what are you thinking now?

Laura: He has . . . I've just forgotten how you say he has . . .

Researcher: What's the choice there – you're hesitating.

Laura: I'm just thinking how I say I have (writes *Il à cheveux* and then removes accent)

Researcher: Why did you take that off the 'a' as a matter of interest?

Laura: Cos when you say I'm in Thame or in Oxford you'd have that there (i.e. *a* with an accent – doesn't fit in).

I'm checking that phrase there from *il porte.*

Researcher: How are you checking it?

Laura: I'm just reading it through and checking it for spelling errors and whether it makes sense . . . looks alright . . .

the weight . . . not sure how to say the weight . . . we haven't really learnt how to describe what you weigh but he weighed I suppose . . .

Researcher: So what are you gonna do . . . look in the dictionary, OK, right . . . so what's the actual word in your head that you're looking up?

Laura: I'm gonna look up weigh and it depends what kind of weigh it is . . . got weigh, uhm, I could say his weight was might be better.

Researcher: So you've made that decision to change and you're looking up?

Laura: His weight . . . it's *poids* . . . *p-o-i-d-s* . . .

Researcher: What's worrying you?

Laura: Whether to add anything else in there (has put *il's*) because it belongs to

Researcher: *Il's*

Laura: Yeah . . . it belongs to it's, his weight is . . .

Using her avoidance strategy in order not to have to deal with something she s not sure of

Here she is using previously learnt language and combining it in a new situation.

Here there is evidence that she is analysing previously learnt chunks and trying to generate a sentence.

This is a previously learnt rule that she has probably noticed rather than been taught.

Two strategies being used here related to meaning and to the graphic form.

Here her strategy of delving back into LTM isn't working and therefore she resorts to the dictionary but she already predicts the kinds of words the dictionary will offer.

However, she then falls between the two options ('he weighs' and 'his weight is' and ends up using a noun with the subject pronoun *Il*. As this causes her a meaning problem 'he weight' she decides to add the apostrophe, allowing a negative L1–L2 transfer.

Researcher: So now you're checking . . . do you normally check after each sentence?

Laura: If it's something I'm not familiar with . . . then yeah . . . I'm describing . . . my name is *je m'appelle*

Researcher: What made you decide to do that?

Laura: What, to give an introduction . . . cos if I just said I left England they wouldn't know who I was . . . My name is Laura and . . .

Researcher: Was *je m'appelle* a set phrase?

Laura: Yeah we learnt that when we first started learning French . . . et *j'habite en Angleterre* . . . uhm

Researcher: What are you thinking?

Laura: Whether to say I'm visiting France or I left England . . . I'm going to say I'm visiting France.

Researcher: Why did you choose that?

Laura: Because, uhm, it kind of gives me, I thought of a sentence like I'm visiting France and I left England no and I arrived uhm whenever I arrived . . . I arrived on . . . I'm thinking about whether I need the word on, cos I don't think you do if you're saying like dates you just say like Thursday.

I'm reading the sentence through . . . I arrived . . . yep that's right . . . I left England . . . I'm thinking of the word to leave which is . . . I can see it in my head but I jus can't think what it is . . . I'll look it up in the dictionary.

Something like retire or something?

Researcher: For leave?

Laura: Yeah, I can see it in a book where we've written it down in a sentence.

Researcher: So you get these visual things, do you?

Laura: Yeah . . . (looks up in dictionary) *partir* . . . yeah, that's right . . . I left from England . . . I left England I suppose I could use either . . .

Researcher: When you put an accent on *Décembre* was it because you'd forgotten or because you always do it like that?

Laura: I always put it on afterwards.

where I'm staying – *j'ai reste* -

Researcher: Do you know that phrase off by heart?

Laura: Yeah, I do.

I'll say I'm staying at a hotel called . . .

There is evidence here of Laura having monitored her strategies in the past. If she generates a sentence, then she monitors it.

Laura monitors her response to the content of the task to see if it makes sense.

Laura writes *J'ai visité France* instead of *je visite la France*. Negative transfer of the L1 structure here is not monitored – perhaps because she is more concerned with thinking through the content. But she successfully recalls that you cannot transfer 'I arrived on Thursday' to French.

It is unclear whether she reads the problem phrase *j'ai visité France* but her auditory monitoring of *j'ai arrivé* and *j'ai parti* does not trigger a correction. The over-extension of *avoir* seems fixed. The choice of three possibilities for 'leave' are not explored sufficiently. She searches in her mind for a visual link to the correct word. Was *partir* the word she was thinking of or *quitter*? She finishes with a back-translation which does not solve the problem either.

She seems aware of this strategy and that it works for her.

She uses the wrong tense here because her formulaic phrase lets her down.

Researcher: You decided to use the phrase *un hôtel qui s'appelle* rather than just the name.

Laura: Uhm, I suppose it's a way of getting out of thinking of something precise.

I'm trying to think how to say I'm going to leave . . . *j'ai* . . . I'm going to look it up . . . or I could just say I am leaving.

Researcher: What was the decision then?

Laura: Cos I don't know the word 'intend' so I'm just going to say I am leaving . . . I'll go back and check that in a minute – *j'ai partir France* a three thirty . . .

three hours . . . whether to write that as a word . . . if it was an exam whether they would look at three and think I don't know how to spell.

I'm leaving France on *Samedi* . . . I'm just looking back here, I don't think the dates match up, I don't think . . . the dates I need to check the dates . . . Monday . . .

I'm just checking the sense . . . I am leaving France at 3 hours and a half on . . .

j'ai means I have but I've left means *J'ai parti* . . . I'm now looking at the word *partir* to see if I need to take the *r* off to make it a different tense but I don't . . . I'm leaving . . . I think that's fine.

I usually go through the whole thing . . . I'd go back to the beginning read it all the way through . . . Uhm, I suppose I'd do it twice, the first time I'd just read it quietly, checking on spelling and accents, uhm, masculine and feminine words whether it needs an extra *e* or an *s* . . .

Researcher: This check list, is it in your head or is it written down?

Laura: It's in my head, I go through and basically check it, sometimes if you've got a word missing it doesn't always sound right, like a linking word.

Researcher: Do you ever translate it back into English in your head as you're going through?

Laura: Sometimes, I suppose, but I don't use that so much because I find it doesn't really help, cos the French sometimes have some of the words back to front . . . If I do do that, it's just to check that I do have everything that I need to speak about.

No, my family don't speak French but if it's a homework that we're working in pairs then we help each other.

Researcher: You looked nervous when you first started and then you were OK – why was that?

Laura: It's cos I didn't know what to expect and when I first saw that, it kinda, I thought I don't know what I'm writing about but then as I thought about it I did and I remembered the things we'd done before and I got into it

---

She could have used *à l'hôtel Molière* but that seems harder than the chunk which she recalls *qui s'appelle* – a kind of avoidance strategy

Again the present tense problem arises.

Another avoidance strategy.

Monitoring for coherence via back-translation.

Sense monitoring by back-translating.

Grammar monitoring by using a visual check – doesn't yield the needed correction.

Overview check using visual monitoring to identify graphic errors.

A second time auditory monitoring to see if it sounds right.

She not only shows an awareness of the pitfalls of L1–L2 transfer but is also able to self-evaluate a particular (back-translation) strategy.

(That is) with a friend.

Laura admits some anxiety but overcomes it by allowing the ideas (L2 items) to flood in but she does this by linking it to previous learning experiences in the classroom.

Laura's strategy use

If any piece of data demonstrates that writing in a foreign language (and learning language in general) requires great effort, it is this. Laura uses a whole host of strategies in order to achieve a piece of work. Again, importantly, many of the strategies are used in combination, usually effectively. In her advance preparation and composition she keeps dictionary use down to a minimum by maximizing known language. This, as in her previous writing task, allows her to keep the writing reasonably accurate but somewhat limited. In order to maintain the high use of known language (but to address the task) she either *recombines*, uses *avoidance* strategies, or tries to *analyse a chunk* to see if it can be reworked. This cluster of support strategies for recombination lets her down when there is an issue of 'tense'. It looks as if 'tense' awareness needs to be conceptualized in L1 at this level of language learning but with some kind of prompting strategy which avoids negative transfer from L1. When she is forced to generate a sentence (as in the description of weight), she sometimes uses the dictionary and occasionally attempts the word for word (*je suis dans en France*). In terms of checking her work, Laura puts in a great deal of effort both as she writes and at the end. She uses the following kinds of monitoring: auditory; visual; sense/meaning; common sense/schemata; coherence; noticing syntax; previous learning experience; content related to task; recall of negative transfer; back-translation. It looks as if it is the checking which occurs as she writes which is the most productive. This would support our earlier finding from the questionnaire cross-tabulation. But Laura also uses a number of indirect strategies which clearly are of benefit to her written output. One of the most interesting of these seems to be her evaluation of past strategies. She has, it seems, evaluated a strategy in the past to do with the amount of checking that non-familiar (or non-recombined) language is going to need. She also seems to have established a pattern of checking whether a word has an accent on it immediately after the word has been written. We can only speculate as to why this is effective for her. One possible reason might be that if she tries to visualize it before it is written she cannot *see* if there are accents and where the accents go. The working memory processing load for this monitoring is reduced once the word has been written. Furthermore, her third option, that of leaving all the accents until the end, does not seem to be her preferred strategy for any type of checking. Laura also tries to predict what a dictionary might offer before turning to it as a resource. This could well be an effective strategy which she may develop over time, allowing her to prompt herself about the pitfalls of dictionary use and the conventions that might help her avoid those pitfalls.

Although this is only a limited amount of data on both students, it is fairly clear to see that Laura is the much more effective strategy user and yet their pre-treatment written work does not present the reader with a huge gap in terms of what they achieve both at the level of content and accuracy. In other words, Laura's better processing is not matched by much better output. We therefore have to ask ourselves if Laura could make much greater progress if she were given tasks with necessitated much greater amounts of generated language; if she were given some training in how to deploy strategies in order to avoid the pitfalls of generating language. We will return to this issue in Chapter 6 and in our concluding chapter.

PAUSE FOR THOUGHT

To what extent do you think you now have a detailed picture of both Laura and Katie before they started the strategy training?

Have you been able to add to your list of strategies that you have been collecting throughout the book?

Think about the learners in your classroom. Is it possible for you, as a teacher, to have this level of understanding of the learners, given the class size and the pressures of time?

Think back to the chapter on methods of collecting data on strategy use. Are there any ideas in the 'looking for traces' section that might allow you at least some insights into individual learners' strategies?

We now come on to the strategy training itself. It will be remembered that only three classes (the experimental or treatment classes) received strategy training. Because of lack of space we can only look at this part of the strategy training cycle in broad terms. Details and materials will be given in Chapter 6. First, let us recap what evidence the researchers and teachers had to go on when deciding what aspects of strategy training to embark on:

1. The test results and the self-report strategies associated with the test.
2. The error analysis of the task and the associated self-report strategies.
3. The think-aloud transcriptions and the task which generated them.

4. Certain features of the questionnaire findings, particularly those related to self-monitoring.
5. The teacher's knowledge of their class.

It was decided that the three broad aspects of training which needed attention were:

1. Making the right decision of when to use L1 and when to use L2 in planning and composing.
2. Dictionary use strategies.
3. Self-monitoring strategies.

The first strategy to be offered to the students was the 'brainstorming strategy'. This was one of the strategies aimed at helping them to make the right decision. What we wanted to avoid was the immediate plunge into word-for-word translation. The precise objective here was to provide them, in the planning stage (that is, in the minutes before they began composing the text) with an awareness that what they would have to achieve is a balance between the use of L2 and use of L1 when composing. In England at this level, typical task types are only about 120 words in length and therefore the content is highly prescribed but not highly demanding in terms of linguistic range. Students were therefore encouraged to brainstorm all the words and ready-made phrases they already knew and were quite confident with, in L2, on the topic in question. They were encouraged, in particular, to brainstorm those they thought they would then be able to recombine in the context of the task. This was quite a difficult strategy to train the students to do as some did not trust the brainstormed phrases and started checking in the dictionary; some started translating word for word in the brainstorming activity. Modelling had to take place a number of times before it was felt that the students were attempting this strategy as it was intended to be used. The importance of slowly making strategy use automatic was again noted. The brainstorming strategy sheet was monitored by the teacher/researcher. It was collected in alongside the finished writing task. It was an additional way of getting inside the students' heads. We could see what phrases they were recombining and the relative success of these.

Once this brainstorming had been completed, students were reminded that not all of the task could be completed using re-combined previously learnt phrases. They would have to generate at least some sentences. Thus the decision-making process was scaffolded by strategy use as follows:

1. What do I already know in L2 on the topic with minimal changing necessary?
2. What do I actually want to/need to say?
3. What is the gap between what I want to say and what I already have in L2?
4. The gap is what I will have to make up by using generated sentences (despite running the risk of L1 transfer).

In order to minimize the L1–L2 transfer problems, it was decided to train them to 'get the tense right first'. The reasoning behind this needs some explanation. All the students had been taught the perfect tense, the imperfect tense and the present tense. Some had been taught the future and conditional while others had only been taught to talk in the future by using *aller* + infinitive, e.g. *Je vais partir*. It was thought from the data that the way that they were making mistakes about tenses (and aspect) suggested there was a branching system of decisions to be made by the learner. Once they made the wrong decision about tenses they went down the wrong route and there was no coming back. The first decision, therefore, was to get the tense/aspect right. The rest (endings; correct auxiliary for the perfect tense) could wait until after this first decision and a connecting rule could be internalized. They were therefore reminded of a simple rule: *all tenses take one verb except the perfect tense which takes two verbs* (they had not been taught the pluperfect tense nor other compound tenses). This was the only grammatical rule related to verbs given to them during the treatment period. Of course, having a rule explained to them was not a strategy. The strategy was to remember to apply the rule at the right time and on every occasion when they might make a mistake, i.e. when generating a sentence. They were therefore given a 'scaffolding sheet' called 'your tenses sheet'. Every time they were to carry out a piece of writing over the next two months they were given this sheet and they were asked to tick each box every time they wrote a sentence and checked it against the rule. At the end of the task, scripts and tenses sheets were collected in by the teacher/researcher. This allowed the teacher/researcher to identify the number of sentences they were generating and feed back to the students about their strategy use.

The third strategy connected to composition concerned the use of the bi-lingual dictionary when generating sentences. This was considered as separate from when they were using the dictionary to check words they 'knew', for example, checking for gender or spelling. A scaffolding sheet called 'dictionary sheet' was provided for the students. Here the objectives were to (a) get the high dictionary users to reduce the number of words they looked up (this in any case was being reduced, hopefully, by strategy number one); and (b) to make them aware of when misuse of the dictionary was affecting their work. In order to do this the students were required to write down which words they had looked up in the dictionary on the sheet. The teacher/researcher was therefore then able to spot easily which 'dictionary words' had led to mistakes in the written text and was able to provide feedback to the students. In turn, when work was handed back, they had to look at the offending dictionary words and try to ascertain why they had made the dictionary-search mistakes or simply why they had not been able to find the word at all.

Now we come on to the monitoring strategies. We were assuming that the bulk of the composing of a sentence had been done. This would have been achieved either through a recombination of L2 items the student already knew as chunks or through a process of generating sentences. Of course we must keep in mind the possibility of both processes being combined. But for the purposes of pedagogical simplicity we felt we should keep the processes apart for the time being. The next strategy therefore concerned the agreement of adjectives. This consisted of inviting the students to stop and check in every sentence all the possible words that the noun in the sentence might have an effect on by drawing a ring around the noun and then sending out octopus tentacles to all the affected words. This strategy was called 'checking the noun clusters'. To remind them to use the strategy, the students simply had a symbol of a circle and some tentacles reaching out to pronouns and adjectives. It was here that it was expected that students would be most likely to check words in the dictionary that they already knew or thought they knew.

The next monitoring strategy was the back-translation strategy. The benefits of this were discussed with the students in terms of why some phrases or sentences didn't make sense when you translated them back into L1. However, some of the disadvantages of back-translation were also discussed such as the possibility of changing something that was in fact right simply because the back-translation didn't make sense. Back-translation seemed to work particularly effectively with omissions (bits of language left out) and additions (bits of language extraneous to the L2 sentence).

The noun cluster and back-translation strategies were introduced towards the end of the project and it is possible that they were not sufficiently scaffolded or practised on sufficient occasions for them to become embedded in their overall strategy use.

Finally, students were encouraged to work collaboratively on their checking and to arrive at lists of mistakes that they made as individuals and lists they detected being made by the whole class. Again this is illustrated in Chapter 6.

Students were not encouraged to read out loud or sub-vocally at the end as many of them already seemed to be doing this and with varying degrees of efficacy.

To summarize the training programme, then, we could say that students were asked to try out and evaluate the following strategies roughly in the following order starting with advanced planning and finishing with an awareness of common mistakes:

1. Brainstorming known language.
2. Focusing on the tense/aspect first when generating sentences.
3. Logging their dictionary problems when composing.
4. Monitoring noun clusters.
5. Back-translating to see that it made sense.

Katie and Laura went through this training programme and we have noted the improvements to their written output. It is not possible to say that the learner training programme was the major reason for these improvements as there are so many factors that can affect causality. However, there are a number of clues in the data that suggest that the way they planned, composed and checked did make an important contribution to the improved output. We will therefore now return to them at the end of the project and look carefully at the data on them.

KATIE'S POST-TREATMENT TASK

Task: Pretend that you have just come back from your first day of work experience. You have been asked by your teacher to write a little report (80 to 100 words), which should include:

(a) A brief description of the workplace (e.g. shop/office), of your boss, Mrs O'Neill, and of Mark, one of your colleagues in the office (in *the present tense* and no more than 30 words long).
(b) An account, *in the past tense*, of what you did which should include the description of something that went wrong while you were working, e.g. a little accident/problem (about 70–80 words).

A translation is provided in the Appendix.

> Je travaille avec un architect compagnie. Le bureau est très moderne et c'est divisé en studio petit. Ma surveillante, Mrs O'Neill, est très compréhension quand je suis confus! Mark est très different, il est très stupide et maladroit!
>
> Huir dans le bureau achevé beaucoup de ~~dossiers~~ dossiersais et conception de immeuble. Quand j'acheverais un dessin je donner le dessin a Mrs. O'Neill. Elle était furieux avec moi parce que le dessin était mal. Mark était ammused avec ma design!

N.B. in this task it would appear that two words highlighted had in fact not been looked up in the dictionary perhaps for lack of time and were left in English.

Now let us look at Katie's attempt to think aloud another piece of text (see Figure 5.5). Translation provided in the Appendix.

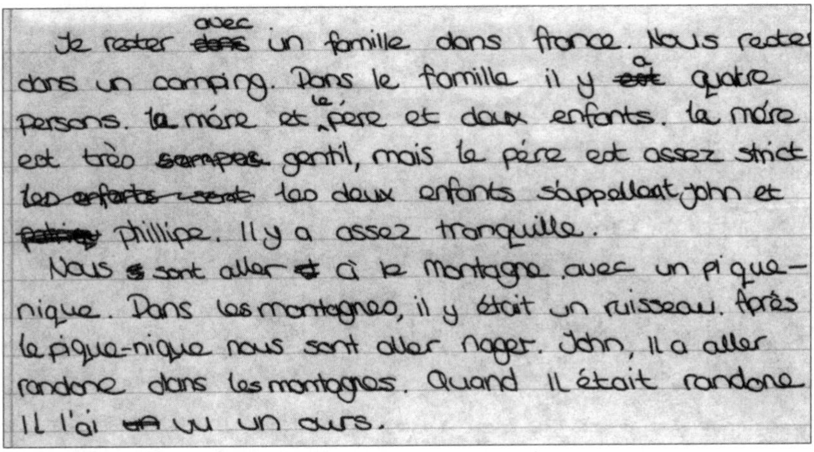

Je rester ~~dans~~ avec un famille dans france. Nous rester dans un camping. Dans le famille il y ~~est~~ a quatre persons. la mére et le, pere et deux enfants. la mére est trés ~~sempas~~ gentil, mais le pére est assez strict ~~les enfants sont~~ les deux enfants s'appellant John et ~~[illegible]~~ Phillipe. Il y a assez tranquille.

Nous ~~s~~ sont aller ~~à~~ à le Montagne avec un pique-nique. Dans les montagnes, il y était un ruisseau. Après le pique-nique nous sont aller nager. John, Il a aller randone dans les montagnes. Quand IL était randone IL l'ai ~~un~~ vu un ours.

Figure 5.5 *Katie's post-treatment writing for think aloud*

Transcription extracts	Commentary
Katie: I am staying . . . that's the present tense so that's one verb . . . *je rester dans une famille* . . . I'm staying in a family . . . oh sorry, I'll put 'with' . . . (changes *dans* to *avec*)	Translating strategy combined with tense prompt. Auditory monitoring and back-translation lead to a change.
'we are staying' so that's the present tense again . . . *nous rester* . . . need something for *rester* . . . it's one verb but it's *nous* . . .	Uses tense strategy correctly and is beginning to turn her attention to endings – the next stage in the interlanguage development.
. . . in a campsite . . . (checks in dictionary) it's masculine so I'll stay with *un camping*	Dictionary checking strategy.
le mere no *la mere* (corrects to *la*)	Auditory monitoring results in a correction.
La mere est très sampas (pronounced like Sampras!) . . . a word I know . . . *sampas* . . . I'll just check . . . it's not the word that I know so I'll change it . . .	Interesting combination of strategies here. Recombination linked with auditory monitoring caused doubt (perhaps she really is confusing the word with the name of the tennis player – July is the tennis season) but she is undecided whether to pursue the dictionary route. Opts for more familiar word although does not remember to make it agree.
leur enfants (but writes *les enfants*) *sont* . . . the children are aged . . . I don't know how to do that . . . one boy and one girl or they could be both male . . . look up 'both' . . . (looks up in dictionary) just looking to see if there's anything I recognize . . . I've got 'les deux' which looks like it means 'the two' . . . uhm, the children . . . the two children . . . I'll start again . . . *les deux enfants* . . .	Back-translation strategy combined with looking up in the dictionary does lead to a correct form (via an avoidance strategy) even though she had not fully understood that 'les deux' actually means 'both'.
Oh, euh *Patrique* . . . euh, I don't know how to spell that . . . *Philippe* (changes it from *patriqu*) . . . *il y a* quiet (writes *il y a assez*)	Avoidance strategy is well justified here. She would have spent time unnecessarily thinking about it and it probably wouldn't have been in the dictionary
Researcher: Where did you get that phrase from?	The recombination strategy doesn't work here (i.e. from 'la maison est assez tranquille' to 'they (the boys) are fairly quiet').
Katie: I remember doing it when we were describing our house.	
Euh, we went . . . past tense . . . two verbs . . . *Nous sommes* or *sont*? It's *nous sont aller* I think . . . two verbs, we went *dans*, no went on a picnic . . . don't know how to say on a picnic . . . have to think of a way round it . . . to the mountains I'll start with . . . *aller à la* . . . I'll work out whether it's masculine or feminine in a minute	Translation strategy combined with tense strategy prompt successful again and she also tries to get the correct auxiliary through auditory monitoring. Clearly the form has not been sufficiently acquired such that it is retrieved automatically.

Avoidance strategy for 'on a picnic' produces an acceptable alternative 'avec un picnic'. Unclear why she writes *le* after auditory monitoring 'à la'.

... in the mountains ... there was *il y etait* cos was, was, there was

Translation strategy not combined with other strategies leads to lack of success. Has not sufficiently internalized the L1–L2 transfer problem.

after the picnic ... we *nous sont aller* we all went swimming *nager* past tense ... no, that's we all went ... swimming ...

Translation strategy combined with tense strategy is successful and she is beginning to grapple with agreement of auxiliary and past participle.

John, he went ... *il est* ... *il a?* it's got to be two verbs ... I find that when it's two verbs the word that follows ... whether it's *a*, *est*, *sont*

Translation strategy combined with tense strategy is successful and is beginning to grapple with agreement of auxiliary but simply cannot apply the correct rule which we know she is quite close to (see above in test self-report).

He went for a walk ... went for a walk, I don't know so I'm trying to think of something to change it to ... walking ... *il a aller randone* (pronounced rondonne) in the mountains *quand* he was ...

Here the tense strategy is only partly successful in that she is not able to isolate the 'two verbs' part (i.e. he went) of the tense.

He saw (looks up)

She consults dictionary and this time looks up the infinitive which leads to greater success than the 'scier' in the pre-treatment think aloud.

Researcher: Which word are you looking up?

Katie: Saw ... see ...

Researcher: Which word are you going to look up?

Reformulation strategy leads to partial success.

Katie: See ... I don't think it's got ... 'saw him running' ... you've got the *voir* which is see ... so that's *je l'ai* (phrase from dictionary) so that will be *il l'ai* ... a bear ...

PAUSE FOR THOUGHT

As you read through Katie's post-treatment writing and the think-aloud transcription you will have noticed a number of changes that have taken place in the intervening months since the pre-treatment work. Perhaps the most obvious of these is that she checks as she is writing.

1. What effect has this change in strategy use brought about?
2. What strategies is Katie now using as she checks?
3. In what way are these strategies proving to be more effective?

At the end of the writing process Katie was asked whether she would now go back and check again through the work she had written. On p. 165 are some of the things she said and some of the ways in which she has changed from before the learner training:

Overall, Katie's approach to writing has changed considerably. Whereas before she was only successful with recombining previously learnt language she is now able to use these in reduced quantity and at the same time to generate some recognizable sentences and in the context of a much harder set of tasks. Whereas before she was very reluctant to check at all for fear of the negative effect this would have on her morale, she now checks both as she writes and at the end. We can now summarize the number and combination of strategies that Katie has been found to be using in the post-treatment data as follows:

1. She uses recombination in conjunction with auditory monitoring and avoidance.
2. She uses translation in combination with tense prompt and endings check.
3. She uses translation in conjunction with tense prompt, auditory monitoring and back-translation.
4. She uses auditory monitoring with back-translation for sense monitoring
5. She uses the dictionary both to generate language and to check language (and more successfully).
6. She uses auditory monitoring in combination with noun clustering.
7. (After composing) she uses auditory monitoring in conjunction with back-translation, tense check and noun clustering.

Transcription extracts	Commentary
Katie: General spelling and then . . . the tenses . . . and I might read it through . . .	This is a shift from her previous position of not wanting to check things because it caused her to find too many mistakes and she would keep doubting.
I stayed with a family in France . . . which makes sense to me . . . in English	Her reading aloud is now making her use a back-translation strategy.
je rester is . . . past . . . it's present cos it's one verb . . . and *nous rester dans un camping* . . . we stayed in a campsite . . . again one verb . . .	Uses the tense strategy to good effect.
in the family there is four people so . . . I'm not sure about the there is . . . I'm not sure how I would try to find it in the dictionary cos it's not like an adjective . . . (looks up) . . . uhm . . . there are . . . *il y a* . . . but would that be there are????	The back-translation strategy picks up the problem and she corrects *il y est* with *il y a* even though she still has doubts caused by the L1–L2 transfer problem (*il y a* can mean both there is and there are).
Ok . . . the mother and father . . . oh *la mère* . . . *et le père* (corrects)	Reading through allows her to spot and correct the gender.
. . . John and Philippe . . . uhm, they are quite quiet . . . *il y a* so that's again they are . . . there are . . .	Here the back-translation, even though it raises the doubt in her mind about 'il y a assez tranquille', doesn't lead to a correction. Perhaps she is just in too much of a hurry at this stage.
He saw a bear . . . I'm still not sure about having that *l'ai* . . . Researcher: Where did that *l'ai* come from . . . Katie: (inaudible) . . . it's in the past and you should have two . . . Researcher: And have you got two? Katie: I think so . . . *l'ai* and *vu*	She doubts the 'l'ai' because it is a phrase that she got out of the dictionary 'je l'ai vu' which she has analysed and reformulated as 'Il l'ai vu'. Fortunately the tense strategy is sufficiently powerful for her to stick to her decision.

Although some readers of her post-treatment work would not, at a glance, declare noticing a big change, there is a marked decrease in noun phrase-related error. Although the verb phrase-related error still exists, it is qualitatively different and in any case occurs in more demanding task contexts.

Let us now look at the progress that Laura has made. We will not examine her post-treatment task in any detail for two reasons. First, there is the problem of lack of space. Second, the written output is substantially better than her pre-treatment task even though the task rubrics require greater complexity of language. However, we do know that she has attempted writing something like this before as a result of doing work experience in a primary school. It is likely therefore that they are largely ungenerated sentences that she is recalling. Nevertheless, we know that the following sentence at least was generated:

> J'ai peinture un tableau avec une petite fille et j'ai renversé les peintures bleues et rouges. J'avais rangé

We know this because she says in her self-report: 'I thought that (b) would be hard because I've never composed a sentence talking about a problem.' We should note therefore the accuracy of this generated sentence and the phrase she crosses out (presumably) for lack of time. We should also acknowledge her more indirect strategy of having taken the opportunity in the past to write in the foreign language about something she had been doing.

PAUSE FOR THOUGHT

Now look at Laura's written output for the post-treatment think-aloud session. Using the list of writing-related strategies that you have been accumulating, can you identify all the strategies (and the combinations) that Laura is using for each of the transcription extracts (see Figure 5.6)? The first two are done for you on p. 167.

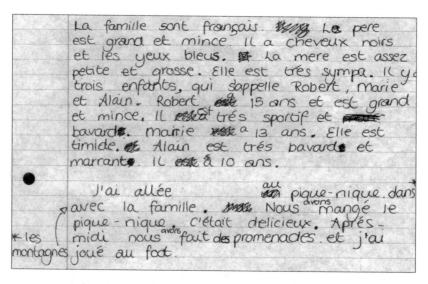

Figure 5.6 *Laura's post-treatment writing for think aloud*

Transcription extracts	Commentary

Laura: Do I need past or present . . . (questioning herself)?

Researcher: Well . . . you're describing what they're like.

Advance preparation. Advance monitoring for coherence ('how is this going to make sense'?).

Laura: The family are French (writes straight down).

There is (crosses out *il y a*) say the father . . .

Researcher: Why did you decide not to say there is . . . I'm not saying it's wrong . . . ?

Probably a recombination of 'ils sont français' rather than a generated sentence.

Avoidance strategy combined with coherence monitoring.

Laura: 'Cos I was going to say . . . uhm . . . I was going to say there was five of them but then I decided not to . . . because it wouldn't have made sense . . . it just wasn't gonna work.

the father is tall . . . and uhm he has . . . brown hair . . . no . . . black.

Researcher: Why did you choose black?

Laura: Cos I wasn't sure of brown . . . *marron* I think . . . but or is it *chatain* . . . no . . . yeah, whatever . . . he has black hair and blue eyes (is going back over the work pointing with the pen).

I want to check about the father . . . the father is masculine so *grand* doesn't need an 'e' . . . and does *bleu* need an 's' because it's plural?

I'm trying to say what his name is now but I don't think I will . . . got to think of a French name so I'll just leave that . . . the mother is quite small . . . short . . . and . . . uhm, she is very nice . . .

I'm pretty familiar with . . . (these phrases)

There are . . . there is . . . five children . . . does that need a change? . . . there are three children.

. . . got to look up that word . . .

Researcher: Have you got a word in your head or nothing?

Laura: No, oh, I could say *petits* . . . no . . . child . . . *enfants* . . . three children . . .

Researcher: So you had no problem looking that up?

Laura: No . . . three children.

Uhm, well, there's . . . actually, I could say what the names are . . . *qui s'appelle*, uhm, Robert . . . Marie and Alan I think, uhm . . . Robert is, uhm, age 15 . . .

Researcher: Why did you cross out *marrant*?

Laura: Cos, I knew the word but then I thought I wasn't sure I think it means . . . *marrant* is . . . I always get them muddled up . . . *marrant* is funny and that (*bavard*) is talkative . . . he is sporty and talkative (back-translation).

Marie is, uhm, 13 years old . . . she is shy, uhm, and . . . she is shy and . . . she could be shy and funny or I might just leave it . . . shy . . . Alan is very talkative and funny . . . now that I know what that word is . . . he is 10 years old . . . (starts going back over the last bit by pointing her pen at Robert) . . . (mumbles the check through in English).

It's masculine so it doesn't need an 'e' and I think I've spelt *sportif* right but I'll check it just in case . . . yep, that's right . . . oh, that might not need an 'e' because I'm talking about . . . Uhm, cos he's a boy.

Uhm . . . that one's right . . .

Researcher: *Timide* is right because it's . . . ?

Laura: Feminine . . . and very talkative that one's wrong.

Researcher: Why's that?

Laura: Because it's got the 'e' on it and it's masculine and so is that (pointing to *marrante*) I think it's alright after that . . . uhm, yeah, OK

. . . well, *aller* is to go, so *aller* is in the past . . . Two verbs.

. . . I went . . . on a picnic . . . don't know how to say picnic . . .

Researcher: And are you looking up the English or the French?

Laura: The English . . . (writes *pique-nique*)

I ate . . . actually it should be we ate . . . which I think is *nous* . . . *nous mange*, uh it's masculine *le pique-nique* . . . and then I'll say *c'était* delicious . . . (as she writes she says something like delichucks) . . . (goes back and translates) we ate

. . . walk is *promenade* . . . *faire un promenade fait*, cos it's past it can't be *faire* (back-translates in whispers), in the afternoon we went for a walk . . .

Laura: Do I need like *des promenades* . . .
des???? but it's *des* cos walks *promenades*
and . . . *et j'ai joué au foot* . . . and I played
football . . . no I'll go back to the beginning and
sort that out (i.e. later), uhm, is it *j'ai allé au
pique-nique* and then would it be alright?

OK I'll just check (at the end) . . . I'm just
reading that (present tense section) in my head
to see if it sounds alright . . . I think it is and
then I'll check the verb rules for this one.

Well, it needs two verbs . . . I've got *j'ai* . . . and
same thing here *nous mangé* . . . oh oh, I
dunno . . .

That means I need it here as well . . . between
nous and *fait* (writes *avons*)

PAUSE FOR THOUGHT

First, let us consider what sort of feedback we should give students in order to bring them on in their language learning in general and writing in particular.

Do you think that Katie's change in her approach to self-monitoring of her work would have come about by the teacher writing a comment at the bottom of her work, such as 'check your work more carefully'? Or: 'Check your verbs more carefully'? What strategy-related targets would you now set Katie? (i.e. not 'just learn the auxiliaries in the past perfect').

What strategy-related targets would you now set Laura? Are these different from Katie's?

Second, what implications does what you have discovered have for managing the languages classroom? For example, is it possible for learners to use the auditory monitoring and back-translation strategies if they are expected to write in silence? Do any of the strategies we have detected in these two case studies on writing suggest to you ways in which learners could work collaboratively in order to make the right decisions when planning, composing and checking their written work?

Finally, have you managed to compile a list of writing strategies which were detected and shared with the students during the course of this project? If you have, check against the list in the summary below.

Table 5.7   *Pre-treatment error analysis of writing task (percentage of errors per phrase)*

	Experimental group	Control group
	NP error 41.8 (Mean)	NP error 34.5 (Mean)
	VP error 39.9 (Mean)	VP error 29.4 (Mean)
whole sample	NP error 38.1 (Mean)	
	VP error 34.6 (Mean)	

Table 5.8   *Post-treatment error analysis of writing task (percentage of errors per phrase)*

	Experimental group	Control group
	NP error 34.1 (Mean)	NP error 33.0 (Mean)
	VP error 32.4 (Mean)	VP error 39.0 (Mean)
whole sample	NP error 33.6 (Mean)	
	VP error 35.7 (Mean)	

We have noted some improvements in two students both with regard to language competence and to strategy use. Clearly, we would not want to generalize from the improvements in just two students. However, if we make a comparison of the experimental and control groups for the whole of the sample in the Oxford Writing project we note the following results. The experimental group appears to have made significant gains[3] over the control group in the task (see Tables 5.7, 5.8), particularly in the area of reduction of verb phrase error.

In addition, the experimental group reported changing their approach to writing. Whereas before the training the experimental group was more likely to rely on teacher materials than the control groups, after the training this was no longer the case. This suggests that they were more independent of the teacher in what they wrote.

Whereas before the training the experimental group reported being 'higher dictionary users' than the control group, there was no such significant difference after the training. The experimental group appeared to use the dictionary more selectively.

Whereas before the training the experimental group described itself as less careful when it came to checking their written work, after the training this was not so. The experimental group now considered themselves less sloppy.

Whereas the experimental group reported enjoying writing French less than the control group, after the training there were no significant differences between the groups.

Although these changes are not dramatic, they do point to some improvement in a number of important areas. Given that the period of training was quite short, we remain optimistic about the effects of the training on their writing strategies.

Summary of writing strategies

What follows is a summary of writing strategies detected and developed in the project which contribute to the learner making better decisions throughout the process of writing:

1. *Advance preparation*: brainstorming all words/phrases you know relevant to the topic.
2. *Getting in the right frame of mind*: not allowing anxiety to block out the brainstorm; working collaboratively with a friend.
3. *Resourcing*: using a dictionary, textbook or previous work done.
4. *Recombining*: constructing a meaningful sentence from two or more (brainstormed) chunks for the new context (topic).
5. *Generating via translation*: using the L1 to produce a phrase or sentence.
6. *Reformulating*: constructing a meaningful (but not necessarily correct) chunk by changing a morpheme from a previous chunk through analysis of form (e.g. 'je l'ai vu' becomes 'il l'ai vu').
7. *Prompting a specific check*: (for example) reminding oneself of the negative L1–L2 transfer of tenses; reminding oneself that in the L2 nouns have an effect on other words.
8. *Avoidance*: deciding not to say something because you predict lack of success from both the brainstorming and the generating strategies.
9. *Common-sense monitoring*: does this make sense against the topic and against my knowledge of the world?
10. *Content monitoring*: is this relevant to the topic or essay title?
11. *Coherence monitoring*: does this make sense with other bits in the text?
12. *Auditory monitoring*: does it sound right to me when I read it out loud?
13. *Visual monitoring*: does it look right?

14. *Back-translating*: does it make sense when I translate what I have written back into L1?
15. *Personalized monitoring*: reminding yourself of the mistakes you know you make frequently.
16. *Evaluating decisions taken*: (for example) was I right to choose that L2 word from the dictionary?
17. *Collaborative monitoring strategies*: two or more students checking each other's work for mistakes.

PAUSE FOR THOUGHT

How did you do with your writing strategy collection? For each of the above 17 strategies (or more if you have detected more), try to categorize them according to whether they are:

(a) cognitive
(b) metacognitive
(c) affective
(d) social

Do you find that the categories overlap?

Use of the target language

In our strategy training should we be encouraging the learner to avoid reference to their L1 or use it in a positive and effective way? We are forced to ask this question again in the light of the Oxford Writing Strategies Research project.

Clearly, at the low to intermediate level of language learning such as the one we have been examining, it will be impossible to exclude the L1 from the process of planning, composing and monitoring. At this level we only have the beginnings of an internalized rule system, vocabulary is still limited to a narrow range of topics and a systematic link between the spoken and written language is still embryonic. As a consequence, the L1 is the predominant language of thought. It could be argued that the L1 has emerged as such because of the artificial nature of the think aloud in that the writer was compelled to report to the researcher their thoughts in their common L1. This objection, however, finds little to support it. Most students self-reported having to think in L1 in order to accomplish the independent tasks and, even when they were able to brainstorm directly in L2, the process by which they went from ideational state (when what they wanted to say still had no language attached to it) to a linguistic state, very likely passed through an intermediate L1 processor. In other words, L2 chunks were still retrieved in a way not dissimilar to the way a computer database operates if the framework of the programme is written in English and the data stored are written in French. It is true that, at this level of competence, the L2 can detach itself from the need to refer back to underlying L1 structures. However, we have to ask what, at this level, this is actually doing to improve the learner's language store. It seems to me that essentially this is a process of, at best, consolidating known language in new contexts, or at worst merely a holistic compensation strategy for lack of language knowledge. By contrast, we see the L1 being the language that helps generate the hypothesis testing that leads to more rapid language development. But there are traps and pitfalls along this route. These the learner needs to avoid by being given and routinely following the crucial strategic signposts and by being provided with carefully targeted feedback.

BEFORE WE MOVE ON

Were you surprised by the strategies that Katie and Laura were applying during the think alouds and the strategies they self-reported in the independent tasks? Was this what you always suspected of this level of learner?

If you do not teach at this level, have your predictions changed about how your students go about the following processes?:

(a)   planning what they are going to write;
(b)   composing
(c)   monitoring as they write
(d)   checking through at the end

What is your reaction to the idea that learners at this level need a decision-making pathway through their writing process?

What is your reaction to the idea that teachers should refrain from correcting more than one or two aspects of pupils' written output?

We have now come to the end of the section of the book which deals with research into strategy elicitation and strategy training. In the next chapter we will be concentrating entirely on practical ideas and materials to use in the foreign language classroom which are designed to train learners to learn more quickly and more effectively.

Notes

1. A comprehensive is a school which does not select its intake by 'ability' at the age of 11 or 12. In England a small minority of schools selects by 'ability' and these are called 'grammar schools'.
2. This is a mnemonic for *être* verbs, i.e. *monter, rentrer, venir, aller,* etc.
3. These statistics are provisional. This is because the mark or rating given to the students' output has not yet been moderated by another person in order to achieve reliability.

CHAPTER 6

Learner Training in Languages Classrooms

In previous chapters we have examined the findings of research carried out which elicited learner strategy use and we have also delved into some findings of research which tried to train learners to use strategies. It is the purpose of this chapter to propose a coherent approach to strategy training that you will be able to evaluate for your own context, together with materials which will help you to 'scaffold' that training. Scaffolding means supporting a course of action that we want learners to take by providing the means by which they are reminded to carry out that course of action, in a controlled way, with the objective that it will become automatic and more autonomously applied once the learner judges that action to be efficacious for their learning or for carrying out a particular task.

Suggestions of how best to use the scaffolding materials are offered. However, I am fully conscious of the vast array of learning contexts that exist and it may be necessary for you to adapt some or all of the suggestions offered here. Moreover, the materials offered in this chapter are intended to be used over a number of years (see Chapter 8) but the exact length of time over which the programme of training will take place will also be best judged by you.

Despite the diversity of contexts, there are a number of issues that need to be considered by all teachers when embarking on a programme of strategy training:

1. What strategies should learners be exposed to and, particularly, what combinations of strategies? Of course, this may depend

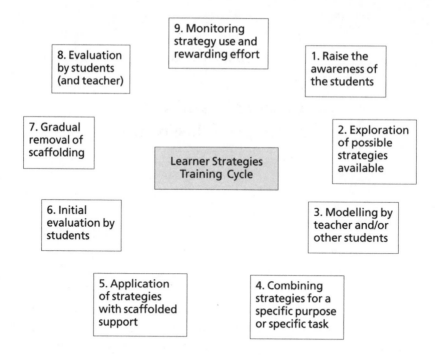

Figure 6.1 *Learner strategies training cycle*

on the problems and deficiencies that the strategy elicitation and the quality of the students' work have revealed.

2. Different task types (and even different texts) may necessitate different strategies or different combinations of strategies – how do we recognize and cater for this?

3. Should the learner training be embedded as part of the language learning or should it be kept separate?

4. If separate, should the training be done at the beginning of a language course or should it run alongside?

5. What language do we do the training in?

6. Should learners be conscious of the strategies they are being taught, with full evaluation of the strategy programme, or should they simply be given random opportunities to practise using strategies?

7. How do we ensure that we do not impose strategies on learners but instead enable them to select the strategies that work best for them?

8. How do we convince reluctant, perhaps unsuccessful, learners that strategy training will be of benefit to them?

I would not claim to be able to provide full answers to all these questions but I hope to be able to offer at least some before we reach the concluding chapter. However, rather than trying to answer each of the above in turn, I will bear the eight issues in mind, as part of the discussion, in proposing a model for strategy training as well as in suggesting ways of using the materials.

The model which I am proposing is cyclical and similar to the model of action research that has been proposed by the chapters of this book. In the Introduction I suggested that the chapters were arranged in order to take you from an identification of the problem, through to being able to evaluate the efficacy of the action that you had taken as a teacher. You would then be in a position (if appropriate) to re-formulate your theories of language teaching and learning and, if necessary begin another action research cycle.

A very similar cyclical model is proposed for your students in a learner strategies training programme and this is represented in Figure 6.1. As we can see, the model has nine steps to it. In this chapter we will essentially concentrate on the first five steps.

Steps 1 and 2 Raising awareness and exploring the range of strategies

When proceeding to raise the general awareness of the learners we should guard against a belief that what we are starting with is a blank sheet of paper or, more appropriately, an empty box. All our learners will have been employing strategies for use with their L1 for many years. Thus, one possible place to start would be to ask them, for example, to think back to when they were in primary school and how they went about improving their reading and writing skills (their literacy). Can they remember, when coming across a new word which they found difficult to read, how they coped with it? Similarly, for spoken language, ask them to think about what is happening when they are listening to an L1 radio programme or a song. How do they describe the language as it enters their heads? What sorts of metaphors do they use? Does their description change (or their metaphors) if the L1 language suddenly becomes a television programme or a rock video? Ask them how they go about planning an essay in their L1 lessons. Do they read through as they are writing, every sentence or paragraph? If so, why do they do this? Finally, ask them to think about when they are speaking in L1 and suddenly can't think of a word or how to put across a particular message. What do they do? Write some of these ideas on a large sheet of paper pinned to the wall. Ask them if any of these strategies are *natural* strategies that they have developed of their own accord (perhaps without even being aware of them until you asked them to think about them) or *taught* strategies (perhaps their primary school teacher taught them how to memorize the spellings of words). It may be an idea to leave the sheet in the classroom for a week or two and then come back to it to see if they have been thinking about the discussion and their L1 strategies. After a week you could even translate some of the strategies on the sheet into the target language using appropriately simplified language.

Now, ask them to make a comparison with their L2 strategies. It's always a good idea to divide them into small groups with a list of open-ended questions to discuss and then get the groups to feed back to the whole class. Start very broadly at first, perhaps with reading and listening. These should draw interesting comparisons and contrasts both between L1 and L2 and between the two modes of receptive skills. At this point you may wish to introduce a short questionnaire.

PAUSE FOR THOUGHT

Look at the list of strategies that you have been building up since Chapter 1. How are you going to devise a questionnaire from this list? Is there a strategy you have thought of that isn't already on the list? If you wanted to include all the strategies that you have collected, the questionnaire would be very long and daunting. Think about all the possible ways in which you could divide up your list of strategies.

What advantages and disadvantages would there be for each division or categorization that you adopted for your questionnaire?

You have a number of options regarding where to start. You could do one of the following:

Option 1 – Select just the metacognitive, social and affective strategies. This would mean that you would be asking them a whole range of questions about the ways that they support and evaluate their learning. It would mean that you could ask them questions right across the range of skills as well as about how they plan their work. It would have the added advantage that, if you were asking them about frequency (using *often, sometimes, not often*, etc.), it would be within the same sphere of context, particularly if you divided up your questionnaire into three sections: *in the classroom; at home; everywhere else*. The disadvantage would be that you would be eliciting only indirect actions to their learning, not the 'brain's contact with the language itself'. Their thinking processes would be indirect thinking processes.

Option 2 – You could just select cognitive strategies – ones that have direct encounters with the foreign language. The same advantages about covering a whole range would apply here as well as the fact that, if you were asking about frequency, it would be in the same sphere of context. The disadvantage of this course of action is that these direct strategies are very difficult for learners to think about. 'How often do I infer meaning from the context? Gosh, it rather depends on the text I'm looking at or listening to! If it's a text using technical language, probably not as much as if it's a newspaper article.'

Option 3 – You could focus on just one process or one skill in language learning such as memorizing, or writing, or 'pro-active strategies for coping with the business of the classroom'. Here you could combine both direct and indirect strategies; primary and support strategies. The advantage here is that the awareness raising becomes tightly channelled. This approach, as an initial awareness-raising exercise, is probably best if you have detected a particular deficiency in a substantial number of your learners, for example, an inability to use the dictionary effectively.

As an initial awareness raising I would personally go for option 1, the metacognitive, social and affective strategies over a whole range of skills and processes.

PAUSE FOR THOUGHT

Well, you've selected your list; you've decided on whether to go for frequency of use or just *yes I do*; *no, I don't*; *not sure*. You've decided whether the questionnaire is going to be totally in L1, totally in L2 or a bit of both.

How are you going to administer the questionnaire? Think about the particular nature of your students. What will their reaction be to the questionnaire task? Do they like ticking boxes? Do they like to tell you about themselves? Will you make the questionnaire anonymous? If not, why not? Are you planning to follow it up with individuals?

> Look at the instructions for filling in a questionnaire below. What issues do they raise about your relationship with your students?
>
> Are the instructions sufficient? What else would you want to say to your students? Do you want to give them the instructions in written form?

Suggested instructions for filling in a strategy questionnaire:

Please fill this questionnaire as best as you possibly can even though you may not find it easy. There are no right and wrong answers and nobody is trying to trick you. Of course, you do not have to do this, and if you feel really unhappy about doing so just hand it in blank or do not hand it in at all. However, as you can see, the questionnaire is anonymous and you have my total assurance that I won't try to find out who wrote which one. I'm not trying to assess you or evaluate you. The aim is simply to get us (the class) to start the process of thinking about the strategies we use when learning a foreign language.

Read through the questionnaire and ask me about anything you don't understand. You may also want to know what is meant by 'often' or 'rarely'. This is very difficult to define accurately. However, if you think that doing something 'often' is doing it nearly every time the opportunity presents itself and when it makes sense for you to do so, then you might have a better idea of what is meant by 'often'. For example, think about 'answer (in your head) questions directed at other people'. If eight times out of ten when I ask a fellow student a FL question you prepare the answer in your head, regardless of *whether I may then ask you*, then that would probably be 'often'. You do that strategy 'often'. If you only 'answer questions in your head directed at other people' once or twice out of ten, then that would probably be 'rarely'. If you only answer them when they are directed at you, then that would be 'never'. In a sense each question is different and requires you to think about the situation in which you would use that strategy.

Fill in the questionnaire individually in class. Don't talk to your friends as you do it. Try to be as honest as possible. Nobody is going to criticize you for not ticking the 'often' column.

You now have a further couple of options. You can collect in the questionnaires straightaway and go away and analyse them, then bring back some results for the class. Alternatively, you can, in the first instance, get them to discuss it in pairs, preferably with a friend they feel comfortable with. You could tell them:

> First, look at all the ones that you have ticked as 'often' or 'sometimes'. Are they the same for both of you? If not, can you think of any reason why they are not? Now look at all the ones you have ticked 'rarely' or 'never'. Are they the same for both of you? If not, can you think of any reason why they are not? If your friend has ticked 'often' for one of the strategies and you haven't, ask him/her how he/she uses that strategy. Is it difficult to do? Is there a difference between doing that strategy in class and at home?

You could then ask them to share what they have learnt about using strategies with the rest of the class and with you.

At the end of the questionnaire you may well have asked the class to list any other strategies (of the type in the questionnaire) that they use. You could therefore try doing a survey of all the extra strategies that students in the class have put down. This would seem to lend itself to being done in the foreign language with support from you. You could collect the results of the survey and put them in descending order (i.e. most used strategies first) on a flip-chart sheet or on the board. Discuss these. Particularly ask how individuals go about doing any unusual ones.

An alternative is to bring the results of the questionnaire to the next lesson and ask them to discuss these in groups. Indeed, you could take the results of the Lingua survey (Chapter 2) and ask them to discuss why there are such differences between boys and girls or the differences between the Italian learners and the English learners.

If you are focusing on a single skill such as writing, you could get them to do a writing task with self-report on strategies similar to the one we looked at in Chapter 2 (page 61). You could then arrange for them to pool their ideas about their approaches to writing . In addition, you could show them Figure 6.2 made up from the analysis of the writing project with 14 year olds. Use the figure to stimulate group discussions about various approaches to planning and composing. If your students were of a different age group, you could ask them to compare their own strategy use with that of the sample of 14–15 year olds.

How often do you look words up in the dictionary?

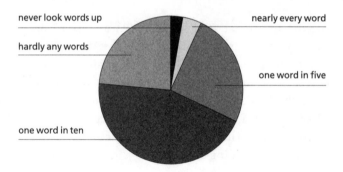

I think of a sentence in English and translate

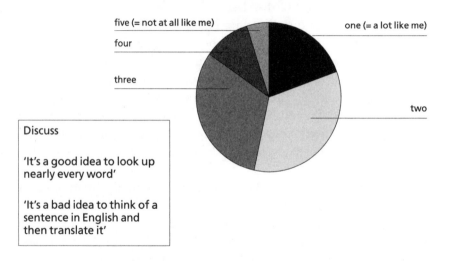

Discuss

'It's a good idea to look up nearly every word'

'It's a bad idea to think of a sentence in English and then translate it'

I only use sentences I know in French
1 = a lot like me; 5 = not at all like me

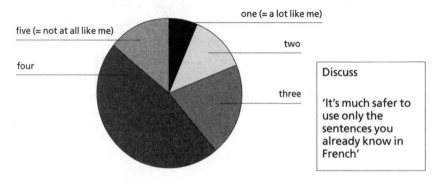

Discuss

'It's much safer to use only the sentences you already know in French'

Figure 6.2   *Pie charts generated by writing strategies questionnaire*

How/when do you check your written work?

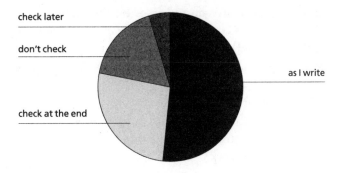

check later

don't check

check at the end

as I write

I read the writing out loud to see if it sounds right

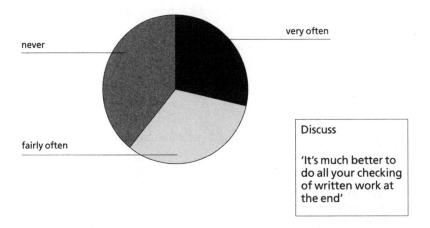

never

very often

fairly often

Discuss

'It's much better to do all your checking of written work at the end'

I check that it makes sense by translating it back into English

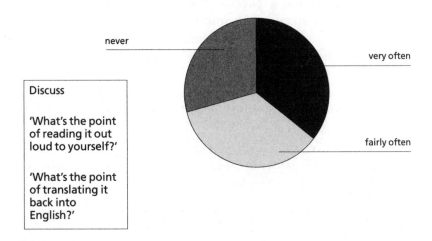

never

very often

fairly often

Discuss

'What's the point of reading it out loud to yourself?'

'What's the point of translating it back into English?'

At this point it will be important to discuss why the use of these strategies might help the students to learn more effectively. Put the following keywords and phrases on the board, overhead projector or flip chart in the class (with younger children these keywords will need to be adapted). Discuss with them why these might be desired approaches that they might adopt with their language learning.

1. Deliberate actions.
2. Take responsibility for your learning.
3. Take control of your learning.
4. Review work.
5. Treat text as a problem to solve.
6. Make learning more systematic.
7. Identify specific skills to develop.
8. Internalize language (Absorb and keep language? Make language your own?).
9. Store language more efficiently.
10. Retrieve language more efficiently.
11. Make learning more enjoyable.
12. Make learning faster.
13. Allow teacher to respond to individuals' needs.
14. Make learning more transferable to other situations.

Now go through each of the strategies in the questionnaire that you used and discuss with the class how the above desired outcomes might be brought about by the use of the strategy. Try to show how the outcomes above are more likely to be achieved if strategies are used in combination and that using only one strategy can, in fact, impede successful learning. You might use as an example how the over-reliance on cognates in reading a text can be detrimental to accessing that text.

You could also discuss with your students the problems of learning a language in the classroom and the strategies that they can use in order to overcome these problems. You might mention that the problems are:

1. A lot of students and only one teacher – teacher can't ask questions to all the students at the same time.
2. Some students are at different levels of knowledge and confidence.
3. If you put together the sum of vocabulary and structures that the whole class knows, it's a lot more than any individual student knows.
4. Some students are more reluctant to speak than others.

5. Some students can concentrate better than others.
6. There is very little time (not enough time) devoted to language teaching in school or college.
7. (In your context perhaps) language learning starts later than other subjects.
8. (As a consequence of 6 and 7) the teacher tries to stay in L2 as much as possible.

You could discuss with them how a number of strategies can be used in combination to overcome this problem. Perhaps you could start off by getting them to match the following strategies to the problems identified above.

1. Look up words in dictionary or coursebook.
2. Ask teacher to clarify or repeat.
3. Practise saying new words under your breath.
4. Practise conversations with a friend at home.
5. Answer questions in your head directed at other people.
6. Make a note of new words (write language down) with a view to finding out what it means (or how to use it) later.
7. Make a vow to read one extra piece of foreign language text per week.
8. Do some pre-task strategies like 'clear the mind of everything else but the language you are about to listen to'.

You could then ask them if these strategies could be used consistently. What might be stopping the students from using these strategies? Can they think of other ways of making the class atmosphere more conducive to language learning?

Another way to raise awareness is to provide the students with examples of what strategies other individual students have said they use, for example, the memorization strategies discussed in Chapter 4. These are highly personalized sequences of strategies and may provoke an interesting reaction (hopefully, one of admiration) from your learners. However, some may say that this isn't their way of learning. If so, they need to be able to articulate why. A variation on this is that some of your younger students are paired up with some older, more advanced learners, and that they go and interview these 'good language learners' about their strategy use.

PAUSE FOR THOUGHT

What sorts of questions about strategy use could they ask the older students? Would they use a highly structured schedule of questions or would they use a semi-structured schedule? Would you ask them to record the interviews or just take notes?

Or, you could divide your class up into groups of three and ask them to carry out a think aloud on a reading comprehension text or a writing task (see Chapter 2 for for guidelines on how to carry out a think aloud). This is not as hard as it sounds. You would have to show them how to do this quite carefully (see *modelling* below). Student 1 would be trying to decipher the text. Student 2 would be asking them the prompt questions (What are you thinking now? How do you know that? What makes you say that?); student 3 could be jotting down notes about how student 1 goes about understanding what is in the text. This activity would probably be best left to older students and adult students but you will know if it is possible with younger ones as well.

You can, if you are very brave, record yourself talking in L2 to the class (for example, when questioning them or providing procedural instructions). You could then watch the video together and ask the students to discuss in small groups what strategies they are using while they are listening to you before feeding back to the whole class. You could particularly focus on what might distract them from the flow of language that is coming at them or distract them from formulating a response to your questions.

Finally, you can raise awareness over time by asking learners to keep the kind of learning diary that was suggested in Chapter 2. Here the main emphasis would be on self-reflection after a period of time has elapsed. This allows the learner to put some distance between themselves and their learning and to treat it with some objectivity. For example, you could simply ask your learners to jot down after each lesson (or major task, or specific skill-related activity) how they felt about it. This would be their immediate 'hot' reaction. You could then ask them (e.g. at the beginning of the next lesson) to provide you with their 'cool' reaction – a more reflective reaction. These reactions could then be discussed in pairs or groups and strategies for dealing with difficulties sought.

All the above are ways of raising the awareness and the consciousness of the existence of strategies with our students and no doubt you will be able to think of other even more creative ways. With the help of symbols and modified input a fair amount can be done in the target language, particularly with intermediate and more advanced learners.

Steps 3, 4 and 5 Modelling, combining and applying strategies

Just making the learners aware of the existence of strategies and exploring the range of available strategies is not going to bring about successful strategy use and, even more importantly, an appropriate combination of strategy use. Learners may need to be shown explicitly and repeatedly the strategies which they can try in order to achieve better learning. In order to discuss modelling we will look at particular strategy combinations linked to specific skills and processes. Sometimes the modelling can be viewed as quite separate from the application of the strategies, at other times modelling, combining and applying strategies overlap considerably. Let us start with reading comprehension strategies. This is one instance of where modelling and application inevitably overlap.

Reading comprehension strategies

An effective way of modelling strategy use in reading is for you to do it in front of them in the same way as you experimented with a text in Chapter 1 where I suggested you tried this with a colleague. Of course you are going to need to use a text which is challenging for you. For example, I have used a Spanish text in order to demonstrate that, although I have never studied Spanish, I can use a lot of strategies which will help me understand quite a lot of it even though it's taken from a Spanish newspaper. So let's just think about using this form of modelling. The first activity is quite simply to take the text (having made copies for the students) and to simulate a think-aloud activity. That is, attempt to translate (or show understanding of) the text while simultaneously describing the thinking processes that you are going through. If you can get the students to call out the 'think-aloud prompts', that's even better. Then ask them to jot down all the strategies that you employed in order to understand the text. They will then get a feel for the sheer number of possible strategies that can be used and the effort that it takes in order to 'crack the code'. Most of the effort resides in the working memory because we need to hold some information in our heads while attempting to retrieve and process other information. Tell them that *you* can use lots of strategies, perhaps like linking to other foreign languages, that they can't. But that should not deter them, there are lots of other strategies that they *can* use.

So, what strategies can we model for them? Let us take the example of a class of 16-year-old French nationals learning English. You have done the think-aloud simulation on your own text. Now you can provide them with an English (L2) (Figure 6.3) text showing them certain things to look for:

The Oxford Times
Friday, 2 Feb 2001 Front page

Cyclist who died under bus 'told to take care'

A CYCLIST who died after being dragged under a bus had been warned several times by colleagues to take better care on the road.

Colleagues at Brasenose College, Oxford, where Mrs Isabel Beckett worked as a silver service waitress, told an inquest on Wednesday that she was known to pay little attention to traffic when cycling. The 47-year-old widow, of Hillsborough Road, Cowley, was crushed under the Barton-to-Kidlington bus as she cycled to work at about 8.10am on August 5.

Ms Shelley Graham, of Littlemore, who was walking along High Street at the time, said that the cyclist swerved in front of the Oxford Bus Company bus without indicating or checking for traffic. She said: "It did not look like she had looked behind her. The bus would not have been able to stop in time and just went over her."

Ms Alexander Saunders, a Brasenose student, saw the accident and ran to the porter's lodge for help. She said: "I had known Isabel for a year. I was aware she had had incidents on her bike before and people had told her she should be more careful."

Ms Angela Everett, Brasenose's porter, said: "I had seen Isabel cycling on several occasions. She paid little attention to traffic. I, and many others at the college, had warned her about the dangers."

Bus driver Mr Aziz Louni said he had spotted a cyclist ahead who looked as if she was travelling straight on. Mr Louni of Curtis Close, Bicester, said: "I expected to overtake the cyclist. Within a split second she came out in front of the bus."

Recording a verdict of accidental death, the Oxfordshire coroner, Mr Nicholas Gardiner, said: "I have to conclude Mrs Beckett, who may have been late for work, swerved across the bus's path. There was no indication she intended to move across the road or that she looked around to check anything was there."

a) Look for keywords in headline

b) Words they should already know

c) Words that look like French ones

d) Words they will need to infer

e) Words which will help them make informed guesses

f) Use of paragraphs and people to tell the story

Figure 6.3   *Accessing a text through strategies*

(a) What items of context their eyes immediately should spot and note – keywords in the headline – cyclist; bus, died. Also the newspaper it comes from is *The Oxford Times*, suggesting this is not a national or international event.
(b) What words they should already know in English.
(c) What words look like French (L1) words, for example, cycliste; bus; collègue; collège.
(d) What words they will have to infer – silver service waitress; coroner.
(e) What information will help them to make informed guesses (inferences) – Brasenose College, Oxford; verdict of accidental death.
(f) Textual and journalistic conventions: use of 'witnesses' to tell the story rather than the author himself or herself and the fact that each witness gets a paragraph.

Try to show how the text above is more likely to be accessed successfully if strategies are used in combination. Ask them to identify a problem in the text – a difficult sentence or a series of unusual lexical items – and get them to try to apply a combination of strategies (at least two at a time) from the list below:

1. Guess what words mean from the context they are in.
2. Use their 'world knowledge' and common sense.
3. Start from words they already know and 'work up' or 'work outwards'.
4. Think about the words that look like L1 words.
5. Look up words in a dictionary (but not so many that it will stop them making any progress at all!).
6. Make a note of some of the new words (perhaps to look up later).
7. Hold an unknown word or phrase in their heads and come back to it later.
8. Predicting what a word might be by guessing what it would look like as different part of speech.

On a number of occasions they can be asked to look at a text and identify a number of problem items of vocabulary or short phrases by putting a circle round them. They can then look around the difficult item for information which will help them infer the difficult item and draw connecting lines to it.

You could, additionally, provide them with the following extended guidelines (in this list I am using examples from French as L2).

Guideline	Commentary
Look for words or phrases you already know.	Constantly try to remind yourself to look for these and to trust them when you feel confident about their meaning. This is something which is often forgotten by students.[1] This should be your most important strategy even though it may take the most amount of effort to remember.
When starting on a text you may hit an immediate problem. Identify and then isolate the problem.	Why are you having a comprehension problem? Isolate the word or phrase that is actually causing you trouble rather than have a 'negative attitude' to a whole chunk of text or even the whole text. This is a way of trying to control your anxiety in a task that's challenging you.
Identify which words you haven't learnt before but which look like L1 words. These are called cognates.	Use this strategy sparingly and in combination with other strategies (particularly *words you know*) not least because of the problem of *faux amis*.
Spot capital letters part way though a sentence. These might well indicate a proper noun (or a noun in German). Try to hold this 'context clue' in your head.	This sounds obvious but teachers often get students telling them that they cannot find a certain word in the dictionary and then it turns out to be the name of a place (complete with capital letter).
Look for verb–noun combinations.	For example, you know the word for washing up and you recognize the imperfect tense and so you are left with an unfinished sentence which looks like this 'he was …ing the washing up' . Well, what can the verb possibly be – eating? driving? smiling?
Identify a verb and then immediately ask yourself 'what tense is it?'; 'who is doing the action?'	Taking this basic step will set you off in the right direction for the meaning of each sentences and, often, each paragraph
Combine dictionary skills with common sense.	The dictionary may give 'XXX' but if the result is nonsense (in terms of what you already know), then it's fairly safe to assume that there is another possible translation.
Look for non-verbal clues	Pictures associated with the text; bits which have been highlighted by the writer or editor; writing/typography conventions.
Try out the phonetics.	How does the word sound when 'read aloud' – or in your head if you are meant to be reading in silence (e.g. an exam)?

See if the written form conforms to what you know.	Or the other way round: you know the sound 'nage' but the written word is 'nuages' – which one should you trust? Trust *what you know* but look for other clues which confirm it.
Break down words into their component bits, then use other strategies such as your general knowledge.	'le championnat de France de football' OK you've got champion (from the 'head of the word') but does your common sense tell you that it can't be a person (a person can't be a French football champion). 'the champions' would need a 'les' and an 's'. It's got to mean something else. Now check with the context and your 'understanding so far'.
Watch out for 'false dawn'! – bits in words which look like words you know.	Are you stuck on 'les huîtres'? You know the word 'huit'- so can it mean 'the eights'? OK, then, try a different tack. What have you been told about circumflexes in French?
Look beyond the obvious and don't get stuck on your pet theory or the first thing that pops into your head.	'le' might not necessarily mean 'the' as in 'je le vois tous les jours'. Anyway you can't have 'the' followed by a verb.
Check if the punctuation makes sense with what you think you have understood.	Questions must have a question mark on the end! This might seem obvious but students don't always spot them. Subordinate clauses (bits that make their own sense in the middle of a sentence) usually have commas at either end of them so that if you lift them out, the rest of the sentence should still make sense.
Go back to the beginning of the text and start again!	Treat your 'cracking the code' of the text as building up layers of evidence. By going back to the beginning you will be consolidating the first layer.

A very effective way of training students to adopt combinations of strategies for understanding written texts is to translate texts with them out loud in class, pointing to clues which they should be spotting and get into the habit of spotting. Translation into L1 may not feature as a teaching strategy in your methodology and/or it may not be a test type in your assessment or examination system. That's fine, there's no need to change your methodology. However, as part of a strategy training programme it is invaluable as the teacher is able to embed the comprehension strategies directly into the L2 activity. As part of a strategy training programme you are obviously not looking for 'style of translation' or accuracy of translation for the sake of it. You are simply exercising and consolidating the combination of strategies described above, guiding the students towards combinations of strategies they may be failing to apply. A teacher should be able to remain in the L2 for virtually all of this activity while allowing the students to make L1–L2 connections.

Listening comprehension strategies

A good starting point in raising awareness of listening strategies is to identify with the class the differences between reading and listening. To a certain extent you may have done this already if you adopted the 'think about your L1 strategies' which was discussed above.

PAUSE FOR THOUGHT

Can you come up with a comprehensive list of differences between reading and listening in the second language? Don't be afraid to mention even the most obvious. Here are a few differences to start you off:

Reading

- You can see squiggles with gaps in between them.

- You can pause and go back.

Listening

- You can hear sounds which may appear continuous.

- You can't always stop the speaker and ask them to go back.

Now model some of the strategies for preparing for listening as in Scaffolding Sheet 6.1. For example, do some deep breathing exercises with the class in order to get them relaxed; provide them with short reading texts and ask them to identify which would be the best strings of words to sample if these were listening texts.

One way of getting them to think about the relationship between their sampling and their scanning for details is to give them a topic and ask them to predict which words or ideas would be likely to come up in a listening text on that topic. You could then give them a transcription of a taped text but with some changes made to the text. As they hear the tape and read the text they have to underline the

Scaffolding Sheet 6.1   *Coping with a difficult listening (taped) text*

Prepare yourself mentally

- Am I feeling anxious? Why? What do I usually do to overcome this?
- Am I concentrating? Why not? What can I do to shut out any distractions?
- I know I've got to try to keep up with the tape. Am I ready to do this?

The task itself

- Is there a topic already indicated? What can I *predict* that the text will include?
- What am I being asked to listen for? The overall meaning ☐ certain items ☐   lots of details ☐

Final countdown

- Activate my world knowledge ☐
- Activate my common sense ☐
- Get ready to identify keywords quickly and hold them in my head ☐
- Get ready to look out for incoming context clues. Tone of voice? Background sounds? ☐
- Get ready to avoid getting stuck on single words for too long ☐
- Get ready to think in chunks of language ☐
- Get ready to 'sample' the language not try to decipher all of it ☐

OK, all systems for listening are go!

differences. Then discuss how they managed to scan for the differences. You could discuss strategies for 're-focusing' if their concentration should go during the middle of a listening activity.

You could then provide your learners with Scaffolding Sheet 6.1 (or something similar) every time you require them to do a taped listening comprehension. They could just think about this sheet for a minute before starting, then turn it over so that it does not distract them.

Interactive strategies

We will now look at some training for interactive strategy use as these follow on rather well from listening strategies. You may need to go back to Chapter 4 to remind yourself of what we mean by interactive strategies or simply consult your strategy list which you have been compiling.

You may find it appropriate to consider interactive strategy training as a longitudinal process. With beginners, in order to keep the conversation flowing, they will need to use many non-linguistic (paralinguistic) strategies such as mime and facial expressions. In addition, beginners will need to deploy (and therefore have to be trained in) a number of strategies which reduce or alter the message that they want to put across: switching to the L1; asking for help in saying something; avoiding a topic; functional reduction; coining words; using the tone of voice to convey meaning. As learners become more proficient in the language, they will be able to rely more on strategies which use knowledge of the language itself such as circumlocution, syntax avoidance and discourse avoidance.

How might you model these communication strategies? To develop effective use of intonation and mime, you might provide two different pairs of students with the following dialogue on p.195 (English L2) with no punctuation. Ask each group to *only use the words* in the left-hand box and use the tone of their voice, mime and exclamations to put across the different meanings provided in the right-hand box. The rest of the class have to guess from their efforts what the message was. An alternative, for more advanced learners, is that they have to write out the two dialogues using all the additional language needed in the written medium in order to convey feelings, mood and assumed action. This strategy modelling would combine well with the listening strategies above.

Student 1: hungry	Student 1 asks student 2 if she is hungry.
Student 2: again	Student 2 replies that yes, as always, she is.
Student 1: empty fridge	Student 1 says: 'Well, that's tough, look, the fridge is empty.'
Student 2: fish and chips	Student 2 says: 'Look, I've got enough money to buy us both fish and chips.'
Student 1: hungry Student 2: again	Student 1 tells student 2 that she's feeling hungry. Student 2 is exasperated because this happens all the time.
Student 1: empty fridge	Student 1 asks if the fridge is empty.
Student 2: fish and chips	Student 2 opens the fridge and pulls out a plate of horrible cold fish and chips.

Another way of developing communication strategies such as intonation, mime and word coinage is to get students to perform role plays and conversations in front of the rest of the class and to provide marks or rewards for those people who, as well as producing good quality language, also deploy communication strategies to keep talking thereby keeping the conversation going. A further variation on this is to video-record role plays and conversations and to play them back to the rest of the class. In order to encourage the performing students to apply these strategies during interaction you might provide the observers with Scaffolding Sheet 6.2 and ask them to identify the strategies being used by the students performing the dialogue. This would act as a model for the application of the strategy for the class.

Scaffolding Sheet 6.2 could then be filled in by the performers themselves *after* they had carried out their dialogues as a way of applying the strategy.

Let us look at some more, slightly different interactive strategies. The scaffolding here, as elsewhere in this book, is designed to get learners into a habit of using a strategy. Here we are encouraging interaction with the teacher in the teacher–whole class situation. In order to model this you might use the approach of 'interactive procedurals' already hinted at in Chapter 4. Let us look at this in more detail. You need to

Scaffolding Sheet 6.2   *Role play*

Role play theme	Strategies used
At the dentist	Mime ☐
	Facial expressions ☐
	Tone of voice ☐
	Exclamations ☐

give your students the following procedural instructions (English L2) for an activity. First of all you word-process the instructions modifying the input such that it is just above the competence level of your students. Obviously, in the example below I'm hypothesizing their competence level.

> OK, we're going to do a role-play activity, working in pairs. We're still on the topic of school: subjects; timetables; likes and dislikes. So we've got partner A and partner B. Each of you has information about school on the sheets and your likes and dislikes. One person at a time has to give the information. The other person has to write down the information on the back of the sheet in the grid provided. I'm going to demonstrate an example first. I want you to speak in English all the time. You have 5 minutes to complete the task. Then I will ask for volunteers.

Then prepare some true/false questions such as:

1. You are going to be working in groups of three.
2. The topic is only about school subjects.
3. You don't have to make up the information.
4. Take turns in giving the information.
5. Write the information from your partner on the sheet.
6. You can start straight away.
7. You can talk for 5 minutes.

Put the true/false questions on the overhead projector or dataprojector. Read out your text and simply ask the students to say whether the statements are true or false. Then do a feedback on what they have deduced in the normal way, asking them to provide you with the correct answers for the false ones. You could also project the same text for them with some gaps in it and ask them orally to fill in the gaps.

By this time they should know what they have to do. More importantly, you have modelled the way in which they can interact with you in order to clarify your message when you are giving them instructions for an activity. You could then do this modelling in combination with Scaffolding Sheet 6.3, Asking for help in saying something. The objective here is not only to involve the students in interaction but to do it using a number of phrases which avoid the easy way out of only using the direct L1 equivalent. These phrases (French L2) would normally be used during interaction with the teacher or a more advanced learner. If students had this grid in the back of their books they could keep a tally of the number of times they asked someone for help in saying something. Obviously it would be best to do this during a moment of reflection *after* the interactive activity but they would need to be reminded of it before the activity began.

Scaffolding Sheet 6.3   *Asking for help in saying something*

Here are some 'asking for help with saying something' phrases. Use them sensibly and note down whenever you have used one by putting a ✓ in the right row. Then do a tally at the end of each term.

Asking for help phrases and their different purposes	Put all your ticks here	Total for term 1	Total for term 2	Total for term 3
Requesting direct equivalent for word or phrase, e.g. *Comment dit-on . . . rucksack en français?*				
Awareness of the possibilities, e.g. *Le samedi je vais . . . au piscine . . . à la piscine? . . .*				
Preparing to speak, e.g. *C'est correcte . . . mes pantalons?*				
Consolidating your learning, e.g. *Comment ça s'écrit?*				

As we have noted, however, interaction strategies also comprise *reception strategies*. Scaffolding Sheet 6.4 (examples given in English L2 and French L2) provides support for developing these. It will be up to you to decide which phrases (and their application) can be expected of which level of students.

Scaffolding Sheet 6.4 *Asking for help and clarification*

This strategy is to help you understand what the teacher or one of your fellow students is saying by actively involving you in 'negotiating meaning' with them. You need to try to avoid letting the language 'flow over you' without at least understanding the important bits. Also try to avoid just saying *je ne comprends pas* (I don't understand) and leaving it at that. Here are some phrases asking for help and clarification. Use them sensibly and note down whenever you have used one by putting a ✓ in the right row. Then do a tally at the end of each term.

Asking for help and clarificationt	Put your ticks in here	Total for term 1	Total for term 2	Total for term 3
I don't understand. *Je ne comprends pas.*				
I don't understand . . . jaw. *Je ne comprends pas . . . mâchoire* (repeating part of text not understood).				
Repeat please. *Répétez s'il vous plaît.*				
Could you repeat please? *Pouvez-vous répéter?*				
I'm completely lost! *Je suis complètement perdu(e)!*				
Could you repeat more slowly? *Pouvez-vous répéter plus lentement?*				
What's that in . . . (L1)? *Qu'est-ce que c'est en . . . (L1)?*				
Excuse me but I haven't understood that. *Excusez-moi mais je n'ai pas compris cela.*				
I didn't quite catch the last phrase. *Je n'ai pas compris la dernière phrase.*				

	Put your ticks here	Total for term 1	Total for term 2	Total for term 3
Could you give me an example? *Pouvez-vous me donner un example?*				
Could you explain that in another way? *Pouvez-vous expliquer cela d'une autre manière?*				

In combination with the grid in Scaffolding Sheet 6.4, learners will become more interactive if they ask for or give confirmation about procedure and even negotiate procedure as in Scaffolding Sheet 6.5 (examples provided in English L2 and Italian L2).

Scaffolding Sheet 6.5 *Useful phrases*

These phrases are intended to help you get involved more with the learning process in the classroom. They should be used in combination with 'asking for help and clarification'. Can you think of any more things you could tell or ask your teacher?

	Put your ticks here	Total for term 1	Total for term 2	Total for term 3
OK, I've understood. *Ho capito.*				
OK, that's fine. *Si, si, va bene adesso.*				
In the back of the book? *Alla fine del libro?*				
Can we start straight away? *Possiamo incominciare immediatamente?*				
I'd prefer to start straight away. *Preferisco incominciare subito.*				

	Put your ticks here	Total for term 1	Total for term 2	Total for term 3
Do we have to change partner?				
Dobbiamo cambiare partner?				
I'd like to change partner now please.				
Vorrei cambiare partner ora.				
We would like to work together.				
Noi vorremmo lavorare insieme.				
I prefer working with a friend, is that OK?				
Io preferisco lavorare con un amico, è possibile?				
How much time have we got?				
Quanto tempo rimane?				
Can I have another five minutes?				
Posso avere altri cinque minuti?				
Can we write on the sheet?				
Si puo scrivere sul foglio?				
I'd prefer to write on a piece of paper first.				
Preferirei prima scrivere su un foglio di carta.				
Can we revise a bit first please?				
Possiamo rivedere un po' prima?				

Coinage or prediction strategies

Students can be asked to try to coin an L2 word or predict what an L2 word might be either from L1 or from L2 respectively. For example, students whose L1 is Italian may not know the English (L2) word for 'tyres'. Rather than stop the flow of a dialogue they might coin from the Italian word *gomme* and come up with an utterance such as: 'I need to change the *goms* on my car'. Students can also try to predict what a word might be in the L2 from their current knowledge of the L2. For example, an English student of French might know that the French word for lemon juice is *citron pressé*. They might therefore predict that the French use the same lexical item for the verb 'to press' and, rather than stopping the dialogue, they might come up with the instruction: 'Il faut *presser* le bouton' when standing outside a building with a French native speaker. L2 speakers are constantly making predictions about the language based on what they already know of the grammar. (I know it's 'I buy' and I've heard people say 'I cried', I predict that it's possible to say 'I buyed'. Let's try it.) Hopefully, in all cases of coinage and prediction, the tone of the L2 speaker's voice (unnatural rising tone on the coined or predicted word) would encourage the person listening to provide the correct form. These two strategies can easily be modelled or practised in the classroom by the teacher asking students to come up with, say, five coined words and five predicted words inserted in spoken utterances. The teacher then provides the correct form as long as the students 'request' a correction by the use of the correct tone on the word they want confirmed.

As we have already intimated in Chapter 4, communication strategies will not help learning directly. It is only when they are used in combination with reception strategies (thereby forming interaction strategies) that the conditions for learning are improved. Although the strategy being developed in Scaffolding Sheet 6.6 is not an interaction strategy, I have placed it here as it would seem to result from those occasions when it is simply inappropriate to interrupt the speaker and ask for clarification.

Scaffolding Sheet 6.6   *Following things up that might slip past*

In a lesson there may be times when you just don't have the opportunity to ask a teacher what something means. This is more likely to happen when you are listening to the tape or the teacher than when you are doing reading work. Don't just give up on it. Make a note on a piece of paper of what it sounded like so you can look it up later. To get you into the habit of following it up, here's a sheet to help you.

It sounded like	In fact it was ... which means ...	Asked teacher later	Asked friend later	Looked in dictionary	Looked in textbook
je neigh pas poo	*Je n'ai pas pu* I couldn't/wasn't able to				

Memorization strategies

First, raise the awareness of your students by getting them to think what type of learner they are in terms of storing language in and retrieving language from their long-term memory. Do they use visual images? Sounds? Repetition? Associations? Or a combination of all these? In order to introduce them to these ideas you might like to show them Figures 6.4 and 6.5 which are ways of memorizing language through some sort of visual imaging. In all these memorization strategies you will need to model how the strategy is to be performed before asking them to try it out themselves.

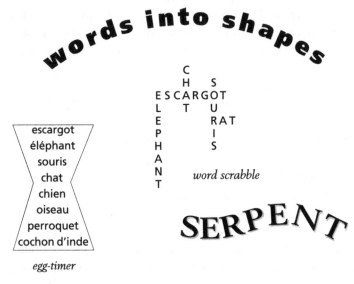

words into shapes

```
          C
          H      S
    E S CARGOT
    L     T      U
    E             RAT
    P             I
    H             S
    A
    N      word scrabble
    T
```

```
  escargot
  éléphant
  souris
   chat
  chien
  oiseau
 perroquet
cochon d'inde
```
egg-timer

SERPENT

Figure 6.4   *Word shapes*

Dictionary definition
(Collins Sansoni):

1. wasp, hornet.
   Nido di vespe – wasps' nest

2. *vespa* – scooter

Figure 6.5   *How to memorize the Italian word for 'wasp'*

Discuss with students how these two approaches to visual imaging can help them to memorize vocabulary. In the case of the word shapes (more suitable for beginners) show them how, after a week, they can still recall the shape and link it to its meaning. Now provide them with an opportunity to make up some of their own visual imaging using these two strategies. A good way to do this is, if possible, to get them to use a computer with clip-art software. As with other strategies, you should encourage your students to try a combination of strategies for memorization. In the case of the visual imaging in Figure 6.5, you could combine this strategy with an initial look at the problems encountered when looking up the meaning of words in the dictionary as is suggested next to Figure 6.5. In order to maximize use of the foreign language, they should, as they move towards a more intermediate level of language learning, try to combine memorizing a word with placing it in some sort of meaning context such as making up a sentence with it or creating sentences from new words or phrases.

Now ask the students to look at the word webs, hooks and chains that were produced by some of the students on the Lingua project (see Figure 6.6).

Discuss how each of these works in different ways to help store and later retrieve language from long-term memory. If they don't come up with many ideas themselves, you could tell them that webs are useful for memorizing tightly bound sets of words, words which fall into a specific category like 'animals'. Hooks allow for a much wider set of meaning associations because they get further and further away from the initial or central idea. Get your students to make up webs and hooks. They could do this at home in preparation for a test. By this I mean instead of simply giving them, for example, fifteen animals to learn, say to them: 'Tomorrow I will test you on fifteen items of vocabulary about animals. You can provide me with a list of any fifteen as long as you hand in a web that you have prepared at home with your test sheet.' Alternatively, you can make it a competition by making students work in groups of about four in order to see who comes up with the biggest 'hook' in a limited amount of time. This activity can once again be combined with 'using a dictionary to expand vocabulary' where learners are taught how to look up (primarily) nouns and adjectives, taking careful note of gender and plurals as appropriate to the language being learnt. This can be taken one step further by making the test a group one. In other words, they hand in their subsequent test sheets in groups (i.e. four lists of words stapled together) and the winning group is the group with the best combined score (N.B. there are social and class management implications to this activity).

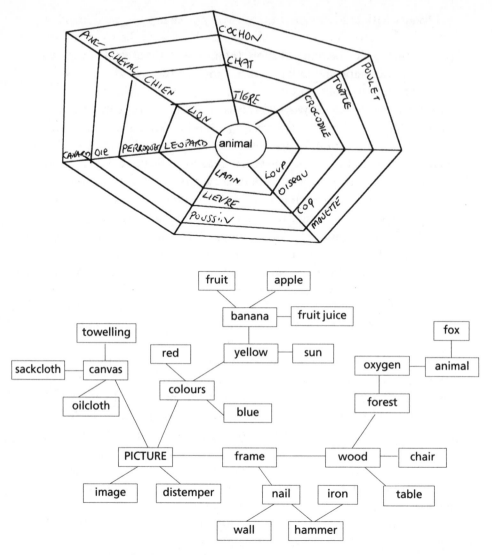

Figure 6.6   *Word webs and hooks*

background – groundsman – man....-...

SCHLOSSGARTEN – GARTENHAUS – HAUSMÄDCHEN – MÄDCHEN-...

Figure 6.7   *Word chains*

Chains can trigger completely unconnected pairs or groups of words and are committed to memory by the 'clashing together' of the different meanings (see Figure 6.7). You should also point out to the students that word chains are very difficult in Italian or French but quite easy in German and English. This language awareness[2] is in itself a kind of learner strategy that can be deployed in many areas of language learning.

Not all mental associations have to be visual, although there is usually a visual element in it somewhere. Some of them can be textual. Ask the students to look at some of the word associations that Italian students of English said they used (Table 6.1) and to think of how this association strategy might work. Then ask them (if appropriate to the language being studied) to do the same with the associations that English learners of French or Italian might make (Table 6.2).

Finally get them to provide in Table 6.3 their own L2 word (column one), their mental association (column two) and get them to ask their partner to fill in column three. You might provide them with some further examples to start them off as in Table 6.3.

Table 6.1   *Word associations in Italian*

English (L2) word	Mental association	Can you comment on how this mental association might work for these Italian students of English?
shopping centre	*compro e 'sento'* (Trans: I buy and hear)	
housewife	*casa + moglie* (Trans: house plus wife)	
scarf	*scaffale* (Trans: shelves)	
thirsty	*triste* (Trans: sad)	
cold	*assomiglia a caldo ma non lo è* (Trans: it resembles hot but it isn't)	
sent	*sentire* (Trans: to hear or feel)	
feet	*la fetta* (Trans: the slice)	

Table 6.2   *Word associations in French or Italian with English*

French or Italian (L2) word	Mental association	Can you comment on how this mental association might work for these English (L1) learners?
soudain (Trans: suddenly)	suddenly in the Sudan	
enfin (Trans: finally)	finally a solution for children! But not quite!	
chercher (Trans: search)	look for a church	
stationner (Trans: to park)	to park your car near the station	
orologio (Trans: a watch)	lots of 'o' look round like a watch	
divertirsi (Trans: to enjoy yourself)	diversion on the road – have a good time	

Table 6.3   *Word associations in French and English*

French (L2) word	Mental association	Can you comment on how this mental association might work?
chips	French sheep eat crisps N.B. (Fr.) *chips* = (Eng.) crisps; (Fr.) *frites* = (Eng.) chips	
je me *réveille*	I wake up to cars *revving up* outside	
je me *lève*	when I get up my tongue feels like *levva*!	
je me *lave*	do I have to wash in the *lavatory*?	
je me *couche*	I go to bed with my *Koosh* ball	

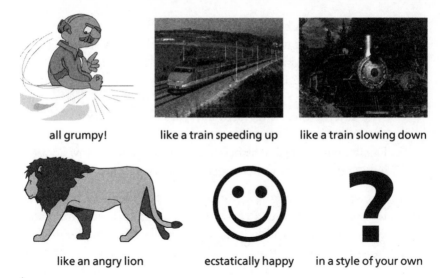

| all grumpy! | like a train speeding up | like a train slowing down |

| like an angry lion | ecstatically happy | in a style of your own |

Figure 6.8   *Styles for repeating with rhythms*

Not all new language can be committed to memory using these techniques. Some of them, like the word association technique, require a fair amount of time and effort. Research has shown that the association technique should be reserved for words which learners have found more difficult to store and retrieve. Much vocabulary can be learnt by using a simple repetitive system which most suits the learner. For example, a system which uses a combination of the written form of the word plus sound and rhythm as in Figure 6.8, which suggests a style of rhythm to try out. This may suit learners who have a good auditory memory or are musical.

The following memorization sequence has been suggested by one teacher on the Lingua project, Robert D'Ambrosio, after discussions with his 13-year-old students of French:

1. Go through the list of words once and tick off words which look like English (L1) words, those that you find very easy to learn, or those that are already known to you. Now tackle the rest!
2. Start by looking at the way the words are written. Start writing the words down by using just the consonants leaving the correct number of gaps e.g. 'souvenir' becomes 's—v-n-r'. Leave the words for 10 minutes and go and make yourself a drink. Come back and then see if you can fill them in.
3. Now use just the first letter but with the correct number of missing letters, e.g. 's———'.

4. Read the words in silence.
5. Read the words under your breath – perhaps try screwing your eyes up as you do this to make the words 'hazy'.
6. Now put the sequence of words to a rhythm. Say the words (without looking at them) out loud in a particular rhythm and style such as those suggested in Figure 6.8 (repeating with rhythm).
7. Finally make a mental association with the word. (How about linking it with that rather superficial girl you know, Sue Veneer?)

This is one way of combining strategies such that the more recalcitrant words to be learnt are gradually whittled away. A further combination of strategies for memorization is the one described in Chapter 4 where vocabulary or phrases are stuck on familiar objects around the student's bedroom and associations are made between the object in the bedroom and the item of language to be learnt. If this is done in combination with one of the rhythmic sequences, it should contribute to a very deep processing of language in the long-term memory.

For those students who have a musical learning style, putting language to music may be a very effective way of learning large quantities of new language. This might be particularly useful for the type of language which the teacher wants students to start using quickly at the beginning of a course in order to get across all the class management and class interaction messages. This language is sometimes referred to as classroom language.[3] For example, I made up this song for a group of 12-year-old learners of Italian because I wanted them to use these expressions when playing language games.

Italian song

tocca a me, tocca a te, tocca a lui, tocca a lei, a chi tocca?
tocca a me, tocca a te, tocca a lui, tocca a lei, a chi tocca?

a chi tocca?
tocca a me
a chi tocca?
tocca a te
a chi tocca

tocca a lui
a chi tocca

tocca a lei

tocca a me, tocca a te, tocca a lui, tocca a lei, a chi tocca?
tocca a me, tocca a te, tocca a lui, tocca a lei, a chi tocca?

English glossary

Tocca a me – it's my turn
Tocca a te – it's your turn
Tocca a lui – it's his turn
Tocca a lei – it's her turn
A chi tocca? – whose turn is it?

This is a tune for very young learners of English that can be sung to the tune of the Beatles' song 'Yellow Submarine':

Listen now, look at the board,
shut the window, open the door,
you can soon go out to play

(chorus)
Stand up, sit down, shake your tambourine, shake your tambourine,
shake your tambourine (repeat)

Can I start my drawing please,
coloured pencils are what I need,
here's a blue and here's a green,
don't forget your tambourine
(chorus)

Finally, here's one made up by Cynthia Martin which learners of French can put to the traditional French tune 'Au clair de la lune':

Entrez dans la classe
Et dépêchez vous
Prenez vite vos places
Bientôt c'est à vous
Ouvrez donc vos livres
Prenez vos crayons
Je vais tout vous dire
Donc, faites attention

You can ask students to put any suitable list of phrases to raps or blues. Many learners will be able to retrieve phrases from memory more easily if they have been stored through a process which involves rhythm, rhyme or music. Figure 6.9 is a blues in French designed to help students learn the classroom language they will need in order to interact with other students on a specific task.

Première strophe

Je vais apporter: les cuillères, les couteaux et les
fourchettes

Tu vas apporter: les verres, la nappe, et les assiettes

Sam va apporter du vin – mais certainement pas les
cigarettes!!!

Deuxième strophe

Moi, je vais jouer le rôle de la serveuse fatiguée

Toi, tu vas jouer le rôle du client énervé

Anne va jouer le rôle de la cliente dégoûtée

Troisième strophe

On va se réunir à onze heures pour pratiquer

Non! On va se réunir à treize heures après le déjeuner

Et si Sam n'est pas là il va payer un forfait!

Figure 6.9   *Organization blues*

PAUSE FOR THOUGHT

Can you think what type of task the group of students were
preparing to carry out in Figure 6.9? If you do not speak French,
what strategies could you use to understand the gist of what this
blues was about?

 Can you think what are the features of a 'blues' which
particularly help with memorization?

Another standard (i.e. often used) memorization strategy you could
propose to them is the system of: look/hide/say/write/check (Scaffolding
Sheet 6.7). You may want to try to get them to log this strategy over a
period of time or linked to a series of tests as in the scaffolding strategy
below. In addition, they could try to combine this technique with a
different technique and evaluate the effectiveness of both strategies.

Scaffolding Sheet 6.7   *Look/hide/say/write/check*

Test number and topic (if applicable)	Look/Hide/Say/Write/Check used? ☑	Combinée avec cette technique:
	Technique: Regarde/cache/dit/écris/vérifie	Combined with this strategy:
1	Oui ☐ Non ☐	
2	Oui ☐ Non ☐	
3	Oui ☐ Non ☐	
4	Oui ☐ Non ☐	
5	Oui ☐ Non ☐	

Finally, we should remember that deep processing will occur most effectively if the new language is used in a context. Here is an interesting technique for developing this process and which can be very effective as a simple form of additional homework. Teachers can vary the number of words an individual student has to find definitions for according to the level of the class. The examples given in Scaffolding Sheet 6.8 are in Italian (L2) and English (L2).

Scaffolding Sheet 6.8   *Creating sentences from new words or phrases*

This strategy is to help you make up sentences and phrases in the foreign language as a way of learning new words in a context. It will also help you develop ways of getting by if you can't remember a word (combine with your interaction strategies). At various points throughout the year different individuals will be asked to choose in secret some new words or phrases from that lesson. Next lesson you should have prepared definitions of each of these using, if necessary, a dictionary to help you. Read your definitions out loud. Your fellow students will have to guess what words you secretly chose from the previous lesson.

Le tue parole segrete (Your secret words)	Le definizioni (The definitions)
1 una gita	una passeggiata in barca, o a cavallo o in bicicletta. Andare al mare. Un piccolo viaggio organizzato.
2 a greengrocer	Someone who owns a shop which sells vegetables
3	
4	

212 LEARNER TRAINING IN LANGUAGES CLASSROOMS

Writing strategies

In Chapter 5 and elsewhere I have already described in some detail the awareness-raising steps that one can take in order to start the process of strategy training in writing. Briefly we can summarize this by saying that we can use questionnaires and the results of questionnaires to present the students with the range of strategies available to them. We can also experiment with task-based think aloud using groups of three students with two of the students researching the writing strategies the third student is using (see above). Finally, we can raise awareness with self-report on a writing task as was exemplified in Chapter 2. We will now look at some materials which were used to encourage students to use a particular approach and series of strategies in the writing process. We need to bear in mind that these materials have been trialled with low to intermediate students using the decision-making branching process I have already described. I am confident that the process can be applied up to intermediate level but it may be that advanced level students would not use quite the same process. Or, at least, I would imagine that the process is much more conflated, proceduralized and intuitive at the advanced level.

Remember, we have said that, in writing, learners are faced with a series of decisions they have to make. Here are some examples:

1. How much shall I use of what I already know (phrases I know off by heart) but which will limit what I want to say?
2. How much new language shall I 'generate' but which risks lots of mistakes?
3. How often shall I consult the dictionary given the task's time frame and the problems associated with dictionary use?

In order to help the students with these decisions provide your students with an example of a brainstorming sheet (Figure 6.10). In Figure 6.10 the task was to imagine an exchange with your ideal school in any country of the world. Students were asked to describe what the school was like and what they did while they were there. The aim here is to train them to brainstorm task-relevant language that they are confident about – language that they are pretty sure is going to be correct grammatically. Perhaps later they might need to check a gender here or a spelling there but by and large it's going to be correct in its 'chunk form'. You will have to model this quite a bit otherwise they might have a tendency to confuse 'chunk language' with 'generated language' and some might brainstorm by doing word-for-word translation – the complete opposite of what is intended. Or they might be using the

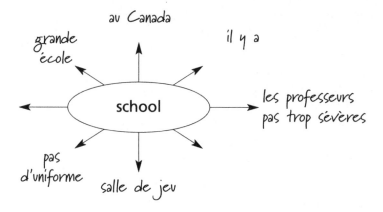

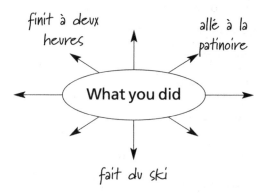

Figure 6.10   *Brainstorming sheet*

dictionary – again incompatible with the kind of strategy that is being advocated here.

Once the students are clear about what language they can use that they already know, they can concentrate on the language they don't know but want to say or need to say to complete the task. In order for them not to be anxious that they will make lots of mistakes with this 'generated' language they need to be prompted to make a number of correct (and I would argue hierarchical) decisions. The greatest problem beginners and intermediate students of French or Italian seem to have is with tenses because of the negative transfer from English (e.g. 'I bought' becomes 'Je acheté'). In order to avoid going down this wrong road, provide them with Scaffolding Sheet 6.9.

Encourage your students to use this form of checking *as they write* because of what the research has suggested to us. Every sentence they should say to themselves: 'What tense is it in the sentence I am trying to generate? How many verbs does that tense have?' They then tick each time they use this monitoring strategy.

Scaffolding Sheet 6.9   *Tenses sheet*

Name:	Date:

Every time you write a sentence
tick to show that you have checked
how many verbs the tense takes:

Have you checked?

Present tense = one verb

Je mange

☐ ☐ ☐ ☐ ☐ ☐ ☐ ☐ ☐

Future tense = one verb

Je mangerai

☐ ☐ ☐ ☐ ☐ ☐ ☐ ☐ ☐

Conditional tense = one verb

Je mangerais

☐ ☐ ☐ ☐ ☐ ☐ ☐ ☐ ☐

Past description
(imperfect tense) = one verb

Je mangeais

☐ ☐ ☐ ☐ ☐ ☐ ☐ ☐ ☐

Past tense
(perfect tense) = two verbs

J'ai mangé

☐ ☐ ☐ ☐ ☐ ☐ ☐ ☐ ☐

The brainstorming strategy sheet is then monitored by the teacher/researcher. It is collected in alongside the finished writing task. It is an additional way of getting inside the students' heads (an example of the awareness-raising step overlapping with the scaffolding step). You will be able to see what phrases they are recombining and the relative success of these. Feedback comments can be provided on this initial process. For example:

> *Un très bon brainstorming* (a very good brainstorming)
> *Quelques erreurs dans ton brainstorming, attention!* (a few errors in your brainstorming)
> *Pas assez de brainstorming* (not enough i.e. I'm sure you've got more)

The tenses check sheet is also collected in with the finished writing task. The teacher/researcher counts the number of sentences the student has written which do not appear on the brainstorming sheet (i.e. the generated sentences), then matches the number of ticks on the check sheet. If there are more sentences than ticks it is possible that the student hasn't checked each one off against the sheet. Feedback comments such as the following were provided:

> *Seize phrases – seulement treize cochets. Pourquoi?* (16 sentences, only 13 ticks, why?)
> *Seize phrases – seulement seize cochets, deux erreurs de temps!* (16 sentences only 13 ticks, and two tense mistakes!)

In other words, the feedback is about *their strategy use*, reminding them that they have not used the check sheet every time and of the possible consequences. All we are interested in is whether the students were using the correct number of verbs needed for each tense used, nothing else at this stage.

PAUSE FOR THOUGHT

If you had decided to carry out a programme of writing strategy training, how onerous do you think that the above 'marking' of students' work would be? Would it be any less onerous *if all you were doing* was this – that is, if you were not underlining/crossing out mistakes and providing correct models of the language?

Could you do this at least once or twice over the course of, say, two months?

What are the workload implications of this training?

Could you enlist the help of anyone else in doing this?

A further strategy that can be used for the 'decision-making process' in the composition phase is a *resourcing* strategy – the use of the dictionary for *generating* sentences. Evidence from the Oxford Writing project suggests that students had problems with looking up 'new' language items in the dictionary, particularly verb-related phrases. If you want to remind yourself of examples of these you could look back to the writing generated by the task-based think alouds in the last chapter. In order to encourage students to use the dictionary but to try to identify where they were going wrong, Scaffolding Sheet 6.10 was provided.

Scaffolding Sheet 6.10   *Using a dictionary with a writing task*

This strategy is to help you use a dictionary more effectively when writing in French. *Every time* you use a dictionary to look up a word you don't know write down the English word you have looked up. Hand it in to your teacher with the written work at the end.

Writing Task 1 (date:)   Writing Task 2 (date:)
(Home – School)   (Home – School)

Words I looked up: Words I looked up:

When you get your work back, identify the mistakes you made using a dictionary. Write down the wrong French word or phrase in the appropriate column and then correct it as in the examples in the box.

too literal a translation?	the wrong choice from the list?	the wrong part of speech?	other:
je suis allant au collège	je mensonge sur la plage	mon frère vente son vélo	

Having dealt with strategies which prompted students to make the right decisions when composing, we now move on to strategies for monitoring. Both the composing processes of using known language and generating language are still likely to give rise to (hopefully minor) mistakes. Students therefore need to apply monitoring strategies both as they write and at the end. In the Oxford Writing Strategies project the noun cluster strategy was modelled for them using Microsoft Powerpoint in order to show them how they should scan for nouns in sentences and then allow the noun's 'tentacles' to reach the words the noun has an effect on. It is impossible to show you how the Powerpoint animation did this here but if you are familiar with the software you will understand. Figure 6.11 shows the noun cluster modelling. After

La semaine dernière je suis allé en Autriche. Je suis allé à Linz.

C'est une grande ville industrielle at commerciale. Linz est à 180

kilomètres de Vienna dans le nord-oest de l'Autriche. Il y a une

très grande université avec beaucoup d'étudiants étrangers.

Je suis resté dans un joli hôtel avec des chambres énormes. Mes

collègues autrichiens m'ont offert un excellent repas dans un petit

restaurant méxicain au centre de Linz (mais le vin rouge était

affreux!).

Figure 6.11   *Noun clustering for the purposes of modelling*

stratégie pour les noms

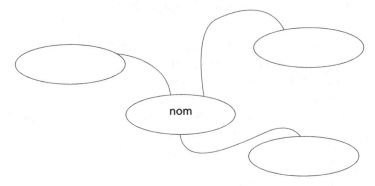

nom

Figure 6.12   *Symbol for prompting the application of noun cluster checking strategy*

Figure 6.13   *Symbol for prompting the application of back-translation strategy*

the modelling session the students were simply provided, on the overhead projector, with the symbol shown in Figure 6.12.

A back-translation strategy can be encouraged in the same way. That is, through a modelling process and then a prompting symbol such as the one in Figure 6.13. On the writing project a Scaffolding Sheet was not used for the noun cluster and back-translation strategies for the simple reason that we feared overloading the students with these sheets in too short a time. If the writing strategy training had been carried out over a longer period of time, it would have been perfectly possible to devise Scaffolding Sheets for these two strategies. The usual mistakes which the back-translation strategy reveals are those resulting from an overload on the processing power of the working memory where attention has focused elsewhere for a moment and omissions seem to have resulted. Sometimes, however, what the student has written just does not seem to make sense and, while this is still probably the result of processing overload, it is difficult to discover the derivation of the 'lack of sense'.

PAUSE FOR THOUGHT

Can you devise Scaffolding Sheets for some strategies? First, have a go at the noun cluster check strategy. If you are a teacher of English as a foreign language (or another language where the noun in a sentence does not have a major impact on other words in that sentence), try to think of a Scaffolding Sheet for a particular syntactic feature of the language that you teach.

Second, the back-translation strategy. This strategy should be applicable to all languages.

Will your Scaffolding Sheets be asking the students to apply these strategies as they write, at the end of the writing, or both?

By the end of the 'application of strategy' stage of the training the students will have practised using a number of strategies for planning, composing and monitoring as they write and checking at the end. They should then be encouraged to use these in combination as well as the other strategies that they are using (refer to list at the end of Chapter 5 on p. 171). As we shall see in Chapter 7, these symbols were used to remind them of the strategies once the scaffolding began to be removed.

Strategy training should attempt to go beyond the planning, composing, monitoring and checking stages. There is a further process resulting from writing even though it is not directly connected to writing itself. This is what the student does with a piece of written work when it comes back from the teacher. We will call these *moving on* strategies because they are used to update the mental models of the target language as a result of feedback. As we shall see below, this feedback from the teacher (and to a certain extent, the other learners) needs to be diagnostic and formative in order to be effective.

Moving on strategies can follow the same modelling, combining and application steps although you could cut out the modelling with certain categories of (older) students. However, these strategies can only be applied by the learners if they are encouraged to think the problems through themselves. As was argued in the last chapter, research suggests that teachers should refrain from writing out the correct model when providing feedback on written work and should also identify only one or two aspects of the learners' *interlanguage* that they wish to develop. There are a number of ways that teachers can do this. In the project, as has been noted, the focus was primarily on tenses, noun clusters and misuse of dictionary. Mistakes relating to these were communicated to the students via feedback on the Scaffolding Sheets themselves. Obviously not all feedback can be as laborious as this. I would therefore propose a simple system of underlining features which you want a student to work on individually or in consultation with a partner and a system of putting a box around features that you want to discuss with the class in plenary. You could use Language practice with a friend below in order to get you started on the process of moving on strategies.

LANGUAGE PRACTICE WITH A FRIEND

Write a message to your partner in the classroom with 10 deliberate mistakes. Ask him/her to discover and underline the mistakes. Now go to Scaffolding Sheet 6.11 and work out *together* 'where did I go wrong?' Scaffolding Sheet 6.11 can then be handed to students for them to work on individually or with their partner.

Scaffolding Sheet 6.11 can then be handed to students for them to work on individually or with their partner.

The next stage is to give students the sheet 'Where did we go wrong?' (p. 221). This is a collaborative way of enabling them to see and act upon the sorts of mistakes that they all tend to make.

Scaffolding Sheet 6.11   *Where did I go wrong? (examples in French L2)*

Write out the mistake here	My English interfered with my French	I thought the rule was always the same	I forgot about the little bits (accents and endings)	I wrote it down the way it sounded	It was a careless spelling mistake	Other reasons for the mistake	The correct version
mon frère est quinze ans	✓						mon frère a quinze ans
j'ai *prendé*		✓					j'ai pris
j'ai un *oiso* à la maison				✓			j'ai un oiseau à la maison
Il porte une *cavate* rouge					✓		Il porte une cravate rouge
les cheveux *noir et frises*			✓				les cheveux noirs et frisés

WHERE DID WE GO WRONG?

As part of your strategy training, a piece of writing you have got back from your teacher has no corrections on it. However, some of your mistakes have boxes round them and some are underlined.

- Get into groups of 6.
- Make lists of any box mistakes that one or more of you have made (i.e write them out as mistakes).
- Now put these in order of the most frequently made mistake to the least frequently made mistake.
- Nominate one person from the group to represent the group and join up with the other five nominees (in the meantime the others check their underlined mistakes).
- The five nominees now make a cumulative list of boxed mistakes with the most frequently made mistake at the top.
- Give this list to your teacher.

You, the teacher, then explain each boxed mistake to the class starting from the most frequently made mistake. An alternative for older learners is to ask the final group to present the list to the class using an overhead transparency or data projector. They take turns in explaining the mistakes to the class and relating it to Scaffolding Sheet 6.11. You then give the class some relevant page references in the text book or support material such as a grammar guide. Some time later the class can be given a similar writing task. The same group work activity is carried out but, having retained the list of frequent mistakes, the class can decide if the mistakes have been ironed out.

From all this process each learner can generate their own *personal mistakes check list* using Scaffolding Sheet 6.12.

Scaffolding Sheet 6.12   *Personal mistakes check list (example Italian L1, English L2)*

My usual or frequent mistakes	Reason why I think I make this mistake all the time
I went in the disco Correct version: I went to the disco	In Italian we say *in discoteca*. I remembered that the English has to have 'the' but not that it has to have 'to' and not 'in'.

You will have noted that in our training for moving on strategies in writing we have gone from the individual to the whole group and then back to the individual. This is an approach that can be adopted for many aspects of strategy training.

Strategies for organizing one's learning

As we noted repeatedly in earlier chapters, research seems to suggest that the most effective learners of a foreign language are those that: (a) use metacognitive strategies to monitor and evaluate their learning; (b) see learning a language as an effortful process; and (c) try to take some control of their learning rather than being passive bystanders. These three features can be targeted by the teacher by the use of the following strategies.

Although good textbooks and language courses incorporate a recycling process of language learning, this appears not to be enough for some learners. There are possibly two reasons for this. The first is that learners are not often aware or understand the way that the course is re-presenting language already learnt but with additional language or in different contexts. All too often, experience and research show (for example, both the reading and writing research projects described in this book) that learners (particularly the least successful) do not use previously learnt knowledge of the language to help them with a current task. The second reason is that all learners acquire/learn new language at different rates and with different levels of in-depth processing. Consequently, a scheme of work or a coursebook which reviews and revises language learnt at its own, as it were, corporate rate cannot possibly hope to 'hit' the precise interlanguage stage of individual learners. A final reason is that some teachers and languages departments do not adhere to a single coursebook but pick and mix from a variety of resource materials. Consequently, learners need to be encouraged to develop their own strategies for re-cycling, revising and reviewing language that they have learnt. The following scaffolding materials are suggestions by which you might encourage your learners to get into the habit of doing this and at their own pace.

You will need to go through the now customary awareness-raising stage with your students with regard to reviewing strategies. You may well have done this already via some of the techniques described at the beginning of this chapter (e.g. questionnaire and group interviews or discussions). Having done this and having promoted the value of some of their best examples of revision, you could offer them the following learner diary (Scaffolding Sheet 6.13). The instructions should be discussed in class as well as being written at the beginning of the diary. The examples can easily be provided in the target language as in the examples below (L2 English and L2 French) but the students are given the choice of whether to keep the diary in L1 or L2. It might be particularly useful, if possible, for learners to set up this diary electronically on a computer. In that way they could do a 'search' to see the last time they learnt a topic or a language point.

Scaffolding Sheet 6.13   *Reviewing language learnt diary (examples in English L2, French L2)*

You may find it useful to keep going back to a topic in order to really learn it once and for all. As you do this, try to think of the way some of the language in the topic is coming up in the work that you are currently doing in class.

Unit: English in the world	Date of first review: 7th October	Date of second review: 12th November
Date Topic Learnt: 1st October	Time spent: 15 minutes	Time spent: 5 minutes
Activity: List of important facts and dates	Activity: memorized facts and dates as whole sentences. Wrote out using look/hide/say/write/check	Activity: brainstormed whole sentences; practised saying difficult dates
	Link with new work: things my parents and grandparents did	Link with new work: An English lesson in Kenya
Unité: Mon collège	Date de la première révision: 7 octobre	Date de la deuxième révision: 12 novembre
Date appris à l'école: 1er octobre	Temps: 15 minutes	Temps: 5 minutes
Activité: écrit une lettre à mon correspondant basé sur les emplois du temps	Activité: lu la lettre une fois; fait un brainstorming des phrases importantes; vérifié avec les corrections du prof	Activité: appris par cœur: *commence à; finit à*
	Lien avec travail actuel? Les matières difficiles et les matières faciles	Lien avec travail actuel? Le concert/disco/la fête commence/finit à

The diary can include a cassette component in order to encourage learners to revise their spoken language using Scaffolding Sheet 6.14.

Scaffolding Sheet 6.14   *Oral revision diary (examples in English L2 and French L2)*

This strategy is to get you into the habit of recording on tape phrases or dialogues you have learnt in class. If possible, record a couple of minutes of the foreign language each week at home. If that's not possible, your teacher will let you do it while you are at school. Keep a tally of the recordings and when you listened to them. Use this strategy in conjunction with the reviewing language learnt diary.

sujet: . . . .   sujet: . . . .

date d'enregistrement: . . . .   date d'enregistrement: . . . .

date de première
séance d'écoute: . . . .   date de deuxième
séance d'écoute: . . . .

heure: . . . .   heure: . . . .

---

topic: . . . .   topic: . . . .

date of recording: . . . .   date of recording: . . . .

date of first listening: . . . .   date of second listening: . . . .

time of day: . . . .   time of day: . . . .

In all these strategies involving logging or keeping a diary of strategy use, you as the teacher will probably need to keep an eye on what the students are doing, on their scaffolding materials, in order to encourage those that are not making the effort. This is an inevitable fact of professional and pedagogical life in most classrooms. In Chapter 7 we will discuss how to slowly remove that scaffolding system. Taking control of one's learning helps to develop a positive attitude to the language. By doing this the perception of the foreign language may slowly change. Hopefully, it will no longer be something imposed by the teacher, or the school, or the exam board but something which the learner has an intrinsic interest in learning. Taking control of one's learning is an essential aspect of developing learner autonomy. In a sense all learner strategies are about taking control of one's learning and, in particular, we have started considering strategies for this in our reviewing language learnt section. Making decisions about when to revise language and doing so at one's own pace are powerful elements in the process of taking control. Another way to take control is to recognize that the foreign language classroom is not the only place where language learning can happen.

Strategies beyond the L2 classroom

In fact, for many learners the foreign language classroom cannot provide sufficient opportunities to offer learners anything but the basis of language learning. For learners of English as a foreign language this problem is getting easier and easier as the media and the Internet are able to provide a rich exposure to English outside the classroom. For learners of other foreign languages, the problem is more difficult but not insuperable. Especially in European Union countries (because of regulations concerning the maintenance of the union's languages), there is a wealth of foreign language outside the classroom if the learner only takes the trouble to go looking for it. Moreover, contrary to popular belief, the Internet is not entirely dominated by English. There are many interesting and quality websites which are updated regularly in French, German, Italian and Spanish as well as the lesser spoken languages of the European Union. The following is a simple activity which will get students into the habit of looking for the foreign language outside the classroom and one which teachers can follow up by collecting a database of foreign language words and phrases that the students have found. First, say to the students, 'Here is some foreign language that learners of English and learners of French found on certain products. Can you guess what the products were?' Then show them Figure 6.14. Then get them to try the same activity using Scaffolding Sheet 6.15. This sheet could be used in combination with the coining and predicting strategies that we discussed above.

> Garnitures non comprises. Renfort.

> Ingrédients: sucre, beurre de cacao, graisses végétales, lait entier en poudre, pâte de cacao, amandes, émulsifiant

Figure 6.14 *Foreign langugage is everywhere*

Scaffolding Sheet 6.15   *The language is out there!*

This strategy aims to encourage you to take every opportunity to use the foreign language outside the classroom. Look at any food products or electrical goods (perhaps when you go to the supermarket) or brochures and other forms of publicity (when you are surfing the World-Wide Web). They often have information on them in the foreign language you are learning as well as your own language. Write down any L2 words that look like words in your own language. Mark these 'c' for cognates. Write down L2 words that you *predict* that you understand for whatever reason. Mark these 'p' for predict. Then write down any phrases that you can see and understand both in your own language and in the foreign language. Then write down all the L2 phrases which are likely to match up with the ones in your own language but which you are not sure of. Hand in your sheet as homework to your teacher on a regular basis for him/her to check through.

Write here 20 words at least	Write here a minimum of 5 phrases (L2)	Write here the L1 equivalents to the phrases

Write here the products or items that you looked at:

Speaking outside the classroom

Not only can learners maximize exposure to the foreign language outside the classroom by reading or listening to language, they can also try to speak the foreign language outside the classroom. Again, this is much easier if they live in an area where there are lots of speakers of that language as the opportunities will be greater. But even in monolingual areas it is possible to find ways. One very interesting approach was carried out by Ros Weller, a teacher involved in the Lingua project. After we had discussed the problem of lack of opportunities to speak the language outside the classroom we concluded that we just had to take the bull by the horns. Let the students speak to people in the foreign language even though those people might not understand. However, some sort of monitoring was clearly needed. But who were going to be those people? Well, why not other teachers in the school! Ros therefore devised an ingenious but simple system of monitoring. She wrote the following message (see Figure 6.15) (followed by the list of students) on the top of a sheet of paper and pinned it on the staffroom notice board:

> The following students are participating in a learning strategies project. One of the exercises involves them in communicating with members of staff in the target language using a simple phrase. Should they speak to you in either French of German please sign next to their name giving the date.

Figure 6.15 shows a selection of students who spoke to other teachers in the foreign language regardless of whether those teachers understood them.

PAUSE FOR THOUGHT

Could you do this in your school or college? Would this be a 'high risk' teaching strategy!? Would your colleagues stop talking to you?

The important thing about this simple activity is that it began to break the mould of the classroom being the only place where short bursts of exposure to the L2 occurred. Figure 6.16 gives examples of a simple Scaffolding Sheet which you could use with students. Illustrated are some examples of 'opportunities to speak' seized outside the classroom in Italy. Even the most geographically isolated students can now communicate with native speakers of the language they are learning through e-mail. Scaffolding Sheet 6.16 allows you to develop and monitor this.

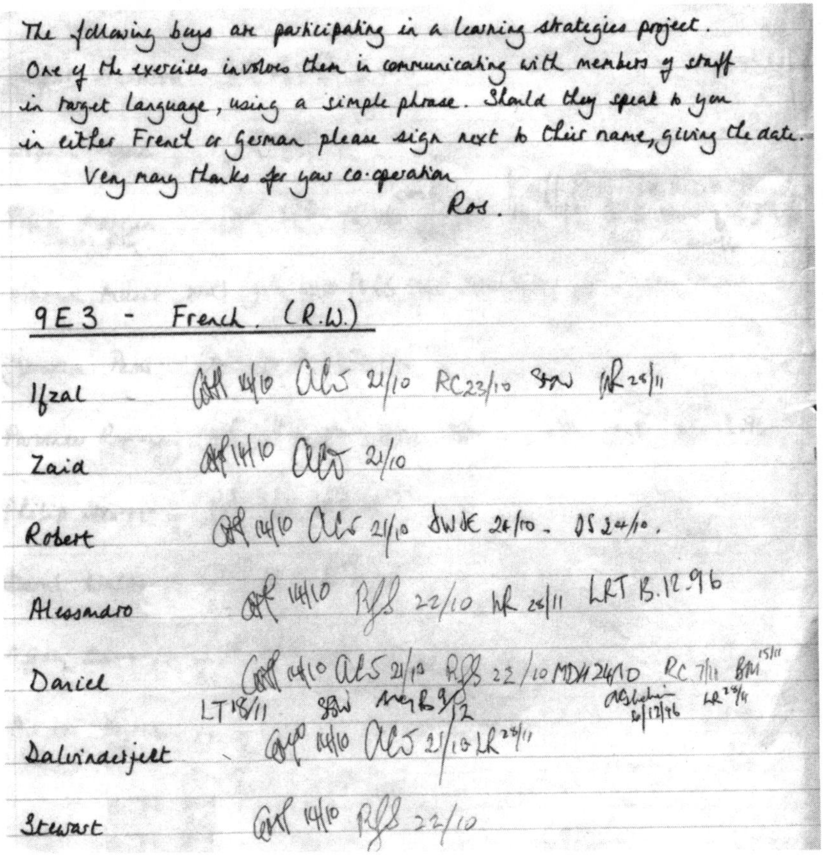
The following boys are participating in a learning strategies project. One of the exercises involves them in communicating with members of staff in target language, using a simple phrase. Should they speak to you in either French or German please sign next to their name, giving the date.

Very many thanks for your co-operation

Ros.

9E3 - French. (R.W.)

Ifzal — 14/10 21/10 RC23/10 28/11

Zaid — 14/10 21/10

Robert — 14/10 21/10 24/10. 24/10.

Alessandro — 14/10 22/10 28/11 LRT 13.12.96

Daniel — 14/10 21/10 22/10 MDH 24/10 RC 7/11 15/11 LT 18/11 2/12 6/12/96 28/11

Dalvinderjeet — 14/10 21/10 LR 28/11

Stewart — 14/10 22/10

Figure 6.15 *List on staffroom wall*

con chi hai parlato UN RAGAZZO quando A FEBBRAIO che cosa hai detto CALCIO	
con chi hai parlato UNA SIGNORA quando MARZO che cosa hai detto DA DOVE VENIVA	
con chi hai parlato UNA DONNA quando PASQUA che cosa hai detto DI MOTORINI	
con chi hai parlato UN AMICO DI MIO PADRE quando APRILE 1 che cosa hai detto SCHERZI	

Figure 6.16 *Using the language outside the classroom*

Scaffolding Sheet 6.16   *Communication by e-mail (Example given in English L2, Italian L1)*

Date	Who I communicated with via e-mail	What we talked about	Some new English words I learnt
15th January	James Calder in Youngstown, Ohio	My latest computer game, the girl he has been seeing!	*Mad* (in America means angry) *Cute* (means *bella* in Italian)

Once students have realized that they can initiate dialogues in this way outside the classroom, they are more likely to do so inside your classroom as well. Again, by scaffolding this strategy, you may be able to encourage your students to initiate more language at appropriate moments as in the suggested approach in Scaffolding Sheet 6.17, with examples given both in French L2 and English L2. You could do this in combination with Asking for help or clarification (p. 198) and also with Developing your memorizing skills or reading strategies as in the example given.

Scaffolding Sheet 6.17   *Taking the lead for a change!*

Classroom talk tends to be started by the teacher. However, I would really like it if occasionally *you* started an exchange of information. A good time is at the beginning and end of lessons so that it doesn't stop the flow of the main part of the lesson too much. Alternatively, you could try this when you have been given some student-centred work to do. In the grid write down the whole dialogue that you had in the foreign language. Of course you will need to take turns in doing this.

Date	Dialogue
☑ Début de la leçon	Moi: Je suis allée voir Sandra hier soir.
	Prof: Ah, elle est sortie de l'hôpital?
	Moi: Oui, dimanche
☐ Fin de la leçon	Prof: Elle va mieux?
	Moi: Je ne comprends pas 'mieux'.
☐ Au milieu de la leçon	Prof: Elle va bien? Mieux ça veut dire 'better'.
	Moi: Ah oui, elle va mieux (*must remember that 'better' in French sounds a bit like the noise a cat makes*).

Date	
☐ Beginning of the lesson	Me: Mr. Thomas, the homework was difficult.
	Teacher: I'm sorry, what was difficult about it?
☐ End of the lesson	Me: The text.
	Teacher: Why was it difficult?
☑ During the lesson	Me: The sentences were too long (*Oops! I can predict what he's going to say: 'Try looking at your list of reading strategies'. Which of course I forgot to do!*)
	Teacher: OK, try looking at your list of reading strategies and let me know which ones you used.

A particular strategy for helping learners to take control is one which I have hinted at on at least one occasion in this book but not discussed explicitly. However, it is, I believe, important as it so closely associated with the problems of lesson management with big classes that teachers face. This is a concentration strategy in that it encourages students to 'stay with the talk' even though they are not talking themselves. Additionally, it is a 'getting ready to speak' strategy in that they may at some point, whether in the classroom or outside, have to utter that phrase or sentence. Scaffolding Sheet 6.18 helps you develop and monitor this with your students. You will need to give out this Scaffolding Sheet when you know that you are going to face a fairly substantial question and answer session.

Scaffolding Sheet 6.18   *Answering questions in your head*

This strategy helps you to maximize the amount of thinking you do in the foreign language. Your teacher needs to ask questions of as many people in the class as possible. So, be patient but try to answer questions *in your head* aimed at *other* people. Your teacher will ask you to record the number of times you do this in six questions and answer sessions over the course of one term. Put ticks in when you answer yourself and when you answer in your head.

première séance	deuxième séance
répondu moi-même	répondu moi-même
répondu dans ma tête	répondu dans ma tête
troisième séance	quatrième séance
répondu moi-même	répondu moi-même
répondu dans ma tête	répondu dans ma tête

Still on the topic of taking control for one's learning, we have an advanced learner's version of the kinds of applications of writing strategies demonstrated above. I say this is for advanced learners for two reasons. First, I personally would only expect advanced learners to be able to articulate L2 rules as explicitly as this (you of course may disagree). Second, with advanced learners especially, where I believe the teacher's focus should be essentially on 'communicating messages', the advanced learner should be empowered to focus on improving the accuracy of written language by focusing on the medium (the form) himself or herself. Scaffolding Sheet 6.19 allows you to monitor their explicit knowledge of the rule system, via this strategy of self-explanation of a rule as it is being applied, without you having to resort to teaching a point of grammar to the rest of the class. In other words, it allows you to adopt a policy of 'if it ain't broke, don't fix it' to the issue of explicit grammar teaching.

Scaffolding Sheet 6.19   *Understanding why I do things*

This is a strategy your teacher might ask you to try out only six times over the course of one year. Choose what you consider to be a difficult phrase from some work you have written as in example 1 or a series of similar phrases as in example 2 (perhaps over the course of two or three pieces of written work). Write down your thinking process as to how you arrived at that form of the element in question.

Example 1	I know the word to get up is *lever* and in the past tense it has to have an
Tous les matins je me suis levé . . .	accent at the end to make it a past participle. Also it's reflexive and it has to have the bits in front of it. I thought I knew that the right bit for *Je* was *me suis* but I looked it up in my grammar guide just in case.

Example 2	After certain phrases which appear to quantify (give an idea of the quantity of) the noun you use *de*. There are
Beaucoup d'étudiants ont décidé de s'abstenir; Trois tonnes de matériel radioactif; Bien des personnes étaient disponibles à;	exceptions, however, as in after *bien des* . . .
Les parents des élèves étaient furieux . . .	It's important not to confuse this with when nouns sort of are related to other nouns – for example, the parents sort of relate to the students – here it's *de* + *les* = *des*.

Social strategies

We have already mentioned practising with a friend earlier in this chapter in the context of modelling what to do when students get some feedback on written work from you their teacher. Scaffolding Sheet 6.20 provides a fuller list of things that students can do with their friends in order to develop this idea that language learning can take place outside the classroom and can involve social activities.

Scaffolding sheet 6.20   *Language practice with a friend*

Language practice with a friend	Date	Success?	Problems?	Collaborative Action Plan?
write a letter to your friend with 10 deliberate mistakes. Ask him/her to underline the mistakes. Now go to Strategy Sheet 6.11 and work out 'where did I go wrong?'				
record a dialogue together				
practise a scene together				
try to work out a foreign language text together				
listen to a foreign language cassette together				
watch a foreign language video together				

Taking notes

Finally, on the theme of taking control of one's learning, we are going to look at a strategy which, as adult learners, we probably all use but which we, as teachers, may not allow our learners to use. I have to confess that I am guilty of not allowing this strategy to be deployed when, in the past as a teacher, I have forbidden learners to take notes during a speaking activity unless it was at a specific point in that lesson that I chose. This may have been due to a view of language learning as being totally natural. I therefore wanted the learners to learn their foreign language in the same way that babies and toddlers learn their first language, by not using any form of the written medium. I am now convinced otherwise. Learning a foreign language at the age of 11 has few natural processes of the kinds that babies and toddlers experience. We should, therefore, allow learners to take notes whenever they want. But what should they take notes about? When I have taught intensive language days to student teachers I have asked them why they felt they needed to write something down. The answer has often been: it helps me to remember or it's when I've spotted something interesting or different about the language. We have dealt at length with the first strategy, memorization. The second strategy is closely linked to the theory of 'noticing'.[4] This theory says that people's interlanguage changes when they notice a difference between their current knowledge (or model of the language) and the input they are receiving. My last strategy in the section on taking control of your learning is about taking notes on noticing something new. You will need to raise the awareness of the learners through some kind of teaching sequence. For example, I use an *implicit* grammar teaching sequence in Italian where the rule for adjectival agreement 'slowly dawns' on the learners. In Italian, adjectives agree either in fours or in twos, for example, the word for red *rosso* agrees both in terms of plural and in terms of gender:

una porta rossa; un libro rosso; due uccelli rossi; due maglie rosse

This works very well until you present learners with an adjective like *verde* (green). This only changes in the plural form. I can guarantee that seven out of ten of these adult learners will reach for a pen and make a quick note because they have *noticed* something. The others either haven't noticed or have stored the noticed element in their heads (using a memorization strategy no doubt!). So, let's see if we can encourage our learners to make a note of new information (I don't mean new vocabulary here but some sort of pattern in the language) and perhaps then move on to storing it automatically via the working memory. Examples in Scaffolding Sheet 6.21 are given in French (L2) and English (L2).

Scaffolding Sheet 6.21   *Noticing something new (examples given in French L2 and English L2)*

In the course of a lesson you may notice something new about the language. A pattern or something which doesn't fit the pattern you've been building up. Make a note of what you have spotted and what you then did with it in order to see how it fitted into your new pattern.

I noticed that with a friend	I asked the teacher later	I looked in the grammar section of the student's book	I asked a friend	I think the new pattern is like this
In French with 'they' the verb changes at the end to 'ent' whereas with he or she it was just 'e'		✓		All verbs with 'they' finish with 'ent'
In English 'I call' became 'I called' in the past tense 'he rolls' became 'he rolled'				All verbs with two 'l's in the present tense take an extra 'ed' on the end in the past tense

Well, let's be patient, shall we, and just give both these learners a little time to get their patterns completely right.

Final remarks

We have been exploring practical ideas to raise the awareness of students about the possible ways that they can help themselves learn and the strategies that they might use. We have also considered a dossier of materials which we can use in order to train learners to use strategies. These materials are designed to 'scaffold' the strategy in question. In many cases the materials merely remind the learners to apply the strategy repeatedly with any given language task. It is hoped in this way that the use of the strategy will become more automatic. The materials have been presented with little reference to practical implementation although some suggestions have been given. This is because of the number of different contexts that readers of this book will be teaching in but also because some of this discussion will take place in the next chapter. Clearly, you would not be able to use all these Scaffolding

Sheets at the same time. You will be best placed to 'stage' the learner training according to the age of the learners and the intensity of the language learning programme. Nevertheless, a proposed timetable for introducing these strategies is outlined in Chapter 8.

There are three things we need to remember. First, learners must evaluate the strategy in order to see if it works for them. We should not try to force learners to use a strategy which they can plainly see does not enhance their learning. Second, we need to monitor their scaffolded strategy use. Especially with younger learners, just because we provide them with a sheet to tick which will remind them about a possible strategy does not mean that they will either use the strategy, record their strategy application or both. Third, they can't use scaffolding materials for the rest of their language learning careers. Sooner or later the scaffolding has to be removed. All these three issues will be discussed in the next chapter.

There is one final point to be made. Much of the research on strategy training gives an impression that all strategies can be applied universally to all languages. The reason for this impression is that the English language dominates at an international level and that most writers are writing with English as foreign or second language in mind. We have seen that teachers of some languages need to explore further sets of strategies (or sub-sets of strategies) because of the relationship between their students' particular L1s and L2s. Both positive and negative transfer from the first language will trigger a need for specific strategy training. This need is particularly prevalent in the development of writing skills.

BEFORE WE MOVE ON

Learning to learn requires a huge amount of effort. How will your students react to these cycles of strategy training?

To what extent do you think you were already *training* your students to use strategies before reading this book and particularly this chapter?

Try to identify the underlying principles behind the strategy training as proposed in this chapter. Do you feel you could now implement some of this training? If not, what sort of knowledge and understanding of the issues and procedures do you think you still need?

What are the practical implications of using scaffolding materials such as the ones proposed in this chapter? Think particularly about:

(a) organizing yourself;
(b) organizing the students;
(c) ensuring there is no over-kill of strategy training;
(d) guarding against there being too many bits of paper at any one time.

Select a handful of these scaffolding materials and decide which could be offered to your students entirely in their L2 and which would have to have at least some L1 in them.

Notes

1. In strategy training manuals this is often omitted. Learners need to be reminded of the words that they already know. Words they already know are in long-term memory and these need to be retrieved via effort!
2. For an introduction to language awareness, see James and Garrett (1991).
3. For a more extensive explanation and analysis of classroom language, see Macaro (1997).
4. For a discussion of the theory of noticing, see Truscott (1998).

CHAPTER 7

Following Up Learner Training

I have now proposed a system of learner training based on a series of nine steps. We considered, first of all, how to raise the awareness of the student and how to explore as many strategies as possible (steps 1 and 2). Then we explored how the teacher can model a particular strategy or how fellow students can describe the strategies that they use (step 3). Modelling is important. It shows the learner that a particular technique is actually possible and that its application can vary according to the different topics or situations they are learning about. It also shows that the strategy application can vary according to a particular skill or language process. Finally, modelling shows how the strategy can be applied in combination with other strategies (step 4). We then went on to examine a number of scaffolding materials which, through a process of reminding students to experiment with the application of a particular strategy, we would hope to get them into the habit of using that strategy as a matter of course (step 5). These are the first five steps in our learning to learn cycle. Our approach to learning how to learn must not, however, end there. To do so would be to suggest a behaviourist methodology (see Introduction) to strategy training where learners repeatedly perform an action until they do so automatically and without considering its effectiveness. Learning to learn must include *choice of action*. Learners must be free, therefore, to monitor and evaluate their strategy use and discard it if necessary. However, to do so, their choice must be an informed choice. They must be able to accept or discard a strategy on the basis of having applied it in different combinations of strategies, with different texts and in a variety of task types.

In Figure 6.1, I proposed that the four steps needed to follow the scaffolded part of the training were: initial evaluation; removal of the scaffolding; overview evaluation; monitoring for maintenance and rewarding effort. In practice, the first three of these four steps may well merge or be conflated into a single activity. Moreover, some of these steps will be taken by the learner independently of the teacher and some in collaboration with the teacher. Nevertheless let's look at each step one by one.

PAUSE FOR THOUGHT

First, though, let's take a combination of cognitive strategies that your learners may be adopting as a result of the scaffolding:

(a) repeating some language over and over (in their heads or under their breath);
(b) analysing across the L1 and the L2 (making comparisons and contrasts between the languages);
(c) noticing something new.

Do you think there would be a process of evaluation going on as they deployed those strategies? If so, on what would that evaluation be based? If you had been deploying the above combination of strategies for learning a foreign language, what would be your criteria for evaluating their effectiveness?

As you do this, think back to the models of foreign language acquisition/learning outlined in Chapter 1. Particularly the theory, based on cognition, that language learning goes through a process from controlled to automatic (or from declarative to procedural).

In which direction would the language processing be going in the above three strategies? Would any be going in both directions? For example, in 'repeating' a language element, could they be *storing* language as well as *retrieving* language?

Step 6   Initial evaluation of strategy training

We could argue that repeating some language over and over is a way of moving the actual text of the language in the direction from controlled to automatic, that is, it would eventually be stored as meaning propositions in the long-term memory to be retrieved (quickly!), as language, when the need arose. For example a learner might use the repetition strategy successfully in order to store the

French phrase *est-ce qu'il y a*. Now, how might a learner have arrived at the conclusion of the effectiveness of that repetition strategy? First, they might say: 'I can retrieve chunks of language like *est-ce qu'il y a* more effectively if I store them through constant repetition.' But more effectively than what? More effectively than not doing anything at all with the language? Well, yes, of course, that is possible. But maybe they were not starting from a position of 'no strategy' use. In fact, it is unlikely that they were doing nothing at all with the language. So (alternatively), they may be saying:

> I now know that I can retrieve chunks of language like *est-ce qu'il y a* more effectively if I store them through repetition than if I store them through the visual images that the teacher holds up in front of me.

In other words, the learner may be dismissing a strategy implied by the teacher's teaching strategies (and used over a period of time) by evaluating the effectiveness of the (possibly) new strategy. Another alternative is that they may be saying:

> I now know that I can retrieve chunks of language like *est-ce qu'il y a* more effectively if I store them through repetition than through the other strategies suggested to me by the teacher and fellow learners.

They might qualify that by saying:

> I tried making a link between *est-ce qu'il y a* and *is it that* and I even noticed something new in the way the *est* comes at the front of the phrase, but that didn't help me retrieve the phrase quickly when the need arose. No, I think that repetition really works best for me in this instance.

Finally, they might be saying:

> I now know that I can retrieve chunks of language like *est-ce qu'il y a* more effectively if I store them through repetition but *only* if I do that in combination with other strategies like contrasting it with English and noticing something new. With some chunks of language, for example, when there's lots of little words, it's even better if I make a written note of the language.

As we can see, evaluating the effectiveness of strategy use is a complex undertaking whether the teacher is involved in eliciting the evaluation or whether the learner alone is doing the evaluating. The important consideration must be, how does the effectiveness of the strategy relate to the cognitive processes involved in language learning? Evaluation of strategy effectiveness needs to be grounded in some sort of theory of language learning. An initial evaluation phase therefore must encourage the learner to reflect on *how* (not just whether) the underlying sub-skills and processes have been enhanced. The learner must be able to reflect not only on 'can I understand (or memorize or interact) better?' but also on 'how is it that I can understand (or memorize or interact) better?'

PAUSE FOR THOUGHT

How might we carry out this initial evaluation? Let us say that you have gone through a short programme of training and your students have used some scaffolding materials created by you or adapted by you (from this book) for improving memorization. You now want an initial reaction to the strategy use. Would you:

1. Ask them as a whole group how effective the strategies were?
2. Divide them into small groups and ask one person to collect views and report back?
3. Get them to jot down on individual bits of paper their evaluations?
4. Provide a section on each scaffolding sheet that allows them to reflect on the effectiveness of their strategy use?

What would be the advantages and disadvantages of the above four approaches? Would you do this immediately after each bit of training or at the end of a certain number of sessions? How would you elicit from them how they came to their evaluative decision?

What sort of terminology might you use in order to put across the concept of 'controlled and automatic' processes?

As an alternative to general discussion of initial evaluation, students may find it helpful to introduce their own individual action plans and use these as a basis for individual or group discussion with you. Here are three strategy action plans as examples of what I mean:

What's the problem?	I can't remember phrases for tests. I'm OK with words but phrases just won't go in
Combination of strategies I've decided to try out:	☐ repeat out loud in a 'chorus style' ☐ try: look/hide/say/write/check ☐ make word associations with the key words in the phrase

Have my test results improved?

☐ yes, I think it's because . . .

☐ partly, I think it's because . . .

☐ no

Have I discussed my problem with the teacher?

☐ yes

☐ no

What's the problem?	Too many mistakes in my writing tasks
Combination of strategies I've decided to try out:	☐ using a dictionary ☐ checking for noun clusters ☐ where did we go wrong? ☐ understand why I do things

Have my writing tasks improved?

☐ yes, I think it's because . . .

☐ partly, I think it's because . . .

☐ no

Have I discussed my problem with the teacher?

☐ yes

☐ no

What's the problem?	Having trouble keeping track of what language I've already learnt so that I can use it as a resource
Combination of strategies I've decided to try out:	☐ make more word hooks with nouns and adjectives
	☐ make more word webs with verbs
	☐ keep a reviewing language learnt diary
	☐ keep an oral revision cassette

Has my use of resources improved?

☐ yes, I think it's because . . .

☐ partly, I think it's because . . .

☐ no

Have I discussed my problem with the teacher?

☐ yes

☐ no

Teacher-led initial evaluations can be carried out through discussion or simply by attaching an evaluation column to the scaffolding sheets I proposed in the last chapter. For example, Table 7.1 could be attached to the look, hide, say, write, check Scaffolding Sheet 6.7 to provide the student with the opportunity to evaluate whether it works well for them, fairly well or not at all well.

Table 7.1 *Evaluation of the strategy*

Évaluation de la stratégie	Further comments on this strategy
Cela marche bien ☐	
Cela marche assez bien ☐	
Cela ne marche pas ☐	

Step 7 Removing the scaffolding

What do we mean by this? Clearly, if the scaffolding materials were there in order to shore up the strategy use over a period of time, then removing the scaffolding suggests slowly removing the supports and hoping that the strategy edifice doesn't topple over and into disuse. However, what we mean exactly by removing the scaffolding needs to be answered both at a psycholinguistic level and at a pedagogical (or even class management) level.

In the same way that knowledge of language becomes automatized (or proceduralized), so can knowledge about strategy use. In other words, the application of a strategy to a particular language task and its immediate evaluation for effectiveness probably go through the same process of moving from a controlled state to an automatized state. We may not be aware of this process. For example, I can remember, many years ago, when I first started sounding out English words on the basis of Italian phonemes in order to remember their spelling, but I cannot remember when I stopped thinking consciously about this and just did it automatically. The problem is that sometimes I do catch myself doing this 'sounding out' and start to think about it consciously. Is it possible that I am re-evaluating it as a strategy? I think it is. So we must be aware that processes are not always linear but they repeat themselves, they are *recursive*. This has implications for when we remove the scaffolding. When should we stop reminding the learners to try out a strategy? The optimal answer would be when each of them has proceduralized the strategy sufficiently for it to have become routine but not so much that the learner is no longer reflecting on its efficacy in different contexts and tasks. As all learners are different and progress at dissimilar rates, this, in practice, is extremely difficult.

In the class management domain, furthermore, there is the issue of learners, at different levels of motivation, needing reminders which vary in length. There is also the question of how not to over-burden the language tasks by too lengthy and too cumbersome a set of scaffolding materials.

In the Oxford Writing Strategies project the scaffolding was removed by simply, at a given point, summarizing with the students all the strategies they had tried out, using a visual (Figure 7.1). This visual was then provided for the learners as a reminder of the strategies available to them when they were planning, composing and checking subsequent written tasks. That is, they were encouraged to keep it on the desk in front of them as they went about their task. However, there was no way for the teacher and researcher to monitor whether they were actually using any of the strategies other than by the results of their efforts –

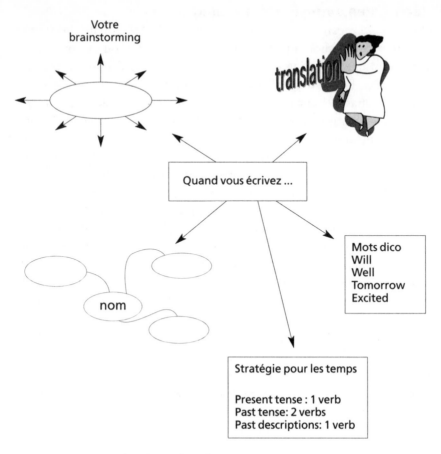

Figure 7.1   *Reminding the student of strategies*

their written work. The removal of the scaffolding in the writing project was probably too abrupt, a consequence of the usual teaching problem – lack of time!

Alternative ways of removing the scaffolding are:

1. To provide the materials periodically, say, half the time compared to the number of times they were offered during the strategy training period.
2. Simply to remind learners of the combinations of strategies they can use when embarking on a task.
3. To give them some scaffolding materials from time to time but not check that they have filled in their tallies.
4. Periodically ask the students before an activity to list which strategies they are going to use to tackle it.

Teachers can, from time to time, re-model strategy use in feedback sessions during this stage of removing the support. For example, when learners have completed and handed in a reading comprehension task the teacher can identify for them all the L2 words that they should have been able to retrieve by ticking them all on an overhead transparency or highlighting them on a computer projection. Similar strategy identification can be done visually with the 'cognates' strategy and with the 'context and common-sense' strategies. All these strategies would be leading to the 'inferencing strategy'. That is, saying: 'From all this information, this phrase must mean this . . .'. This retrospective strategy reminder can be particularly useful in that it enables learners to reflect on why they may not have deployed the strategy or, indeed, why the strategy was not effective. This can lead to a greater awareness of other combinations of strategies. For example, why did some learners find it difficult to retrieve a word they already knew? Was it because they could not isolate it in its new context? Was it because they felt they had not sufficiently processed it in the first place? Was it because they had failed originally to find out its full meaning (by asking for clarification, for example)?

Step 8   Overview evaluation

The next step in the cycle is to ask the learners for an overall impression of the strategy training programme. This can be done in a number of ways as follows:

- through teacher-led discussions;
- through group discussions with feedback;
- through questionnaires;
- through summaries at the end of a period of diary keeping;
- through interviews with the learners either individually or in groups.

PAUSE FOR THOUGHT

What are the advantages and drawbacks of each approach to overview evaluation as listed above?

In 1996 I carried out, in collaboration with teachers in four schools in the south of England, a pilot study on learner strategies used by year 9 and year 10 pupils. There were, in microcosm, the three usual phases to a learner strategies study: an awareness-raising stage; a strategy training stage and an evaluation stage. The first phase involved administering a questionnaire to 194 pupils at the end of the summer term. The questionnaire asked them to estimate the frequency with which they used a number of strategies in the same way as the Lingua study. After completing the questionnaire, pupils were asked to discuss the strategies they claimed to use and share their ideas with others. The second phase – a strategy training phase – consisted of encouraging pupils to use more strategies and more often than they previously had done. This was attempted by devising a strategy training booklet and using it throughout the following Autumn term. The third stage evaluated whether pupils had felt this awareness raising and training had been beneficial to their learning. This was done by a questionnaire in the following Spring term. Results of this pilot study are documented in detail in Macaro (1998). The important thing to note here is that girls claimed to use strategies much more than boys in the phase 1 questionnaire. In fact, only in one strategy, the use of computers to redraft written work, did boys score higher than the girls. However, after the strategy training, boys reported having found the whole process more useful than the girls. This would confirm my earlier suggestion that some high strategy users do not find strategy training as useful as low strategy users. They are simply being told to do something they already do. Perhaps, therefore, strategy training, like language learning, needs to be differentiated.

The overview of strategy training was framed by questions such as those in Tables 7.2 and 7.3 where the latter asked learners to respond to specific training materials.

The results of these evaluation materials have already been documented in Macaro (1998). The general response to strategy training was positive although not overwhelmingly so. For example, we can see from Table 7.4 that only 9.3 per cent of students felt that the strategy training made a big difference to their language learning. However, 61.7 per cent did say that it made *some* difference. What was even more encouraging is that of those students who reported a positive reaction to the strategy training, a higher percentage was from male respondents than from female respondents. In fact only 1.6 per cent of the males in the sample said that the strategy training, made no difference to their language learning. Given that these were English students of foreign languages (we have noted that adolescent females in England outperform boys in language exams), this again suggests that strategy training may be more beneficial to those who start from a lower base. This is the kind of tendency that we would want to look for in strategy training results.

Table 7.2   *Overview evaluation of strategy training*

Generally, what difference did the strategy training make to your language learning?	
a big difference	☐
some difference	☐
not much difference	☐
no difference at all	☐

Table 7.3   *Evaluation of specific scaffolding materials*

Strategy: word hooks, word webs and word chains
Did you enjoy doing these activities?
☐ yes, a lot   ☐ they were OK   ☐ not much
Did the activities help to increase your vocabulary store?
☐ yes, a lot   ☐ to some extent   ☐ not much
Please comment if you wish:

Table 7.4   *Student self-report on the effectiveness of strategy training*

	Whole group (%)	Males (%)	Female (%)
made a big difference to language learning	9.3	11.5	6.5
made some difference to language learning	61.7	63.9	58.7
did not make much difference to language learning	23.7	23.0	23.9
made no difference to language learning	5.6	1.6	

Note: N = 194

Evaluating the Oxford Writing Strategies Project

We have already seen in Chapter 5 that strategy training appeared to lead to better results in terms of two learners' production of the written language (task and test results). In that chapter we analysed to what extent the strategy training appeared to have helped the experimental group make progress with their use of strategies and with their language learning. In this chapter we will look at what the students said about the strategy training as a whole, what their feelings were about it and in what way the learner training altered the learners' perception of writing in French.

PAUSE FOR THOUGHT

Study Table 7.5. What conclusions about the effectiveness of the strategy training would you draw from the statistics which summarize the learners' responses? Now look back at the results of the analysis of the first questionnaire in Chapter 5, that is, what the students in the experimental group said about the way they approached a writing task.

Then study Table 7.6. This describes the students in the experimental group's reaction to the scaffolding materials. What inferences might you draw from these two tables of figures? Compare these to the analysis I have provided below. Do they differ? If so why?

A further piece of information which may provide an insight into the students' development is that, whereas in questionnaire 1 the students in the experimental group said they enjoyed writing in French less than those in the control group, by the end of the strategy training there were no significant differences between them.

Tables 7.5 and 7.6 clearly demonstrate that the writing project seems to have had an important impact on many students in the experimental group. Of course we do not necessarily need to have a majority of students saying that it impacted on them. This is because within the sample there may have been students who were already adopting appropriate strategies which they felt were leading to successful learning as far as they were concerned. For example, let us take approaches to checking. Let us consider the following three pieces of data:

Table 7.5   *Changes to work caused by strategies*

	Yes (%)	No (%)	No comment (%)	Possible inference from pre-treatment questionnaire
Has the way you go about doing a written task changed as a result of the writing project?	47.9	38.4	13.7	
Has the way you go about checking your work changed as result of the writing project?	32.9	43.8	23.3	
Has what you check changed as a result of the writing project?	31.5	26.0	42.5	

Note: N = 73

Table 7.6   *How helpful were the following materials and strategies that we suggested?*

	Positive response (%)	Negative response (%)	Didn't use/ attempt the strategy (%)	No comment made (%)
The brainstorming scaffolding sheet	69.9	16.4	5.5	8.2
The tenses sheet	49.3	35.6	5.5	9.6
The dictionary sheet	39.7	41.1	8.2	11.0
The noun cluster checking strategy	31.5	30.0	17.8	20.5
The back-translation checking strategy	43.8	21.9	16.4	17.8

Note: N = 76

1. In the pre-treatment questionnaire the 'as I writers' (those that checked their work as they wrote) were most likely to be more careful with their written work and, possibly, to consider themselves more successful writers.
2. In the pre-treatment questionnaire 49 per cent reported *not checking* 'as they wrote'.
3. In the post-treatment questionnaire 32.9 per cent of learners said that the way that they checked their work *had changed*.

We can therefore infer that a good proportion (perhaps as many as 75 per cent) of the students who did not check as they wrote may have switched to being 'as I writers' as a result of the training. This is of course an inference, but it is a reasonable one.

Similarly, we can infer that if 69.9 per cent had found the brainstorming scaffolding sheet a successful strategy to use and 47.9 per cent had changed the way they went about writing, then it is likely that they were brainstorming language that they felt confident with first rather than launching straight into word-for-word translation. However, we should tie this in with other aspects of the data. For example, the experimental group commented (in open-ended questions) on their use of the dictionary in a number of ways. Some students said that:

1. They now used it more often to check phrasing and spelling.
2. They were more confident with finding correct meaning equivalents.
3. They took greater notice of the symbols.
4. They looked up infinitives rather than conjugated verbs.

This meant that they now knew how to use it more efficiently, perhaps by being able to find words more quickly and in the correct context. The experimental group provided more open-ended comments in general than the control group. They also provided more comments related to strategy use rather than teaching strategies or simply what they had been taught. The analysis and evaluation of the enormous amounts of data collected for this study are still going on and I hope to publish more comprehensive results elsewhere.

Step 9   Monitoring strategy use and rewarding effort

Teachers who have carried out a programme of strategy training will want to monitor strategy use over the longer term. They can do this by:

1. Listening in on students during oral interaction (pair-work or group work) to see what interaction strategies they are still using.

2. Observing the frequency of dictionary use, by individuals, in reading or writing tasks in order to monitor whether certain students are changing their dictionary use habits. For example, are any of the students going back to the strategy of looking up every word instead of inferencing (in reading) and using a combination of language already learnt and generated sentences (in writing)?
3. Discussing after the end of a topic or an assessment whether some of the principles of combining strategy use are still being adopted.
4. Detecting, in the skills development of the learners, whether combinations of strategies are still being used.
5. Monitoring the general enthusiasm of the class as a whole.

We have noted in earlier chapters that the research evidence seems to suggest that language learning is not an effortless process. Teachers often provide feedback evaluations of work which not only comment on what was achieved linguistically but also on the effort that the individual student has put into the work. It is not always clear to the student (and perhaps to the teacher) what is meant by effort. Taking the time to deploy a combination of strategies during a language task is a clear manifestation of the effort that a learner has put into that task. It would seem logical, therefore, that feedback on both oral and written work should include comment on strategy use. We will remember that this was a teaching strategy adopted in the writing strategies project (see Chapters 5 and 6). With younger children it is often a reward system that produces the greatest effort. If this is so, then why not reward strategy use as well as providing feedback on its use, not only during the training but also during the monitoring stage? Of course, strategy use is hidden beneath the surface of the task and you will need all the knowledge that I have (hopefully) managed to put across in this book in order to detect it.

PAUSE FOR THOUGHT

If you have not yet embarked on a strategy training cycle, look back over this chapter at the suggestions for following up the strategy training. Can you think of any other ways that you might be able to evaluate and monitor the strategy use of the students that you teach?

If you have already embarked on a strategy training cycle, write down what you think are the ways that you have evaluated and monitored your students' strategy use. What have you noticed about your students? Are they, for example:

(a) more aware of themselves as learners?
(b) more independent in the way they go about certain tasks?
(c) more conscious of what works and what doesn't work for them?

Try to stand back from the training cycle and write down your own feelings and beliefs about its effectiveness and its feasibility.

By way of comparison with your own conclusions, we will end this chapter with the 'voices' of some teachers on the two projects. In a way this means going back to the beginning of the book. We started our exploration of learner strategies with the problems that teachers encounter in the languages classroom. We began thinking about our beliefs about language learning and teaching. First, the writing study. At the beginning of the project all six teachers (those of both the experimental groups and control groups) were interviewed to find out what approaches they had to writing in the foreign language.

Well, I suppose in a sense writing is the last skill that I would look at with a class . . . first thing I would do is sort of present it to them in writing and let them look at it, let them read it – then I might do an exercise where a kind of gap filling exercise . . . that kind of thing, then I think we would probably go on to everybody writing the same kind of thing and then going on to everyone being able to use hopefully the grammar they knew, to be able to write what they needed to say, and hopefully at that stage dictionaries would come into play. (Anna)

I always like to start off with a model of some description but I like to see if they can see where structures are coming from . . . after having had examples in their books, I would then expect them to be able to go away and produce their own sentences with a similar structure all on the same topic. (Ben)

First thing is just to make good use of the vocab we've been learning together . . . as well of the structure we've been learning together . . . I do actually ask them to focus a lot on what they actually read and making good use of the reading they have got in front of them and apply the same sort of pattern and be re-using and . . . able to try . . . I don't want them to think in English, but just like thinking of the syntax in French. (Clare)

Well, basically, a lot of it is copying and . . . what we call 'panel writing' where you get them to basically copy and to just change the odd little bit . . . I don't feel they are good or confident enough to do actual free-writing, it has to be quite guided, quite structured (Interviewer: What importance do you give to writing?). Not that much, to be honest. I think writing can be useful as an aide-mémoire but when it comes to actual everyday life you don't actually need to write in the language you're learning . . . I try to emphasize that they should write what they know they can write which is correct and lie, tell lots of lies rather than insisting on telling the truth. (Daniel)

Well, I try as far as possible to incorporate all four skills in every single lesson and I try to give as many writing homeworks as possible. I think, usually, once I've taught a grammatical structure, the very first thing I get them to do is usually a task involving them filling in the blanks, for example, a letter or filling in blanks in sentences and then I move them to a more autonomous open-ended task where, for example, they have to write a letter themselves. So, first of all, I start with quite a lot of support and then I gradually withdraw the support [but I tell them] stick to the structures we are learning today! Don't try to branch out too much, because what you'll find is you'll create a whole line of mistakes for yourself. (Geneviève)

I think with the less able group we tend to do stock phrases rather than them working tenses out for themselves so, in other words, it's more receptive . . . but that's sort of the bottom 'B' group[1] . . . ahem . . . with the 'A' band it's definitely more independent, they . . . I expect them to find out things for themselves like the genders, the agreement of adjectives and so on – yes, everything is taught in proper terms and they know that they know what it refers to, so we can use those terms over and over again. I get them to find out the rule first, I never tell them the rule, I show them what happens and they tell me the rule and we have done things like we've done poems about rules. (Joan)

They were also asked at the beginning of the project how they would describe their general approach to *marking* written French:

I try not to correct everything because I don't want to see a page of corrections but what I try and do is to say, right, I'm going to be looking at the verbs . . . I'm going to be looking at the tenses here or it might be I'll be looking at adjective endings . . . the rest is not perfect but we're just going to focus on one thing. (Anna)

Uhm, I like to mark everything that I see. All the mistakes . . . I prefer not to leave things uncorrected . . . because I don't think I'm doing them justice. I would feel I was letting them down if I didn't mark something that was incorrect and if there's a chance of them being able to use it again incorrectly . . . I give them the correct model . . . if there's a recurring mistake . . . I don't correct it every time but I'll underline it. (Ben)

When I am marking the writing, if it's like an essay or a paragraph to write, I would take into consideration the accuracy of the grammar and the vocab, the content. (Clare)

Right, well, I mark almost all writing tasks on the basis of three criteria: content, language and accuracy. Each one of those is equally important in the writing task. It's difficult to come down on one or the other. Sometimes you get pieces of work that have fantastic content but are poorly written, conversely, sometimes you get pieces of work where the language is very good but the content is poor . . . I'll just underline the word or the letter so that they know what they've got to do [to put it right]. (Geneviève)

I tend to write comments rather than marks unless I'm doing, like, I am counting the right amount of verbs. I've done that before at GCSE[2] or counting the correct number of agreements or whatever . . . I tend to write comments on the bottom. I try to write [things like] look at this because you are falling down on your agreements or you need your verbs or the subject and verb doesn't match or whatever. (Joan)

PAUSE FOR THOUGHT

In the above quotations which describe a number of different approaches to marking written work there would appear to be four issues:

1. What the expectations of a piece of written work might be (i.e. content, quality of language, accuracy of language).
2. How much to mark.
3. What aspects of writing to mark.

4. How to provide feedback to the learner.

Looking back to our analysis of writing strategies in Chapter 5, which approach to marking and feedback would you say would most likely to be in tune with the promotion of effective strategy use on the part of the learner? You will find some thoughts on these issues in the concluding chapter.

We will now listen to the three teachers who took part in a programme of strategy training to see in what way their perceptions, attitudes and beliefs about learners have changed. These were the three teachers of the three experimental classes who agreed to take part in the programme of learner training. At the end of the learner training period the three teachers of the experimental group were asked if their approaches to writing had changed as a result of the strategy training and the study in general. Unfortunately it was only possible to conduct formal interviews with two of the experimental group teachers. The third provided some brief feedback in an informal conversation.

Lots [has changed] – the different things that they were checking in their written work. Normally I would just say check your work and it was broken down into specific things and also I have never really focused very much on accuracy and using the dictionary . . . it's tended to be a case of 'use your dictionary more carefully' rather than the guidance that we've been giving them . . . and I think including two tenses was totally appropriate because in all their GCSE items they have to use two tenses . . . Yes, I will focus a lot more on them checking their work and also I intend to spend more time on them looking at their corrections when I give back their work . . . it was something that was very important when I was learning French at school . . . the teacher did spend a lot of time on corrections . . . I've done it sporadically when I felt there was something I needed to do more vigorously at the end of piece of writing . . . I [still] tend to correct things that I don't think they're going to be able to correct themselves or a recurring mistake I'll correct once and underline it but I will give them the time in the lesson in order for them to do that . . . otherwise there's no value in it because most of them don't go home and then spend time . . . I must admit I did find it . . . it's probably something from within . . . when I marked pieces for the writing project and just focused on those [few] I found I had to pull myself back from marking everything . . . I think there's part of my brain that agrees entirely with focusing on one point which is going to hopefully make them better but I feel I'm doing them a disservice by not marking everything in the way . . . it's a conflict . . . I do agree with that more because I've seen that students have been more focused on those specific areas of their work by developing and using the strategies . . . probably more inclined to focus on specific aspects of their writing. (Ben)

Before I tended to do sort of brainstorming together and not as systematically as you've been doing it . . . uhm . . . I didn't get them brainstorming as such on their own which I think is a good thing to do . . . .the mnemonics to remember verbs, e.g. two verbs for the past . . . that was new to me as, well, yeah, my normal approach to doing a writing activity would be to do a similar sort of text, give them a similar text, and get them to do a similar one where they have to change a few things . . . parallel writing, that's the way I tended to do it with them but there are, I think I've realized that there are, a lot more approaches than I've been using . . . before I would concentrate on one [tense only], I would give them a writing task which involved talking about the future or talking about something happening in the past or doing a descriptive one or present tense, I didn't tend to mix them up much . . . [mixing them up] is a very good thing . . . because, to be honest, I don't like the textbook. I think I'm gonna have to go off the textbook quite a bit and . . . you know, get them to use their own resources and for me to provide them with other resources rather than the textbook, well, I think the methods are very useful and I will certainly use some of them. I'll probably try them all . . . I think my marking is similar [to what I was doing before] anyway. (Daniel)

I think definitely give them more writing to do than before, more difficult tasks to work out on their own . . . it tends to be lots of bits of writing and assessed for their coursework so, yes, I suppose it is at the end of a period of work [that I used to do it] but . . . it is better to go back to tasks that go back to earlier topics to get them thinking more. (Clare)

A number of themes arise from these teachers' comments that were underlying the writing study's rationale. First, there is the theme of persuading pupils to retrieve words from their long-term memory language that they already knew and recycling them in imaginative ways in a new context. In order to do this the students need a new context in which to do the recycling. If written tasks always appear at the end of a topic where new language has been learnt but don't involve a transfer of previously learnt language, the students will not develop the cognitive and metacognitive strategies necessary for language retrieval. Consequently, and as we have seen in earlier chapters, they will not have the tools to overcome the anxiety of 'not appearing to know what to say' in a new task involving a new context. The second theme is that of encouraging the students to check their work more carefully and (although the teachers do not say this explicitly) as they write. The project seems to have convinced the teachers of the need to develop strategies in their students to do this more systematically. The third theme is that of marking the written work. Here there is some divergence. Whereas Daniel feels he was already applying the technique of not providing the correct model, Ben still feels that he is letting the learners down if he does not correct everything and provide the correct model at least once. For Ben, this seems to stem from a gut feeling about what he should do, even though, at a rational level, it would make sense to refrain from doing so.

The teachers were also asked about specific materials used in the strategy training programme:

I think the tense checking sheet they still found difficult, they still . . . particularly with the perfect (passé composé) they couldn't always identify two verbs . . . especially with j'ai, they'd see that as one word . . . uhm, with the other tenses not so much of a problem as with the perfect tense . . . I thought the brainstorming was a very good idea to use but the lines round the bubble, they felt compelled to write something on each one, which probably slowed them down a lot . . . the tense sheet . . . I thought it was a good idea and gave examples of each one but I sometimes think they found it hard to relate to writing on a separate piece of paper.
Interviewer: Too many bits of paper?
I think there can be too many bits of paper sometimes, yeah, and when I got them to just write on the sheets I think they found that easier but that was a check at the end . . . I think there's a time pressure as well, it felt that we were rushing to get things finished so they probably weren't checking as well as they could have done . . . the dictionary sheet . . . I think it helped . . . it made them think more about their use of the dictionary . . . I think it was good to get them to write down the English of the word they'd looked up instead of French. I think it helped us to know where they were coming from . . . I think they used the dictionary less, I think they are prepared to rely on their instincts [more]. (Ben)

Back-translation for instance . . . after something has been written that was a new one, yeah, checking and being aware of what they are checking and how they are checking.
Interviewer: The brainstorming sheet . . . what is your impression of that?
Excellent . . . Brilliant! (Daniel)

The tenses [sheet] I thought was very useful. I think they've made a lot of progress with the perfect tense . . . even now they still seem to remember when to use it a lot better. (Clare)

Finally, they were asked to comment on what they thought the learners' reaction had been to the training in general and whether they thought it was feasible to do the strategy training without the help of a researcher attached to the class:

I've seen that students have been more focused on those specific areas of their work by developing and using the strategies . . . probably more inclined to focus on specific aspects of their writing . . . I'm hoping to use the strategies next year with my year 10 class and I'm hoping to encourage members of my team to also use some of the strategies if they think their groups will cope with it . . . I think the materials could be used . . . I really want to try and introduce some of the strategies next year . . . I used the tense check with my year 8 last week when I introduced the perfect . . . making them identify that there were two verbs in every sentence we did and it was very positive in fact . . . yeah, I think they could be used by every teacher . . . obviously they would need to have the training to use them . . . you have to teach the children how to learn a language . . . you have to train them to know what they're actually doing. It's been very enlightening, I think I've learnt a lot, it's given me ideas . . . the brainstorming idea is very good at the beginning of the lesson . . . the back-translation as well . . . a lot of them, I think, learnt a lot by doing that. (Ben)

I think they have taken it quite well . . . at least with the dictionary they know where to look for things . . . with the textbook they often don't know where to look for things, you know, if they look words up, it's got a limited vocabulary at the back, it's limited in that a lot of time what they are looking for is not there. In many ways the dictionary is a much more whole resource than the textbook . . . I was impressed by the amount of work they have done . . . [the] approach could be feasible, even with these kids . . . although some

of the other problematic ones might [still] not do any work.
Interviewer: Their reactions?
Better than I expected . . . I knew what we hoped would happen
and I was quite surprised it worked out as well as it did . . . I think
they are much more independent, you know, you can now give them
a task and a dictionary and they'll know how to deal with it, they
will not be as dependent on the teacher . . . I think it's a good
thing . . . I think it was too rushed at the end. (Daniel)

Clare said that she felt the students were taking their writing more seriously now. Interestingly, the informal discussion with Clare occurred some two months after the project had finished with the summer vacation in between. An issue that is always in the minds of researchers in strategy training is whether strategies and motivation for effort are maintained not just during the period of removing the scaffolding, but much later when, perhaps, other work pressures jostle for prominence in the minds of the students. That is why the final step in our strategy training cycle, monitoring of strategy use and rewarding effort, is so important.

PAUSE FOR THOUGHT

What are your impressions of these extracts from the teacher interview transcripts? Are they generally positive about the strategy training and its ability to improve the quality of the writing of their students? What reservations do they have?

Compare what the teachers said with what the students appeared to be saying in the questionnaire analysis (above). Do their impressions coincide?

We will give the final word to Mary, from the Lingua project, which, we will remember, mostly focused the training on memorization and reading strategies. She stood back from it all and wrote this about the class that she had been experimenting with in terms of learner training:

I feel that over the course of the year the class has become a lot more
aware of what it needs to do itself to help its own learning. I have
made them more aware that they can learn as long as they give
themselves the chance. The learning we have done together in class
has been very effective and in future I will bear in mind their need
for confidence in the pronunciation of the words. For a group like

this, monitoring of work is essential in that they will try to get away with the minimum amount of work if allowed to. It was important therefore that the monitoring was consistent throughout the year . . . I sense that the group is more confident and I know that the girls are no longer a chatty little bunch. They have become more motivated and focused and last week when I had to test the class on an oral presentation (a task I was half-dreading as I felt we had not really had sufficient time to prepare it), I was very pleased with the standard of their work and impressed by the painstaking way in which they had prepared themselves for it. I now need to focus on the issue of raising awareness lower down the school as these [strategies] should be in place in Key Stage 3 [11 year olds to 13-year-old learners]. Parents could also be made aware of how they could help and encourage. Members of this class took part in the taping of the interpretation of a text in German [think-aloud task on a text]. This exercise I have found particularly helpful for myself and I have since given my classes more reading exercises that do not have as their outcome comprehension of gist. I am finding two advantages to this. The first, a growing awareness of the grammatical structure of a sentence and, the second, a greater widening of vocabulary as all sorts of interesting words and phrases are learnt that could never be presented in pictorial form on an overhead transparency or on flashcards. (Mary)

BEFORE WE MOVE ON

Read again through Mary's overview of the year's involvement with learner strategy training. Can you make a list of all the keywords in her text which relate to themes which we have explored in this book?

Notes

1. Perceived to be of low ability ('A' group would be of higher ability).
2. National exams in England at the age of 16.

CHAPTER 8

Conclusions

In this concluding chapter I have resisted the temptation to provide a holistic reformulation of all that has gone before. I have come to this decision because of the different approach that this book has taken and the style of writing that it has endeavoured to maintain. I have tried to invite you, the reader, to discover things about your beliefs and practice and about your students and how to research their learning rather than simply be told about how teachers teach and how students learn. In order to do this I have had, on many occasions, to refrain from giving what I thought was the right answer to the questions I was asking. Right answers, in any case, rarely exist. All we can hope for is a steady movement in the right direction. However, as a consequence of this lack of author prescriptivism and, because of the limitations of this particular distance learning experience (i.e. sadly, we will not be able to interact further), I feel that the Conclusions need some clear statements from me about what is now known with some level of confidence with respect to 'learning to learn' and to make some recommendations. You will, I anticipate, have arrived at your own set of conclusions and formulated personal or collective recommendations which are directly related to whatever language teaching context you are working in. With this knowledge and increased understanding 'in the bag', I trust, therefore, that you will not find what follows too dramatic a shift towards methodological prescriptivism.

Conclusion number 1

The research evidence suggests that some learners are using more strategies and more effectively than others. This may be because the former's response to the methodology being used by the teacher is more in tune than the response of the latter. Or, they may simply do better, because of their deployment of strategies, whatever the teacher's pedagogical approach. Future research may be able to tell us whether obstacles to strategy use stem from some learners' inability to handle complex cognitive loads in working memory. Whatever the reasons for ineffective strategy use, one thing seems to be increasingly clear and that is that, across learning contexts, those learners who are pro-active in their pursuit of language learning appear to learn best. Thus, a question still to be fully answered is: do some students come with the motivation to learn and therefore deploy the 'obvious' strategies that any keen learner would deploy? That is, is the (what appear to be) complex set of combinations of strategies simply what any keen learner can bring to the languages classroom, as a result of a kind of general past experience? Or, is it the case that effective combinations of strategies are difficult to discover and/or proceduralize? In which case, the ineffective and/or de-motivated learner is simply the learner who has not been able to discover them and/or proceduralize them?

Recommendation number 1

Teachers and researchers should work closely together to discover the role of working memory and the role of motivation in learner strategy use. Teaching approaches need to be analysed to ensure that they are compatible with promoting effective strategy use. An interesting practice-related avenue to pursue is whether what we mean by *effort* when doing a language task simply means the effective deployment of a range of strategies in a task.

Conclusion number 2

Partly in answer to the above, the research evidence suggests, on balance, that strategy training is effective in promoting a greater predisposition towards language learning and a framework which enables the learner to take more responsibility for their learning in the immediate, medium and long term. Strategy training, however, is not without its problems and pitfalls. Consequently, programmes of training have to be carefully evaluated in order to justify the time taken out from the daily exposure to and interaction with the second language.

Recommendation number 2

The most effective and lasting educational changes occur when there is impetus and involvement at grass-roots level. It should be teachers themselves, by working with other teachers and preferably with dedicated researchers in this field, who drive forward the shift in focus from teacher methodology to working *with the learners* in order to bring about improved language skills. Nevertheless, policy-makers should be closely involved in supporting teachers' efforts by facilitating local and national programmes of strategy training and by creating resources such that these programmes can be carried out in a coherent manner and evaluated for their effectiveness.

Conclusion number 3

The dilemma of when and how much strategy training to carry out is likely to remain unresolved. Clearly, one would wish that all language learners came to the very first lesson already with the knowledge of how they best learn a language and that they were proficient in strategy use. But it is highly unlikely that this will ever be so. It is even difficult to make a case for this 'learning how to learn' to occur in other lessons, in other subjects or even in a special subject such as 'study skills'. Some prior awareness raising may be possible but the language teacher will continue to have to play a pivotal role. The reason is that although a core of metacognitive skills and strategies could be universal for all academic subjects, the more cognitive, direct strategies are so interlinked with what we might call the 'the brain's interface with the second language' that they have to be experienced, attempted and evaluated in the second language classroom by language learners working in conjunction with language teachers. Again, and for the same sorts of reasons, it would not appear to make sense for a language teacher to embark on a programme of strategy training *before* beginning their language teaching programme. There are strategies in all four skills which need to be developed as the contact with the second language becomes more complex and as reliance on the first language becomes less evident. We are again reminded of the often made assertion that the content of our subject is the same as the medium (the language of instruction) through which that content is being taught.

Recommendation number 3

In terms of situating a programme of strategy training within an overall language curriculum therefore, all I can recommend is what are, to me, a series of compromises. Nevertheless, Figure 8.1 is a programme of strategy training which takes into account the following:

1. Strategies have to be experienced, evaluated and taken on board *in combination*.
2. Strategies may service a number of language skills and processes simultaneously.
3. Strategies have to be linked to type of task and to the task's cognitive and metacognitive demands.
4. Too much strategy training will lead to a disconnection from the actual process of learning a language.
5. Too much strategy training over a short period of time will be logistically difficult for the teacher to administer and monitor.
6. Most strategy types should have been addressed in some limited form *before* learners reach the advanced stage.

Figure 8.1, therefore, provides an indication of when a particular aspect of strategy training might be introduced. It is to be understood that these are then re-visited throughout the duration of the course particularly if the teacher's monitoring reveals a reduction in strategy use and/or the learner identifies a problem in their learning. In addition, they should be revisited in order to combine them with other, newly developed strategies. Figure 8.1 also suggests that this programme is set against a framework of language learning (a language curriculum) which starts with the dependence on the teacher as a language resource and moves towards dependence on multiple and varied resources (textual, electronic, human, etc.) which the learner can access and learn from with increasing autonomy. Above all, Figure 8.1 contains a belief that strategy training is a gradual, recursive and longitudinal process.

Conclusion number 4

Strategy training is more likely to be effective if it is clearly articulated and explicitly modelled by the teacher. Strategy training *can* be partly embedded once the initial awareness and modelling steps have been gone through but research seems to suggest that some learners will not develop their strategy use in combination without an initial conscious and controlled exploration of the mental processes and actions involved.

Recommendation number 4

Teachers who are attempting strategy training for the first time should follow as closely as possible the cycle outlined in Chapter 6 and summarized here as: initial awareness raising; exploration of possible strategies available; modelling by teacher and/or other students; combining of strategies for a specific purpose or specific task; application of strategies with scaffolded support; initial evaluation by students; gradual removal

Beginner ——→ Intermediate ——→ Advanced

Dependence on the teacher ——→ Dependence on resources of all kinds

Beginner →	→	→	→	→	→ Advanced
Memorization of vocabulary and chunks via visuals; graphics; song; mental associations	Reviewing speaking and listening	Brainstorming the writing you know	Reviewing language learnt	Noticing something new (taking notes)	Following things up that might slip past / Understanding why I do things in writing
Noun cluster checking		Making the right decision with tenses	Negotiating procedure		
Developing own vocabulary store via hooks, webs and chains	Talk to a teacher outside the classroom	Taking the lead in starting to talk		Talking to native speakers at every opportunity	
Initial reading strategies					
Multilingual packaging ('the language is out there!')	Using a dictionary to understand	Listening strategies	Predicting what words might look like		Talking outside the school
Answering questions in your head	Using a dictionary to create language	Providing the teacher with confirmation		Negotiating procedures with the teacher	
Practising with friend	Interactive strategies (role play)	Advanced reading strategies	Memorization via 'creating sentences'	Where did we go wrong?	Where did I go wrong?

Figure 8.1   *A programme of strategy training*

of scaffolding; further evaluation by students; monitoring of strategy use by teacher and the rewarding of effort. I am not convinced that an *ad hoc* approach to strategy training can ever be effective.

Conclusion number 5

Strategy training needs to be presented to the students as a serious undertaking. It has to match the importance of the language learning process itself. Yet it has to cater for individuals' learning styles and personalities.

Recommendation number 5

In order for this to happen, teachers have to carry out a difficult balancing act. On the one hand, they have to go beyond the 'tentative hands off' approach that some may advocate in order to redress some of the deficiencies in an individual's learning patterns. On the other, they have to ensure that individual strategies which may be inappropriate for certain individuals are not being imposed on them. What we want to improve is their ability to simulate, evaluate and then use a combination of strategies. We should beware of merely leading them to the situation where they demonstrate for the teacher's benefit that they are using one particular strategy consistently but, as it turns out, ineffectively.

Conclusion number 6

Taking a 'bird's eye view', Communicative Language Teaching has done a great deal to further the direct application of language learning to learners' needs and aspirations, to enable many learners to become confident speakers of the language and to expose the myth that language learning is only suitable for an intellectual elite. However, some extreme interpretations of CLT have sought to exclude the learner from the learning process. At a national level these interpretations have led some policy-makers, apparently not informed by empirical research, to set up a framework of learning (curriculum, assessment, training, inspection) which places obstacles in the way of the teacher to adapt their teaching to the strategy-related needs of their learners.

Recommendation number 6

Further work needs to be done to ascertain how individual interpretations of CLT as well as local and national interpretations have an effect on strategy use. For teachers in England it is particularly important as success in language learning continues to lag behind most of our European counterparts.[1]

Conclusion number 7

Research suggests that we have ignored the value of reading and writing in the process of learning and that the strategies underlying these two skills are interlinked. In the case of reading we are ignoring its vital contribution to input. In the case of writing we have looked on the skill as an end product, a final stage in the communicative pedagogical goal. The two main projects described in this book attempt to rectify that situation somewhat. The data on reading show just how lacking in any form of independence some of the students are when it come to accessing a written L2 text. The writing project is only one of many that shows that the cognitive processes involved in planning, composing and checking the written language are likely to be extremely fruitful in reformulating mental models of the language and in facilitating storage and future retrieval. Moreover, the use of the dictionary as a tool for expanding vocabulary, generating sentences, truly understanding meaning and checking for accuracy is likely to be facilitated by more emphasis on the reading and writing processes at all stages of learning. Finally, it looks as if we need to reappraise the value of providing overt corrective feedback to written mistakes.

Recommendation number 7

Much more research needs to be done on reading and writing strategies at the beginner and intermediate level. National curricula and exam syllabuses should reflect the value in the process of accessing text and in producing writing and how these contribute to speaking and listening. In addition, we should not allow structural requirements to impede the use of valuable learning resources such as dictionaries. The one major advancement in reading (and reading for pleasure in particular) would come about if we taught learners *how* to read instead of trying to test what we feel they should have understood. The one major advancement in writing proficiency would be achieved if teachers stopped correcting everything that was wrong, focused on one aspect of interlanguage at a time and provided the correct model only on very rare occasions. Both these measures would have the added benefit of cutting down on teacher marking time and would proportionally increase the likelihood of teachers allowing students to experiment with generated language rather than limiting them to pre-formulated phrases.

Conclusion number 8

Although research suggests that it is the range and combinations of all strategies that ineffective learners lack, it is the metacognitive, social and affective strategies which seem to be the strategy types most lacking in the arsenal of the less successful learners.

Recommendation number 8

The strategies which plan and evaluate learning and the strategies assumed by the learner who goes out and makes contact with the language outside the classroom are the ones that teachers should increasingly turn their attention to. The kinds of action plans suggested in this book, the form of diary keeping which encourages the learner to consolidate, transfer and review their learning over an extended period of time, should be built into every language learning syllabus alongside the content of what is to be taught.

Conclusion number 9

I have argued elsewhere (Macaro 1997, 2001) for a reappraisal of the role of the first language in second language learning. This reappraisal could find no better grounds for exploration than in the field of learner strategy research. Here it is not only the cognitive processes that need continued examination for the value of L1–L2 connections but also whether the declarative knowledge involved in strategy training is best filtered through the medium of the L1. My conclusion is that in both processes there needs to be a balance struck by the teacher between L1–L2 connections and L2-only re-modelling of the language. I have a fairly strong gut feeling that, in formal classrooms at least, L2-only re-modelling can occur only when the language transfer carried out by the learner has been reduced to a minimum by the learner, i.e. in advanced classrooms. Since this is a theme which I have traced throughout the book, let me allow myself a further observation on the use of cognates as a learning strategy. The practice of focusing on cognates is not limited to when students are responding to text which has been composed either in written or spoken form. It is not a strategy limited to authentic text accessibility. Teachers use cognates, especially at beginner and intermediate level, as one of the key elements of their input modification. If the teacher is doing so in order to expose learners to some new language for the purpose of intake, this seems justifiable. What I mean by this is that, because of the finite capacity of the working memory, the teacher might reduce the load by providing cognates which are more easily processed for meaning, thereby leaving space for the working memory to process the new bits of language that the teacher wants the learners to learn. This seems highly sensible and good practice. But if the teacher, perhaps as a result of methodological dogma or curriculum requirements, uses cognates merely to avoid using the L1 regardless of any new language that might be processed and acquired, then it would seem that the range of lexical items that the learners could possibly acquire will be limited. It could be that use of cognates leads to such a reduced level in the quality of teacher oral input that in fact it would be more beneficial to use L1–L2 lexical contrasting. Learners might in fact learn more if the word or phrase were provided in both languages because lexical contrasting, skilfully handled, might well lead, paradoxically, to a richer target language input.

Recommendation number 9

Teachers should not feel guilty about using the L1 for the purposes of strategy training. Wherever comprehension is the issue, the decision should be in favour of comprehending the strategy training and not teaching a random set of vocabulary and structures brought about by the language of that training. As there is nothing in the literature to suggest that codeswitching is harmful to language acquisition, there is absolutely no reason why training materials could not contain a mixture of L1 and L2. Moreover, teachers should beware of the possible deleterious role played by cognates. The use of cognates as a strategy should be subordinated to (or at least modelled in conjunction with) strategies that increase lexical variety.

Conclusion number 10

Learner strategy training is merely a number of small steps which lead the learner towards autonomy. But the autonomy of learners mirrors the autonomy of teachers. As teachers are increasingly given the tools with which to understand their classrooms and research their learners, so they become more autonomous teachers, able to make research-informed decisions at many levels of classroom practice. Simultaneously and consequently, teachers who are autonomous in this sense are much more likely to seek to develop autonomy in their learners. This *loop input approach* (Woodward 1991) to language teacher development is a powerful one.

Recommendation number 10

Language teachers need to be given the time and the training to analyse their own practice in relation to what they can discover about their students. Professional development must be based on what research tells us about second language acquisition.

A good place to start to implement these ten recommendations, it seemed to me, was with a book which tried to help teachers find out what learners do to help themselves learn. But it would be wrong to claim that I had these recommendations in mind when I started to write. In writing we learn about the world because it helps us to organize and synthesize our thoughts. In writing the book, with the reader in mind,

I too have gone though a process of professional development. All teachers are different and have construed teaching and learning through the lenses of countless experiences. They operate in a multitude of language learning contexts. My own development in the writing, therefore, included trying to expand my pedagogical range beyond my immediate and limited geographical experience towards every type of reader. This I may have failed to do and what I have concluded may seem strange or parochial to some readers. The above recommendations may be incorporating all the bias of having experienced learning a language, teaching languages and training language teachers through the lens of my own beliefs. I feel justified in not writing a book which merely tried to describe an aspect of educational reality or provided simple answers to complex problems. Again, it may not have achieved the lofty aims that I had set it. I hope that it did generate in you, however, the enthusiasm to start digging for answers in your own backyard and provided you with some suitable and hard-wearing tools for the task.

Note

1. A number of researchers (notably LoCastro 1994; Oxford and Burry-Stock 1995) call for further research into the effects of teaching and learning environment on strategy-related issues.

Appendix

Translations of some non-English texts in the book. Content or accuracy mistakes are not reflected in the translations.

Figure 3.1 (p. 89)

Dear Friends,

We are sending you this brochure because last year we spent a marvellous holiday in this region. We rented a holiday home which was really well equipped: a very pleasant small apartment. The children loved it because they could go swimming every day; it was free, which was good and moreover, there was a lifeguard on duty, so I had peace of mind. They could also have done other sporting activities, but it was a bit difficult because they weren't in the same village, so it would have meant driving them there and fetching them . . . anyway, on the whole, it was good; what we liked the most were the evenings: we had the choice of activities near our apartment or we could go to neighbouring villages and see entertainment of all kinds, but really, during the holidays, we avoid going anywhere by car. We do enough driving for our work!

Katie's pre-treatment task (p. 143)

Hello! I'm really happy that you can come to visit in April.

My house is in a town called Thame, it's near Oxford, and an hour from London. My house is fairly big. On the ground floor there's a kitchen, a living room and a dining room. Downstairs is my parents' bedroom, my bedroom and the guest bedroom. My room is fairly big but I've got a lot of furniture. I'm an only child. The guest room is fairly small and there's a desk as well with a computer. My garden is very big and there is a pond. In the holidays I visit my aunt in Lincolnshire. I went cycling and swimming. It was tiring but lots of fun. And you? Did you have a fun holiday?

Lots of love
 Katie

Figure 5.2 (p. 144)

Katie's pre-treatment writing for think aloud

I saw him leave the shop at ten o'clock. He is very big and was wearing black trousers and a yellow jumper. His hair was brown and his eyes were brown too. He was between 28 and 30 years old. I'm staying in a town with a friend. I arrived in France in March. I'm leaving France in a year's time. I'm leaving for England in March 2000.

Laura's pre-treatment task (p. 149)

Hi

I've received your letter and I'm very excited that you are going to visit England. I can't wait to see you.

I live in the countryside in a big house. There are five rooms and you have to stay in the friends' bedroom. The room is quite big and very fashionable (???). There is a bed, a desk, a wardrobe and a chest of drawers and a chair and two mirrors. It's comfortable. The garden is quite small but there is a big park near me. There is also a shop and a swimming pool near me. I have a dog called Pidgeon and she's really nice. Do you have a pet?

Last week I went to the cinema and to the restaurant. It was very nice. Do you want to go to the cinema with me in England?

Figure 5.4 (p. 151)

Laura's pre-treatment writing for think aloud

I'm in France. The thief is tall and thin. He has short, straight brown hair. He is wearing grey trousers and a white shirt and a black jacket. He weighs approximately 70ks.

My name is Laura and I live in England. I visited France and I arrived on Friday 23 December. I left England on Tuesday 20 December. I'm staying in a hotel called . . . in Paris. I'm leaving France at half past three on Saturday 25 December.

Katie's post-treatment task (p.161)

I'm working for a company of architects. The office is very modern and it's divided in small study rooms (???) My supervisor, Mrs O'Neill, is very understanding when I get confused! Mark is very different, he is stupid and clumsy!

Yesterday in the office I finished lots of files and drawings of buildings (???). When I finish a drawing I give it to Mrs O'Neill. She was furious with me because the drawing was bad. Mark was laughing at my drawing!

Figure 5.5 (p. 161)

Katie's post-treatment writing for think aloud

I'm staying with a family in France. We are staying on a campsite. There are four people in the family. The mother, the father and two children. The mother is very kind but the father is very strict. The two children are called John and Philippe. It's (???) fairly peaceful.

We went to the mountains for a picnic. In the mountains there was a stream. After the picnic we went swimming. John went for a walk in the mountains. During his walk he saw a bear.

References

Anderson, N.J. and Vandergrift, L. (1996) Increasing metacognitive awareness in the L2 classroom by using think-aloud protocols and other verbal report formats. In R.L. Oxford (ed.) *Language Learning Strategies Around the World: Cross-Cultural Perspectives*, Manoa: University of Hawaii, Second Language Teaching and Curriculum Centre, 3–18.

Bacon, S.M. (1992) The relationship between gender, comprehension, processing strategies, and cognitive and affective responses in foreign language learning, *The Modern Language Journal*, 76, 2, 160–75.

Baily, C.A. (1996) Unobtrusive computerized observation of compensation strategies for writing to determine the effectiveness of strategy instruction, in R.L. Oxford (ed.) *Language Learning Strategies Around the World: Cross-Cultural Perspectives*, Manoa: University of Hawaii, Second Language Teaching and Curriculum Centre, 141–50.

Beaton, A., Gruneberg, M. and Ellis, N. (1995) Retention of foreign language vocabulary learner using the keyword method: a ten-year follow up, *Second Language Research*, 11, 2, 112–20.

Bedell, D.A. and Oxford, R.L. (1996) Cross-cultural comparisons of language learning strategies in the People's Republic of China and other countries, in R.L. Oxford (ed.) *Language Learning Strategies Around the World: Cross-Cultural Perspectives*, Manoa: University of Hawaii, Second Language Teaching and Curriculum Centre, 47–60.

Bernhardt, E. B. (1991) A psycholinguistic perspective on second language literacy, *AILA Review*, 8, 31–44.

Block, E. (1992) See how they read: comprehension monitoring of L1 and L2 readers, *TESOL Quarterly*, 26, 2, 319–43.

Brown, T. and Perry, F. (1991) A comparison of three learning strategies for ESL vocabulary acquisition, *TESOL Quarterly*, 25, 655–70.

Bügel, K. and Buunk, B.P. (1996) Sex differences in foreign language text comprehension: the role of interests and prior knowledge, *Modern Language Journal*, 80, 1, 15–28.

Campbell, I. (1997) A question of language awareness: using English to support second language learning, *Babel (AFMLTA) (Victoria), Australia*, 32, 2, 10–13.

Carrell, P.L. (1989) Metacognitive awareness and second language reading, *Modern Language Journal*, 73, 2, 121–34.

Carter, R. and McCarthy, M. (1988) Word lists and learning words: some foundations and developments in the teaching of vocabulary, in R. Carter and M. McCarthy (eds) *Vocabulary and Language Teaching*, London: Longman.

Cavalcanti, M. (1987) Investigating foreign language reading performance through pause protocols, in G. Faerch and G. Kasper (eds) *Introspection in Second Language Research*, Clevedon: Multilingual Matters, 23–50.

Chamot, A.U. (1987) The learning strategies of ESL students, in A. Wenden and J. Rubin (eds) *Learner Strategies in Language Learning*, Hemel Hempstead: Prentice-Hall, 71–85.

Chamot, J.M., Barnhardt, S., El Dinary, P. and Robbins, J. (1996) Methods for teaching learning strategies in the foreign language classroom, in R.L. Oxford (ed.) *Language Learning Strategies Around the World: Cross-Cultural Perspectives*, Manoa: University of Hawaii, Second Language Teaching and Curriculum Centre, 175–88.

Chamot, J.M. and Küpper, L. (1989) Learning strategies in foreign language instruction, *Foreign Language Annals*, 22, 1, 13–24.

Clarke, A. and Trafford, J. (1996) Return to gender: boys' and girls' attitudes and achievements, *Language Learning Journal*, 14, 40–9.

Cohen, A. (1998) *Strategies in Learning and Using a Second Language*, London: Longman.

Cohen, A.D. and Aphek, E. (1981) Easifying second language learning, *Studies in Second Language Acquisition*, 3, 2, 221–35.

Cohen, L. and Manion, L. (1994) *Research Methods in Education*, London: Routledge.

Dadour, S. and Robbins, J. (1996) University-level studies using strategy instruction to improve speaking ability in Egypt and Japan, in R.L. Oxford (ed.) *Language Learning Strategies Around the World: Cross-Cultural Perspectives*, Manoa: University of Hawaii, Second Language Teaching and Curriculum Centre.

Dickinson, L. (1987) *Self-Instruction in Language Learning*, Cambridge: Cambridge University Press.

Ehrman, M. (1990) The role of personality type in adult language learning: an on-going investigation, in T. Parry and C. Stansfield (eds) *Language Aptitude Reconsidered*, Englewood Cliffs, NJ: Prentice-Hall.

Ehrman, M. and Oxford, R.L. (1989) Effects of sex differences, career choice, and psychological type on adult language learning strategies, *Modern Language Journal*, 72, 253–65.

Ellis, N. (1995) Vocabulary acquisition: psychological perspective, Vocabulary Acquisition Research group, University of Wales, Swansea, Virtual Library: http//www.swan.ac.uk/cals/vlibrary/ne95a.html.

Ellis, R. (1994) *The Study of Second Language Acquisition*, Oxford: Oxford University Press.

Ericsson, K.A. and Simon, H.A. (1987) Verbal reports on thinking, in G. Faerch and G. Kasper (eds) *Introspection in Second Language Research*, Clevedon: Multilingual Matters, 24–53.

Erler, L. (forthcoming) Oxford: University of Oxford, Department of Educational Studies.

Evans, M. (1993) Flexible learning and modern language teaching, *Language Learning Journal*, 8, 17–21.

Faerch, G. and Kasper, G. (1983) *Strategies in Interlanguage Communication*, Harlow: Longman.

Faerch, G. and Kasper, G. (1986) Strategic competence in foreign language teaching, in G. Kasper (ed.) *Learning, Teaching and Communication in the Foreign Language Classroom*, Aarhus University: Aarhus University Press, 179–94.

Fleming, F. and Walls, G. (1998) What pupils do: the role of strategic planning in modern foreign language learning, *Language Learning Journal*, 18, 14–21.

Friedlander, A. 1(1990) Composing in English: effects of first language on writing in English as a second language, in B. Kroll (ed.) *Second Language Writing: Research Insights for the Classroom*, Cambridge: Cambridge University Press, 109–25.

Gathercole, I. (1990) *Autonomy in Language Learning*, London: CILT.

Graham, S. (1997) *Effective Language Learning*, Clevedon: Multilingual Matters.

Grenfell, M. and Harris, V. (1999) *Modern Languages and Learning Strategies: In Theory and Practice*, London: Routledge.

Harbord, J. (1992) The use of the mother tongue in the classroom, *ELT Journal*, 46, 75–90.

Harris, V. (1998) Making boys make progress, *Language Learning Journal*, 18, 56–62.

Harsch, K. and Riley, L.D. (1998) Language learning strategies development and use: an ESL/EFL comparison, paper given at the Second Language Research Forum University of Hawaii at Manoa, USA, October 1998.

Hawras, S. (1996) *Towards Describing Bilingual and Multilingual Behaviour: Implications for ESL Instruction*, Double Plan B Paper, Department of English as a Second Language, University of Minnesota, Minneapolis.

Holec, H. (ed.) (1988) *Autonomy and Self-Directed Learning: Present Fields of Application*, Strasbourg: Council of Europe.

James, C. and Garrett, P. (eds) (1991) *Language Awareness in the Classroom*, London: Longman.

Kellerman, E. (1991) Compensatory strategies in second language research: a critique, a revision and some (non-)implications for the classroom, in R. Phillipson, E. Kellerman, L. Selinker, M. Sharwood-Smith and M. Swain (eds) *Foreign and Second Language Pedagogy Research*, Clevedon: Multilingual Matters.

Kern, R.G. (1994) The role of mental translation in second language reading, *Studies in Second Language Acquisition*, 16, 4, 441–61.

Kobayashi, H. and Rinnert, C. (1992) Effects of first language on second language writing: translation versus direct composition, *Language Learning*, 42, 2, 183–215.

Krapels, A.R. (1990) An overview of second language writing process, in B. Kroll (ed.) *Second Language Writing: Research Insights for the Classroom*, Cambridge: Cambridge University Press, 37–56.

Little, D. (1994) Autonomy in language learning: some theoretical and practical considerations, in A. Swarbrick (ed.) *Teaching Modern Languages*, London: Routledge, 81–7.

LoCastro, V. (1994) Learning strategies and learning environments, *TESOL Quarterly*, 28, 409–14.

Lynch, T. (1995) The development of interactive listening strategies in second language academic settings, in D.J. Mendelsohn and J. Rubin (eds) *A Guide for the Teaching of Second Language Listening*, San Diego, CA: Dominie Press, 165–85.

Macaro, E. (1997) *Target Language Collaborative Learning and Autonomy*, Clevedon: Multilingual Matters.

Macaro, E. (1998) Learner strategies: piloting awareness and training, *Tuttitalia*, 18, 10–16.

Macaro, E. (2000). Learner strategies in foreign language learning: cross-national factors, *Tuttitalia*, 22, 9–18.

Macaro, E. (2001 forthcoming) Analysing student teachers' codeswitching in foreign language classrooms: theories and decision making, *Modern Languages Journal*, 85, 4.

McDonough, S.H. (1995) *Strategy and Skill in Learning a Foreign Language*, London: Edward Arnold.

McDonough, S.H. (1999) State of the art article: learner strategies, *Language Teaching*, 32, 1–18.

Naiman, N., Frohlich, M., Stern, H. and Todesco, A. (1996, new edition) *The Good Language Learner*, Clevedon: Multilingual Matters.

Nyhus, S.E. (1994) *Attitudes of Non–native Speakers of English Toward the Use of Verbal Report to Elicit their Reading Comprehension Strategies*, Plan B Masters Paper, Department of English as a Second Language, University of Minnesota, Minneapolis.

O'Malley, J.M. and Chamot, A.U. (1990) *Learning Strategies in Second Language Acquisition*, Cambridge: Cambridge University Press.

O'Malley, J.M., Chamot, A.U. and Küpper, L. (1989) Listening comprehension strategies in second language acquisition, *Applied Linguistics*, 10, 4, 418–37.

O'Malley, J.M., Chamot, A.U., Stewner-Manzanares, G., Russo, R. and Küpper, L. (1985) Learning strategy applications with students of English as a foreign language, *TESOL Quarterly*, 19, 557–84.

Oxford, R.L. (1990) *Language Learning Strategies. What Every Teacher Should Know*, Boston: Heinle and Heinle.

Oxford, R.L.(1996) Why is culture important for language learning strategies?, in R.L. Oxford (ed.) *Language Learning Strategies Around the World: Cross-Cultural Perspectives*, Manoa: University of Hawaii, Second Language Teaching and Curriculum Centre.

Oxford, R.L. and Burry-Stock, J.A. (1995) Assessing the use of language learning strategies worldwide with the ESL/EFL version of the strategy inventory for language learning (SILL), *System*, 23, 1, 1–23.

Oxford, R.L. and Nyikos, M. (1989) Variables affecting choice of language learning strategies by university students, *The Modern Language Journal*, 73, 3, 291–300.

Parry, K. (1991) Building a vocabulary through academic reading, *TESOL Quarterly*, 25, 4, 629–53.

Parry, K. (1993) The social construction of reading strategies: new directions for research, *Journal of Research in Reading*, 16, 2, 148–58.

Rees-Miller, J. (1993) A critical appraisal of learner training: theoretical bases and teaching implications, *TESOL Quarterly*, 27, 4, 679–89.

Rost, M. and Ross, S. (1991) Learner use of strategies in interaction: typology and teachability, *Language Learning*, 41, 235–73.

Sarig, G. (1987) High level reading in the first and the foreign language: some comparative process data, in J. Devine, P. Carrell and D. Eskey (eds) *Research in Reading English as a Second Language*. Washington, DC: TESOL, 105–20.

Saussure, F. de ([1916] 1966) *Course in General Linguistics*, London: McGraw-Hill.

Silva, T. (1990) Second language composition instruction: developments, issues and directions in ESL, in B. Kroll (ed.) *Second Language Writing: Research Insights for the Classroom*, Cambridge: Cambridge University Press, 11–23.

Skehan, P. (1989) *Individual Differences in Second Language Learning*, London: Arnold.

Skehan, P. (1998) *A Cognitive Approach to Language Learning*, Oxford: Oxford University Press.

Spada, N. and Lightbown, P.M. (1999) Instruction, first language influence and developmental readiness in second language acquisition, *The Modern Language Journal*, 83, 1, 1–22.

Stern, H.H. (1987) Foreword, in A. Wenden and J. Rubin (eds) *Learner Strategies in Language Learning*, Hemel Hempstead: Prentice-Hall, xi–xii.

Tarone, E. (1981)Some thoughts on the notion of 'communication strategy', *TESOL Quarterly*, 15, 3, 285–95.

Thompson, I. and Rubin, J. (1996) Can strategy instruction improve listening comprehension?, *Foreign Language Annals*, 29, 3, 331–42.

Truscott, J. (1998) Noticing in second language acquisition: a critical review, *Second Language Research*, 14, 2, 103–35.

Vandergrift, L. (1997) The Cinderella of communication strategies: reception strategies in interactive listening, *The Modern Language Journal*, 81, 4, 494–505.

Weinstein, C. and Mayer, R. (1986) The teaching of learning strategies, in M. Wittock (ed.) *Handbook for Research on Teaching*, New York: Macmillan.

Wenden, A. (1987) Incorporating learner training in the classroom, in A. Wenden and J. Rubin, *Learner Strategies in Language Learning*, Hemel Hempstead: Prentice-Hall, 159–68.

Woodward, T. (1991) *Models and Metaphors in Language Teacher Training*, Cambridge: Cambridge University Press.

Index